BRITISH BUSINESSMEN
AND CANADIAN CONFEDERATION

British Businessmen
and Canadian Confederation

Constitution-Making in an Era
of Anglo-Globalization

ANDREW SMITH

McGill-Queen's University Press
Montreal & Kingston · London · Ithaca

© McGill-Queen's University Press 2008
ISBN 978-0-7735-3405-6

Legal deposit third quarter 2008
Bibliothèque nationale du Québec

Printed in Canada on acid-free paper that is 100% ancient forest free
(100% post-consumer recycled), processed chlorine free.

This book has been published with the help of a grant from
Laurentian University.

McGill-Queen's University Press acknowledges the support of the
Canada Council for the Arts for our publishing program. We also
acknowledge the financial support of the Government of Canada
through the Book Publishing Industry Development Program
(BPIDP) for our publishing activities.

Library and Archives Canada Cataloguing in Publication

Smith, Andrew, 1976–
    British businessmen and Canadian confederation:
    constitution-making in an era of Anglo-globalization /
    Andrew Smith.

    Includes bibliographical references.
    ISBN 978-0-7735-3405-6

    1. Investments, British – Canada – History – 19th century. 2. Great
    Britain – Colonies – America – Economic policy. 3. British North
    American Association. 4. Canada – History – Confederation, 1867.
    5. Capitalism – Great Britain – History – 19th century. 6. Great Britain
    – Colonies – America – Administration. 7. Canada – Economic
    conditions – 1763–1867. I. Title.

    FC474.S62 2008   971.04'9   C2008-901372-7

This book was typeset by Interscript in 10.5/13 Palatino.

Contents

Acknowledgments

I have been assisted by countless librarians and archivists. Several individuals stand out as particularly helpful. John Orbell and Moira Lovegrove of the ING Baring Archives in London, England, took an active interest in my project and went far beyond the call of duty. I am indebted to the guidance of Phillip Winterbottom of the Royal Bank of Scotland Archives in London. The staff of the Manuscripts Room of the British Library fielded a number of stupid questions from me and I tried the patience of the staff at the Library and Archives of Canada (formerly the National Archives) for two summers. I also need to thank the staff of the Local Studies section of the Manchester Library and Archives; the Public Record Office (now the National Archives of the United Kingdom); the Borthwick Institute at the University of York; and the University of Nottingham Library. For many years, I have been helped by the staff of the D.B. Weldon Library of the University of Western Ontario in London. Among other things they have arranged interlibrary loans, tracked down misplaced rare volumes, and advanced word of electronic resources about to be acquired by the library.

I express my appreciation for permission to use several manuscript sources. Archives of the Royal Bank of Scotland and ING Baring were made available to me, in the case of ING Baring without any restrictions on how I quoted the material. Research in Canada and the United Kingdom was supported by a doctoral fellowship from the Social Science and Humanities Research Council of Canada (SSHRC), a doctoral fellowship supplement from the Federalism and Federations Initiative of SSHRC, and travel bursaries from the Department of History at Western. The fellowship from the London Goodenough Association of Canada allowed me to spend the 2003–04 academic year at Goodenough College in London, England, in close proximity to archival materials. The writing was assisted by an Ontario graduate fellowship.

The publication of this manuscript was assisted by Laurentian University. I would also like to thank the *Journal of the Canadian Historical Association* for permission to reprint material that appeared as "The Reaction of the City of London to the Quebec Resolutions, 1864–1866."

This book is partly about Canadian debts owed in London, England. I owe tremendous academic debts to Professors Hall and Thompson for all their help during my six years at Western. I owe similar debts to David Cannadine, my postdoctoral supervisor. I would like to thank Professor Michael Piva of the University of Ottawa for the time he took to discuss Canadian government finances in the 1860s with me, a topic for which few other people have much enthusiasm. Ged Martin and Peter Cain provided much useful advice. I would also like to thank the two anonymous readers at McGill-Queen's for their thoughtful comments on an initial draft of this work. My editor, Joan Harcourt, has been outstanding, as has copyeditor Claire Gigantes.

It is difficult to express in written words the immense gratitude I feel to my father for his constant interest and assistance. The help of my brother is also warmly appreciated.

BRITISH BUSINESSMEN
AND CANADIAN CONFEDERATION

1

Introduction:
Canada's Heritage in the City

British businessmen played a crucial role in the achievement of Canadian Confederation. Without the support of a small but influential group of investors, Confederation would not have occurred in 1867, if at all. Studies of the making of British colonial policy usually focus on politicians and civil servants, an approach to the writing of imperial history that has been summed up by the phrase "Whitehall and the Wilderness."[1] But in looking at the coming of Confederation, it is instructive to expand our purview from the Colonial Office to include the City, London's financial district. On the eve of Confederation, British people had extensive investments in the core of the future Dominion of Canada: Upper and Lower Canada, New Brunswick, Nova Scotia, and Rupert's Land.[2] The scale and nature of these investments in a rapidly modernizing region were important factors shaping British colonial policy in the 1860s.

At the beginning of the 1860s, a crisis in British North American investments threatened the economic well-being of some of the most important financiers in London, then the world's financial capital. As a result of this crisis, prominent men with investments in Canada came to support both the political unification of British North America and the construction of the long-awaited Halifax-Quebec railway. In early 1862 they formed an organization to lobby the British government to support these twin measures. This organization, the British North American Association (BNAA), lies at the heart of the political narrative told in the following pages.

In the years leading up to 1862, the Colonial Office had been indifferent if not hostile to the idea of Confederation. A shift in policy came soon after the BNAA's public call for "colonial union" and because of the application of political pressure by its members. In July 1862 the Colonial Office invited the colonies to consider federation. Colonial politicians responded positively to this encouragement and the famous conferences at Charlottetown and Quebec were held. The delegates at the Quebec conference drafted an outline constitution that was eventually embodied in the British North America Act.

When the details of the proposed constitution arrived in London, the investment community reacted positively. The attitude of the City was crucial; for investor hostility would have been a substantial if not insurmountable obstacle to implementing a project so dependant on British support and financial guarantees. British investors welcomed the proposed constitutional change because the existing constitutional order in Canada had ceased to work in their interests. Discussions of underperforming investments in the colony were often infused with the language of class, the implication being that Canada was too democratic. The Canadian electorate was much wider than the British and it was natural that attitudes about social class would inform investors' views of Canada.

Some British observers with conservative political leanings connected colonial federation with a tendency in the colonies towards stiffer voting requirements. More stringent criteria for voters would have reduced the proportion of adult males with the electoral franchise. While most investors probably knew that it would be difficult to roll back the democratic tide in this way, the transfer of power from the local legislatures to a more distant level of government appealed to those seeking to qualify democratic rule. At first, London's investment community was disturbed by the fact that the draft constitution produced at Quebec envisioned the continued existence of separate provincial legislatures. The general attitude was that a unitary state would be preferable. However, this feature of the scheme ceased to bother British investors once it became clear that the provincial governments would be little more than glorified municipalities under the firm control of the central government. As they watched the drafting of the Canadian constitution, the British investors displayed a consistent and strong centralizing bias that was connected to their class ideology.

The debate over North American colonial policy in the 1860s exposed deep divisions within the British business class. Some businessmen supported the British policies necessary for Confederation while others vehemently opposed them. The opposition was led by Richard Cobden and John Bright, two cotton manufacturers who were strong proponents of classical liberalism. Cobden and Bright denounced the spending of British tax money in the colonies, whether it was on garrisons or the Intercolonial Railway. These radicals for capitalism disliked the British Empire, an entity they saw as a vast system of outdoor relief supporting the aristocracy, the military, and other perceived social parasites. Admirers of the decentralized and democratic institutions the United States, they did not think Britain should exert itself to keep Canada as a colony. Cobden died in 1865 (he had travelled to London against doctor's orders so that he could vote against spending on Canadian fortifications).[3] Bright, however, remained on the political scene and in 1867–68 he championed Nova Scotia's right to remain apart from Canada, a polity he regarded as both corrupt and protectionist.

This study of the role of interest-group politics in the making of British colonial policy is a contribution to a revisionist interpretation of Confederation. The reinterpretation of Canada's birth began in 1995 with the publication of Ged Martin's *Britain and the Origins of Canadian Confederation, 1837–1867*. In this important work Martin challenged the pro-Confederation bias of much of the existing literature, methodically disproving the arguments used by the advocates of Confederation and their twentieth-century apologists.[4] By establishing that the arguments of the anti-Confederates were, in many cases, quite reasonable, Martin undermined the existing explanations for the causation of Confederation: uniting the colonies was not an inevitable or even logical response to the problems facing British North America.[5]

Confederation is sometimes attributed to the Fenian threat and the need to unite against the power of the victorious northern states. The Fenians were an Irish-American paramilitary force that believed that attacking British North America might help bring about Ireland's independence from British rule. In 1866 the Fenian Brotherhood staged several inept crossborder raids. Martin demonstrated that the defence-related arguments used by Confederation's supporters were extremely weak and that Confederation and the Intercolonial Railway did little to make the colonies stronger militarily.[6] The spectre of Fenianism may have encouraged some contemporaries to accept Confederation, but according to Martin such thinking was an illogical panic response. Historians of Confederation have long pointed to the existence of "political deadlock" in the Province of Canada as proof that fundamental constitutional change was necessary. Martin took issue with this theory by arguing that the issue of representation by population might well have been resolved within the context of the existing union of the Canadas (i.e., without Confederation).[7] He also pointed out the illogic of the commercial justifications for political union; for a *Zollverein*; or free-trade zone, of the sort proposed by the Canadian government in March 1864 would have liberalized trade without the necessity of political union.[8]

Martin's approach was innovative because he emphasized the role of Britain in Confederation. By challenging the inward-looking bias of the older historiography, he helped to resituate Confederation in the contexts of British and comparative imperial history. He did not argue that British power over the colonies was overwhelming and indeed demonstrated that it could be quite limited. Martin argued that the British government had a number of levers for advancing its long-discussed goal of colonial federation. These pressure points included provision of colonial garrisons, the ability to underwrite colonial borrowing in the London market, and the eagerness of elite colonists to stay at aristocratic country houses and participate in the British honours system.[9]

Martin's path-breaking interpretation is marred by one major omission, namely, the role of businessmen. For Martin, Confederation was an episode of high politics best understood in relation to the ideas and actions of a small group of political leaders. Martin has dismissed the idea that British support for Confederation was the result of business pressure, claiming that "historians who habitually emphasize economic factors tend to portray unidentified capitalists whispering in the ears of British ministers in the mid-1860s, urging them to create a unified British North America."[10] In other words, Martin believes that business played little or no role in driving the Confederation agenda.

Martin's view rests on the problematic assumption that policy making is best understood with reference to public opinion and the ideas of disinterested statesmen.[11] But Confederation was not created in an interest-group vacuum and economic forces help to explain why Canadian Confederation happened at all and why it took place when it did. The unification of the British North American colonies was a perennial idea that had been proposed as early as the 1790s, but it was implemented in the 1860s because it suited the interests of British investors at that point. The proposals for British North American federation in earlier decades did not get past the concept stage because they were irrelevant to the economic interests of the day. In looking at the birth of the unnatural geographical entity called the Dominion of Canada, the role of the investment community needs to be acknowledged.

Confederation was a complex phenomenon that involved many interest groups on both sides of the Atlantic. The British businessmen who influenced Colonial Office policy were very aware of the many constraints facing British North America's politicians. The Fathers of Confederation had to manage pressures that ranged from ambitious office seekers to bishops anxious to protect the interests of the Catholic church under the new constitutional order.[12] Looming in the background were the colonial electorates. All of these groups had agency and it would be foolish to maintain that iron-fisted British financiers dictated the course of events in a unilateral way. So simplistic a view would be unsustainable in light of the secondary literature highlighting the limitations on the power of financiers and the relative autonomy of the state. But the investors' part in this drama is an important one that historians have largely ignored up to now.

Candid contemporary observers believed that interest-group pressure played a crucial role in the making of policy: many policies were proposed and debated by politicians, but only a few received enough business support to be implemented. In *The Prime Minister*, an 1876 novel dealing with the connections between politics and the City and featuring an overseas railway scheme, a somewhat jaded Anthony Trollope observed: "It is acknowledged in politics that any measure is to be carried, or to be left out in the cold ... according to the number of deputations which may be got to press a Minister of the subject."[13]

Trollope was referring to the deputations of businessmen that periodically visited Downing Street. He knew what he was talking about because of his long tenure at the British Post Office, a government department heavily involved in the politics of transportation subsidies. Because of his obsession with balanced budgets and resistance to the demands of special interests, Trollope's fictional Chancellor of the Exchequer, the stern Mr Monk, bears a remarkable resemblance to William Gladstone, the real chancellor discussed below. Moreover, the dubious railway investments that appear in Trollope's novels have definite parallels with some of the projects discussed in this book.

After focusing on the cultural aspects of the British empire for several decades,[14] historians are returning to the empire's economic dimensions, a topic that preoccupied many historians in the 1950s.[15] In thinking about the political economy of the British Empire, a useful starting point is the concept of "Anglo-globalization," a term introduced by Niall Ferguson.[16] Ferguson maintains that in the years 1815 to 1914, the British Empire promoted the worldwide rise of capitalism in much the same way that the current *Pax Americana* has facilitated the interrelated phenomena known collectively as "globalization." By arguing that the British Empire was the institutional foundation of globalization in the nineteenth century, Ferguson posits a close link between bourgeois hegemony, free-market capitalism, and British imperialism.

The Canadian experience forces us to modify parts of Ferguson's thesis. Proud membership in the empire did not prevent successive Canadian governments from pursuing protectionist policies detrimental to the interests of British manufacturers or from passing other laws that were anathema to classical political economy. John A. Macdonald's anglophilia did not extend to the free trade ideas of Adam Smith, David Ricardo, and John Stuart Mill.[17] Moreover, anti-imperialism was most prevalent within the ranks of Manchester Liberalism, an intellectual tradition that produced the most dogmatic proponents of free markets, tax cuts, and retrenchment in government spending (especially spending on the military and in the colonies). In other words, the section of the British middle classes with the strongest attachment to unadulterated free-market capitalism tended to support the "Little England" position that colonies were useless encumbrances.[18] Ferguson fails to examine whether the attitudes towards empire of the British middling classes were different from those of the old landed aristocracy or the bankers of the City, groups with markedly less enthusiasm for the radical individualism and cosmopolitanism espoused by Manchester Liberalism.

There is a large body of literature that views British colonial policy in terms of social classes or interest groups within British society. This approach dates back to Jeremy Bentham.[19] In the early twentieth century, J.A. Hobson advanced an interest-group explanation of imperial expansionism that focused on capitalists, maintaining that the maldistribution of incomes in British society created a surplus of savings that necessitated the existence of overseas colonies as fields for investment that would serve as vents for superfluous capital.

Lenin modified this idea by arguing that advanced capitalist states acquired colonies because it was in the interests of governing classes faced with a growing socialist threat from below.[20] Some non-Marxist students of the economic history of the British Empire also adopt an interest-group approach. In the 1950s Ronald Robinson and John Gallagher founded a school of interpretation that suggested that British colonial policy was dictated by the needs of manufacturers.[21] More recently, cliometricians operating on broadly neoclassical assumptions have argued that having a costly overseas empire enriched particular groups within Britain at the expense of the country as a whole.[22]

The interest-group approach that is the point of departure for this book is the "gentlemanly capitalist" thesis of empire. Because it provides a theoretical framework for understanding the making of British colonial policy, the gentlemanly capitalist thesis is useful in bridging the gap between generalizations about social class and imperialism and the details of policy making in a complex political environment.[23]

Two economic historians, Peter J. Cain and Anthony G. Hopkins, introduced the concept of gentlemanly capitalism as an aid to understanding the political economy of the empire.[24] Their thesis has several key components. Drawing on the well-established distinction between Industry and City in the Literature on British political economy,[25] Cain and Hopkins argue that the British Empire was run primarily in the interests of the financiers of the City at the expense of other sectors of the community, including the industrialists Robinson and Gallagher saw as major beneficiaries of imperial policy. In refuting the Robinson-Gallagher thesis, they point out that Britain's overseas possessions took a consistently low percentage of her total exports of manufactured goods and that the possession of overseas colonies conferred few benefits on manufacturers. In their view, the involvement of manufacturers in setting colonial policy was very limited.

Cain and Hopkins supply a complex explanation of the City's influence over colonial policy that incorporates the research findings of social historians and that is reminiscent of Anthony Sampson's classic studies of the British elite.[26] They argue that the City was linked to Whitehall by much more than geographical proximity, although that was important. Financiers were intermarried with the governing class, the aristocracy, for more than the owners of factories were. In the British mindset, finance had much greater status than manufacturing and there was a shared ethos that united senior civil servants and finance capitalists. A tight nexus of private banks, the Treasury, the Colonial Office, and the Bank of England coordinated policy.

According to Cain and Hopkins, this sociological reality was the underpinning of the favouritism that the makers of colonial policy showed towards the City at the expense of industry. In their eyes, the growth of the empire in the first place, the manner in which it was governed, and even the way in which decolonization was managed were all intended to further the interests of the City.

Cain and Hopkins see the British response to the higher revenue tariff imposed by Canada in 1859 as an example of gentlemanly capitalist policy making. Although they concede that the actions of the Colonial Office were influenced by constitutional considerations, Cain and Hopkins argue that its decision not to interfere in Canada's progressively higher tariffs, despite the outcry from British manufacturers, served the interests of British financiers; for while adverse to the interests of exporters, the higher customs duties gathered the revenue needed to meet Canada's obligations to railway bondholders in Britain.[27] Similarly, Cain and Hopkins argue that British support for Confederation was dictated by the needs of the City, although they do not develop this idea at much length. Cain and Hopkins describe Barings' Bank, the Grand Trunk, and the Hudson's Bay Company (HBC) as the British firms most involved in Confederation.[28]

Cain and Hopkins support their thesis with a large number of historical examples drawn from every corner of the empire and their research helps to set the British North American experience in a global context. Another virtue of their synthesis is that it helps to explain why anti-colonialism was most popular with British manufacturers and relatively uncommon in the City of London. In the 1860s Manchester and the other manufacturing towns were centres of the belief that the colonies should be made independent because they were costing the taxpayer too much.[29] In contrast, the City tended to believe in retaining and acquiring colonies.

Although the gentlemanly capitalism thesis is generally sound, there are weaknesses that will be addressed in this study of the role of British business in Confederation. In the following pages, it will be shown that Cain and Hopkins have made too much of the distinction between the manufacturing sector and the pro-imperial City. We shall see evidence of people in the manufacturing centres supporting the colonialist pro-Confederation policies endorsed by the gentlemanly capitalists of the City. The career of Edward Watkin, for example a man from a manufacturing family steeped in Manchester Liberalism who nevertheless supported assertive and interventionist imperialism, shows that the Cain-Hopkins paradigm must be refined. For various reasons, a number of British manufacturers rejected the conventional wisdom in Britain's manufacturing towns, i.e., the Little England argument that the colonies should be discarded.

Some critics of the gentlemanly capitalism thesis argue that Cain and Hopkins go too far in emphasizing the power of financiers over colonial policy and government policy in general.[30] The limitations on the political power of financiers will become especially apparent in the sections of this work dealing with the sale of the Hudson's Bay Company lands to the Dominion. At the time of Confederation, several factors had eroded the influence of the City over British government policy. One of them was a Chancellor of the Exchequer, William Gladstone, who was deeply suspicious of its power and determined to free the state from the grip of the financiers, as he saw it.[31] Gladstone's preferred means of doing this included retrenchment in spending, increased income tax, accelerated debt repayments, and new ways of raising capital that did not involve City intermediaries, such as though the Post Office Savings Bank.[32] Gladstone, a powerful force within Palmerston's cabinet, was opposed to granting imperial aid to the Intercolonial Railway, a project desired by Thomas Baring, George Carr Glyn, and other titans of finance.

One fundamental problem with Cain and Hopkin's analysis of Confederation is that it rests on the writings of R.T. Naylor, a Canadian whose ideas have been hotly contested by other scholars. Naylor sardonically remarked that Baring Brothers were the true Fathers of Confederation. By dramatically overstating a case based on limited primary source research, Naylor brought a plausible thesis into disrepute.[33] The evidence presented below will be used to support a more moderate version of the business influence thesis that Naylor advanced.

The correspondence from investors to be found in the papers of the Colonial Office is extensive but essentially routine: there are many pro forma letters from Baring Brothers enclosing cheques for small sums and the like.[34] Although various cranks wrote to the Colonial Office to express their views on the proposed Canadian constitution,[35] the Colonial Office papers are largely silent about the constitutional views of the major British investors in Canada.

In looking at the making of British policy in the era of Confederation, we are therefore forced to shift from the well-organized files of the Colonial Office to the more haphazard world of scattered private papers. Once we do so, however, the nexus postulated by Cain and Hopkins is very much in evidence. The non-official correspondence allows us to explore the connections between the Colonial Secretaries and investors. The key individual here was the fifth duke of Newcastle, Colonial Secretary in the crucial 1859–64 period. Newcastle's immediate predecessor, Sir Edward Bulwer-Lytton, had poured cold water on the idea of colonial union in 1858–59. By the time illness forced Newcastle's retirement in April 1864, Britain was committed to Confederation and colonial politicians had responded to the invitation to discuss colonial union.

Newcastle's successors (Edward Cardwell, Lord Carnarvon, and the duke of Buckingham and Chandos) merely had to manage a process that was already underway. Management was sometimes tricky (as when dealing with such thorny problems as George-Étienne Cartier's baronetcy, New Brunswick's mercurial lieutenant-governor, or the Nova Scotia Repeal agitation) but the basic thrust of policy had been set.[36] Although Newcastle's immediate successors did not have strong personal ties to the British investors in the North American colonies, Cardwell[37] and Carnarvon made colonial policy in the same gentlemanly capitalist context. As we shall see later, there are several recorded instances of investors discussing the proposed British North American constitution with Cardwell.

The duke of Buckingham and Chandos, Colonial Secretary from March 1867 to 1868, had very close ties to those leading capitalists who were interested in Canada. The son of a wastrel father, Buckingham had repaired his family's fortunes through lucrative directorships in British railways. For many years, he had served as chairman of the London and North Western, a railway controlled by George Carr Glyn, who was also a major investor in Canada's Grand Trunk.[38] Neither Buckingham nor any of the other Colonial Secretaries would have intentionally sacrificed the public interest to help their investor friends, but their definitions of the public good were largely congruent with the aims of the gentlemanly capitalists of the City. British legislators in the 1860s liked to believe that they were far less corrupt than either their eighteenth-century forebears or contemporary colonial politicians. But as Joseph Howe correctly pointed out in 1862, "interest" (i.e., personal pecuniary considerations) was as much a part of law making in the mother country as in the colonies.[39]

The attitudes and personal connections of the Colonial Secretaries' subordinates at the Colonial Office can be dealt with more briefly. In 1859–64, Newcastle was assisted by a parliamentary under-secretary, a Liberal MP named Chichester Fortescue, and a small staff of civil servants. While some parliamentary under-secretaries were very actively involved in their assigned departments, Fortescue was not.[40] Fortescue and Newcastle were rivals for the hand of Frances Lady Waldegrave, whose marriage to Fortescue in 1863 helps to explain why his involvement in the Colonial Office was close to nominal.[41] Because Fortescue was not involved in Colonial Office decisions at that juncture, it would be pointless to ask whether his ties to the gentlemanly capitalists who were interested in Canada were as close as those of Newcastle. Even if the investors had had any influence over Fortescue, he could have done little to assist them as long as his relations with the Colonial Secretary were strained. When Newcastle was replaced by Edward Cardwell, Fortescue was simultaneously shuffled out of the Colonial Office.

Fortescue's replacement was W.E. Forster. Although Forster later became interested in Imperial Federation and other issues affecting the settlement colonies, he was not a major figure in the Colonial Office in 1864–66 and left most of the work to his superior, Cardwell.[42] When the Conservatives took power in July 1866, Forster was replaced by C.B. Adderley, a noted author on colonial matters. Although he was sometimes accused of being a closet supporter of separation from the colonies,[43] Adderley believed in retaining overseas colonies and merely thought that the colonists should pay for their own defence. He saw colonial federations as a way of promoting military self-reliance.[44] Because the policy of Confederation had already been set by the time he reached the Colonial Office, Adderley's chief importance was his speech during the debate on the British North America bill.

As for the Colonial Office's small permanent staff, they guarded their personal opinions in the course of discharging their official duties. Rumours abounded that the top staff were Little Englanders who believed that the settlement colonies should be forced to become independent. We know from memoirs that in some cases these rumours were quite true,[45] but the civil servants appear to have left their opinions at home. Newcastle, a visionary imperialist committed to retaining the colonies, saw no evidence of Little Englander ideas in their work. In 1861 Newcastle replied to Palmerston's accusation that there were "theoretical Gentlemen in the Colonial Office who wish to get rid of all colonies" by remarking that "if there are such, they have never ventured to share their opinions to me."[46] Because Newcastle's subordinates adhered to the principle that civil servants should assist the elected government in implementing its desiderata, their beliefs and personal connections (to investors or anyone else) are far less important to this story than the ideas and connections of their chief, the duke of Newcastle.

An up-to-date steam-age aristocrat who took an active managerial role in the development of his coalfields, Newcastle was comfortable in the world of business. In the early 1850s Newcastle's properties had led to his first substantive meeting with Edward Watkin, the railway executive who went on to become a major player in the British North American Association. Out of this chance encounter a close friendship blossomed. Both men were interested in colonies and railways. Newcastle once made an offhand comment about investing personal funds in Canadian securities,[47] but the loss of much of the duke's correspondence by fire means that the full extent of his own colonial holdings is now impossible to ascertain. What is clear from Newcastle's surviving papers is that he was in frequent contact with both Watkin and Watkin's colonial associates. These included Sir Allan Napier MacNab, the Canadian Tory who famously declared, "My politics now are my railroads,"[48] and who was later a long-term guest at Newcastle's country house in Nottinghamshire.[49]

It appears that Newcastle's attitude to colonial enterprises was influenced by whether or not Watkin was involved. Before it was taken over and reorganized by Watkin's syndicate in 1863, Newcastle was distinctly hostile to the territorial claims of the Hudson's Bay Company. Newcastle had condemned the HBC as hopelessly antiquated and adopted a view perilously close to the confiscation policy advocated by Upper Canadian Reformers.[50] Not surprisingly, Newcastle had not been on good terms with the leading figures in the HBC. In fact, the great fur-trading magnate Edward Ellice had complained in 1862 about being *persona non grata* with the Colonial Office.[51] But once a syndicate led by Watkin was in charge of the HBC, Newcastle's attitude to the company changed, and he stopped seeing it as a barrier to progress.[52]

Edward Ellice and Edward Watkin were both, in the terminology of Cain and Hopkins, "gentlemanly capitalists" and their relations with Newcastle suggest the relevance of their interpretive framework. Recently, the political power and influence enjoyed by nineteenth-century British investors has been the subject of extensive historical research. Some scholars see parallels with present-day issues such as globalization and Third World indebtedness. Important works on the political economy of nineteenth-century sovereign indebtedness include Michael Costeloe's study of the political activities of the Mexican Bondholders' Committee,[53] Frank Dawson's work on the Latin American debt crisis of the 1820s,[54] and a recent paper on the Corporation of Foreign Bondholders, a powerful body established in London in the early 1870s to coordinate lobbying activities.[55]

Because mid-Victorian Britain did not engage in gunboat diplomacy whenever the aggrieved holders of foreign bonds asked for it, the rare occasions on which Her Majesty's Government did decide to intervene on behalf of a particular set of investors are especially interesting episodes in political history.[56] One lobbying victory was represented by the British decision in the 1850s to use naval power to intimidate Buenos Aires into giving up its dreams of independence from the Argentine federation. The reversal of the general non-intervention policy in this instance is attributed by historian Henry Fern to pressure by the Buenos Aires Bondholders' Association, an organization that included Thomas Baring, who was prominent in the City and who had important ties to Canada.[57] Coming a decade before Confederation, this incident suggests that the City's preference for larger rather than smaller political units was already firmly established. By the 1850s, British capitalists had come to see centrifugal forces and the multiplication of countries as bad for business. By the end of the 1860s, political unification appeared to be the wave of the future in the New World as in the old.

The lobbying efforts of the foreign bondholders' organizations closely paralleled those of the BNAA. Like many of the organizations that represented foreign bondholders, the association held its meetings at the London Tavern on Bishopsgate Street. More importantly, its membership frequently overlapped with that of the other organizations.[58] Thomas Baring, head of the most powerful interest represented by the BNAA, was also the agent of the Mexican Bondholders' Committee, an organization that influenced British policy during the French Military intervention in that country in the 1860s. France, it should be noted, had invaded Mexico after that country had defaulted on bonds held by investors in Europe. France's efforts to install a puppet monarchy in Mexico were tacitly supported by Britain, which was home to many of the aggrieved investors.[59] Another similarity stemmed from the fact that debtor governments typically raised most of their revenue from customs duties: investor groups such as the BNAA and the Mexican Boudholders' Committee sometimes collided politically with British exporters who wanted other countries to have the lowest possible tariffs.

The British businessmen and politicians discussed in this book worked closely with the so-called Fathers of Confederation in bringing about colonial federation. There is a sizeable literature devoted to the economic ideas of the Fathers.[60] My work helps to contextualize their motives, which were characterized by a mixture of self-interest and genuine concern for the public good.[61] It also helps to dispel a widespread but entirely inaccurate view of Confederation. As Barbara Messamore has noted, many Canadians inaccurately believe that Confederation was a step towards Canadian autonomy along the lines of the 1931 Statute of Westminster, which marked the effective legislative independence of Canada.[62] Canadians need to be reminded that the Fathers and the British businessmen who supported Confederation acted in the belief that a federation would cement the ties linking the individual colonies to the British Crown.

The first of July 1867 was not some sort of peaceful equivalent of 4 July 1776. The constitutional convention of 1787 provides a better American parallel to Confederation because it replaced a loose union with a functioning federation. Even here the comparison is problematic, because the issues of political economy at stake during the Philadelphia Convention were largely internal ones relating to the economic relations between and within American states.[63] Canadian Confederation involved intracolonial and intercolonial wealth transfers, but it was also about the financial web linking British North America to London, the world's financial hub.

The term "Anglo-globalization" had not yet been coined, but it sums up a number of the issues important to the Fathers of Confederation. Confederation promoted the transatlantic flow of British capital. Of the seventy-two resolutions agreed by the Fathers of Confederation at the Quebec Conference in the autumn of 1864, the first five dealt with the relationship of the colonies to the mother country. The very first of the resolutions declared the delegates' belief that the "present and future prosperity of British North America will be promoted by a Federal Union under the Crown of Great Britain."[64] The connection the delegates drew between the colony's ties to Britain and prosperity is telling and speaks to the centrality of economic issues to Confederation.

Peter J. Smith has advanced an interesting ideological interpretation of Confederation, arguing that it was the product of a pro-capitalist "Court Party" ideology that favoured centralization as a way of promoting the development of a capitalist economy. According to him, the opponents of Confederation were motivated by a pre-capitalist "Country Party" ideology that valued decentralized political authority as more consistent with communitarian restrictions of economic freedom. Smith suggests that the 1860s saw the re-emergence in the colonies of a centuries-old pattern in Anglo-American politics that reflected different attitudes to capitalism.[65]

Smith's interpretation is plausible for several reasons. First, the British businessmen who supported Confederation displayed a preference for a relatively centralized federation. Moreover, the desire of the Fathers of Confederation to see the British connection preserved was entirely consistent with their interests as individual economic actors. The influx of British capital into the colonies in the 1840s and 1850s had been, in part, due to the colonies' status qua formal colonies rather than independent republics.

Colonial politicians, many of whom were businessmen themselves, had compelling economic reasons to see the British connection preserved. In the ideal world of the Fathers, the colonies would have continued to enjoy reciprocity with the Americans and privileged access to British capital markets. Although many of the Fathers of Confederation later became protectionists, in the 1860s they were friends of comprehensive globalization who wished to promote the international flow of goods as well as of capital. Macdonald later implemented a tariff designed to exclude foreign goods, but he always supported the inflow of outside capital.

The desire of British North Americans to remain part of the British Empire is usually interpreted in light of a monarchical political culture,[66] the history of political thought,[67] and the North American colonists' membership in an imagined community called "the British World."[68] These studies of culture and identity provide one way of understanding why the Fathers of Confederation were so determined to remain part of the empire. But there is a more straightforward materialist explanation: many of the Fathers of Confederation were personally involved in projects that were dependent on the continued inflow of British capital.

In the 1850s George-Étienne Cartier, a former rebel against British rule, became the well-paid solicitor of the British-financed Grand Trunk.[69] John A. Macdonald's attachment to Britain of was undoubtedly heartfelt, but his lucrative employment by the British-controlled Trust and Loan Company of Upper Canada[70] also needs to be taken into account when explaining his desire to preserve the constitutional link with the "old country" (and its capital markets). The Fathers of Confederation in the lower provinces had similar projects on the go. For instance, Charles Tupper acquired a stake in coalfields near the projected route of the Halifax-Quebec railway. Not surprisingly, he loudly advocated British government assistance for the line.[71]

None of the Fathers of Confederation did anything that violated the standards of the era: conflict of interest legislation lay far in the future. But the strongly pro-imperial ideology articulated by most of the Fathers was entirely congruent with their own pecuniary interests. For the Fathers, it was important to keep British capital flowing into British North America. Because colonies enjoyed a privileged position in British capital markets relative to sovereign borrowers, remaining part of the British Empire was crucial. Political options that threatened to disrupt the inflow of investment, notably republicanism and independence, were anathema to the Fathers.

Most people in British North America in the 1860s saw some benefit in remaining part of the British Empire. However, a segment of public opinion feared that being subjects of Queen Victoria meant subjection to the financiers of the City of London. Hostility to British high finance flared up in the period 1862–64, when Sandfield Macdonald was premier of Canada West.

Peter Baskerville has characterized the Sandfield Macdonald ministries as pursuing an agenda of decolonization. Drawing on Ronald Robinson's "excentric" theory that the willingness of local elites to collaborate was the basis of colonialism, Baskerville argues that during Sandfield Macdonald's time in power a section of the Canadian elite tried to escape from the collaborationist system and to probe "the limits of human agency at the periphery of the Empire."[72]

Baskerville's description of this time is flawed because he does not distinguish political decolonization (i.e., pulling down the Union Jack) from opposition to an economic order centred on the gentlemanly capitalists of London that involved borrowing and subsidization on a massive scale. Under Sandfield Macdonald the government did not seek political decolonization and its program implied that Canada could continue to be a British country without remaining a gentlemanly capitalist economic satellite. To the political leaders of Canada West, cooperating with the British government and its personnel was distinct from collaborating with a clique of bankers.

The economic agenda of the Sandfield Macdonald's government was strongly supported by George Brown's *Globe*, which saw no contradiction in upholding the British political connection while supporting efforts to free the colony from the influence of British capitalists. The *Globe* felt that Canadians should be tied to the mother country through the Governor General and other political institutions rather than by a web of credit mediated by politician-bankers.[73] George Brown had no objection to British capital coming into Canada (indeed, he sold his Bothwell property to a Scottish investment syndicate), but he firmly distinguished such unaided enterprise from the subsidy-guzzling Grand Trunk.[74] Thus, while Brown attacked Governor Sir Edmund Head as the pawn of London's bankers, he also used the *Globe* to "cultivate a national feeling, national in the broadest sense of the term, embracing Great Britain and all her colonies."[75]

George Brown and Sandfield Macdonald's second minister of Finance, Luther Hamilton Holton, believed that the best way to escape from the grip of the City of London was through retrenchment, balanced budgets, and the eventual repayment of the public debt. Neither man was an advocate of pure laissez-faire (as Elisabeth Wallace showed long ago, there were none in British North America and few elsewhere)[76], but both had drunk deeply at the well of classical political economy. Their ideas were in keeping with those of Gladstone and the Radicals who joined him in demanding "liberty, retrenchment, and reform" in Britain. Because of their Gladstonian aspect, the British classical liberal ideologue Robert Lowe much preferred the Sandfield Macdonald governments to the borrow-and-spend ministries that had been headed by Macdonald and Cartier. Lowe described these previous ministries as "the imperson-ation of evil" and denounced their "great servility to the moneyed interests in England."[77]

The thesis that British investors played an important role in the making of Confederation is hardly a new one and dates back to the time of Confederation itself. One theme common to the anti-confederate argument in the four original provinces was that Con-federation was a scheme to enrich certain British investors at the expense of the colonial populace.[78] In January 1867 the *Montreal Witness* denounced Confederation as something that would "put a couple of millions, more or less, into the pockets of London bankers and speculators" connected to the Grand Trunk and the Hudson's Bay Company. In return for supporting this corrupt measure, the British government had promised to put "all our prominent men into governorships or at least into a sort of order of nobility."[79]

The *Rouge* paper *Le Pays* of Montreal, organ of the radical liberal party in Canada East, made similar accusations regarding the influ-ence of the Grand Trunk, identifying its general manager, C.J. Brydges, as the chief culprit behind Confederation. *Le Pays* thought that Confederation would lead to a mountain of debt and skyrock-eting taxation that would enrich a few London bankers at the ex-pense of Canada.[80] In the Canadian parliamentary debates on the Quebec Resolutions, Benjamin Seymour had lashed out at the Grand Trunk as a venture "planned by English capitalists" at the expense of Canada's taxpayers. Seymour condemned both it and Confedera-tion as incompatible with "retrenchment and financial reform."[81]

In effect, the opponents of Confederation presented the London bankers as the corporate welfare bums of their day. The fact that such allegations were being levelled in the colonies helps to explain why the Province of Canada's London financial agents, Thomas Baring, MP, and George Carr Glyn, MP, remained silent during the debate at Westminster on the British North America bill. When the anti-confederates discussed the role of the bankers in Confederation, they did so to condemn them for interfering in colonial political af-fairs. Their tone was frequently hysterical. In the twenty-first cen-tury, it is possible to assess the role of the bankers in a more detached fashion. Indeed, the involvement of financiers in Confederation was simply a logical outcome of the vast scale of British investment in the colonies. The colonists had chosen to develop their economy with borrowed money rather than with local savings: this money came with political strings attached.

It would be hard to underestimate the economic and political importance of the capital flows between Britain and Canada. The colonies abounded with investment opportunities but were chronically short of capital. Savings were relatively plentiful in Britain, where returns on investment were generally lower. As a result, there was money to be made through arbitrage. The societal consequences of the transatlantic flow of money were massive. Borrowing abroad allowed newly settled societies to develop more rapidly. The impact on Britain was also significant. John Stuart Mill believed that the price of money in old countries had a tendency to fall towards zero but that "the perpetual overflow of capital into colonies or foreign countries, to seek higher profits than can be obtained at home ... [has] been for many years one of the principal causes by which the decline of profits in England has been arrested."[82] Capital exports changed the terms of trade between the owners of capital and other groups in British society.

Before the political role of the investors can be explored, it is necessary to survey the economic ties that linked Britain to her North American possessions on the eve of Confederation. At the time, the products of Britain's Industrial Revolution were everywhere, from the coarse and colourful blankets traded in the Far North to the fine textiles that adorned the ladies of Montreal. British investors controlled significant sections of the British North American economy. Their interests ranged from the wooden stockades of Rupert's Land to the bricks and mortar of Montreal. The influence of the London bankers pervaded colonial life and touched everything from the smallest coin in the pocket of a Nova Scotian fisherman to the massive span of the Victoria Bridge. In the decades before Confederation, a wave of British capital had transformed the fabric of British North American life and all of this money had been supplied in the expectation of eventually seeing a dividend. In the following pages, a story will be told that involves trade and investment, greed and disappointment, hope and resistance, politicians and priests, oligarchy and democracy, and the financial systems that shaped the daily lives of millions of British North Americans.

2

An Empire That Did Little for Manchester but Much for the City of London

In the 1840s Britain broke with centuries of tradition and announced that it would no longer give preference to its colonies in matters of trade.[1] The abolition of colonial preference placed the British subjects in Canada and Nova Scotia on the same level playing field as the citizens of Ohio and Massachusetts, and in the 1860s people were still trying to come to terms with this radical change in policy. The new economic environment shaped British reactions to both the separatist ideas articulated by people such as Goldwin Smith and the rival plans for a British North American federation. A classical liberal who deeply admired the United States, Smith emphasized the cost savings that would come from severing the political connection with the settlement colonies: Britain's colonies should be made independent whether they liked it or not. Smith saw Canada as a financial sinkhole and a particularly good candidate for compulsory independence.[2]

Not all British people thought that a Little England policy was in the national interest. Many of the opponents of Goldwin Smith's agenda rallied to the standard of Canadian Confederation. Moreover, people's private interests coloured their reactions to the debate over whether Britain should continue to have colonies in North America. Many British manufacturers supported the idea of colonial independence, while the country's financiers were generally opposed to the policy advocated by Smith. This chapter explains why people in different sectors of the British economy responded differently to the prospect of British North American independence. Subsequent chapters will show that while the manufacturers had able spokesmen, the financiers enjoyed privileged access to the corridors of power and were able to shape British policy in the 1860s. The investors fought against the Little England concept and warmly supported the unification of British North America. However, before we can understand the clash of interest groups discussed below, it is necessary to examine the state of Anglo-Canadian economic relations as they existed on the eve of Confederation.

A weak trading relationship between countries does not preclude a strong investing relationship. Nations can exchange vast volumes of goods without people in one country owning assets in the other. Similarly, the importance of the capital flows between two countries can dwarf their trade in visible goods. The economic bonds between Britain and her North American colonies in the 1860s can be summarized as "little trade, much investment." This underlying economic reality shaped British attitudes to Confederation, a measure that many viewed as tending to preserve the bond between Britain and her sprawling North American possessions.

Under a system of mercantilism, countries generally reserve colonial markets for producers in the parent state, an arrangement that gives exporting manufacturers a compelling interest in the maintenance and even expansion of the boundaries of the colonial empire. Britain's shift in the 1840s to free trade changed the dynamic and meant that British manufacturers no longer had the same stake in the preservation of empire. On the other hand, the flood of British capital into the British North American colonies in the 1850s owed more to their status as British possessions than to their inherent attractiveness as fields for investment. British financiers rather than British manufacturers were the primary beneficiaries of Britain's colonial political relationship with the North American colonies. Because the military, naval, and other costs of empire were born by the average British taxpayer, one could say that those who invested in the colonies benefited from a hidden subsidy.

British imperialism has been represented as a quest to obtain raw materials and to capture markets for British manufacturers,[3] but the figures for British trade with British North America on the eve of Confederation call this view into question. Relative to total imports and exports, trade with British North America was of minor importance to Britain. In the period 1856–60, just 2.74 percent of British exports went to the North American colonies; the figure for imports, 3.3 percent, was only slightly more impressive.[4] The modest extent of this trading relationship was consistent with a broader trend, namely, the relative unimportance of trade with colonies as a proportion of overseas trade. Three-quarters of UK exports went to independent countries and only one-quarter went to British possessions, a ratio that remained roughly constant over the next few decades.[5] In the same period, just twenty-one percent of imports came from British colonies.[6]

For many British manufacturers in this era, European markets were far more important than overseas ones, so much so that one historian of intra-European trade speaks of the decades after 1860 as the era of the "First Common Market."[7] The United States, a sovereign country, was Britain's most important extra-European customer in that period.[8] Looking at the overall trade statistics helps us to see why many British manufacturers thought that the Little Englander viewpoint was reasonable. After all, why pay taxes to defend a colony that took relatively few British goods? Why not let Canada be absorbed by the United States, which was Britain's best overseas customer?

One thing that kept the North American colonies from being totally irrelevant to Britain's merchants and factory owners was their moderate importance as suppliers of several commodities fish,[9] timber,[10] and wheat.[11] These commodities have been the subject of extensive study by Canadian economic historians working within the framework of the staples thesis, a theory that held that the production of raw materials (stables) for export was the central fact of Canadian economic and political history.[12] But while this trade was very important to the North American colonies, British North America was only one of many suppliers that served the United Kingdom's needs. The importance of Canada to British wheat consumers, for instance, was actually quite modest. Although Canada's share of the British wheat market increased during the Crimean War, it quickly fell back to pre-war levels with the coming of the peace. In 1858 the United Kingdom's wheat imports totalled £9 million. Of this amount, only £230,000 came from British North America, whereas £1.29 million came from Russia, £1.46 million from Prussia, £1.46 million from the United States, and £1.78 million from France.[13] In 1860 the Board of Trade considered the Province of Canada to be one of the United Kingdom's significant sources of wheat and flour, but listed it after the United States, Spain, France, and the Hanseatic Towns.

British North America was more important as a supplier of timber and in some segments of the wood trade its producers were dominant. In 1858, for instance, forty-five percent of the deals and battens and twenty-six percent of the staves imported by the United Kingdom came from the North American colonies.[14] In general, however, British North America was only one of several tributary regions that satisfied industrial Britain's voracious appetite for raw materials. Moreover, there were no signs that a change in British North America's political status would disrupt the flow of raw materials. If France and the United States exported wheat to Britain, would not an independent Republic of Canada continue to do likewise?

Commercial considerations of this sort help to explain a striking feature of the British politics of Confederation, namely, the near total apathy of Britain's timber, wheat, and fish merchants. In the 1840s organizations representing people in these lines of trade had been actively involved in the struggle over the end of colonial preference,[15] but in the 1860s those who imported raw materials from British North America were indifferent bystanders in the political struggle over the region's constitutional future. When we look at the petitions and meetings associated with Confederation, the names of the great timber merchants discussed by Arthur Lower rarely appear. J.C. Sim of the timber company Churchhill and Sim attended a few meetings of the BNAA, but his involvement was atypical of the London timber merchants as a whole, and he soon stopped coming.[16]

By all accounts, the merchants who imported raw materials were similarly uninterested in the Little England ideas propounded by Manchester manufacturers disgusted with Canadian protectionism. There is no record of the timber and wheat merchants doing anything to either oppose or support the proposals to get rid of the colonies or to federate them. Politically, they were like an inert gas. Under mercantilism, it had really mattered to importers whether or not the Union Jack flew over a territory. The apathetic attitude to Confederation displayed by the commodity merchants suggests that by the 1860s they had realized that the boundaries of formal empire no longer mattered that much to their businesses.

The aggregate export and import figures lent credence to the Little Englander argument that commercial Britain gained little from retaining colonies of white settlement. Confronted with these statistics, contemporaries who defended the political connection to the colonies were forced to use other numbers. Archibald Hamilton and J. Beaufort Hurlburt, two writers who were strongly committed to the colonies, made much of figures showing that the average person in the North American colonies used more British goods than the average American. In their eyes, the per capita figures proved that trade still followed the flag.[17] Judging by the winning entry, the old association between formal political dominion and trade was very much alive in 1862, when an essay competition asked manual workers to explain the benefits to the working classes of retaining overseas colonies.[18]

Others, however, were less convinced. For one thing, the average Canadian, unlike the average Australian, did not purchase markedly more British goods than a typical American.[19] The fact that the tariffs of the United States were generally higher than those of the settlement colonies was sometimes used as an argument for keeping the colonies. However, the advent of colonial fiscal autonomy meant that this argument no longer worked as well as it once had. The incendiary Canadian tariff of 1859, which was widely perceived to be protectionist in intent, was frequently mentioned in British discussions of colonial defence expenditure during the American Civil War.[20] British manufacturers could see little profit in paying to defend colonies that leaned towards American-style protectionism. Even the *Economist*, a newspaper that wanted Canada to remain part of the empire, conceded that Canada's status as a colony made little difference in the hard-nosed world of trade and exports.[21]

While some Little Englanders wanted to get rid of all of Britain's colonies, others placed the North American possessions squarely in their sights. Tax-averse manufacturers had excellent reasons for focusing on this region of the empire; for the North American colonies took fewer goods than the much less populous Australasian colonies.[22] Moreover, the North American colonies were protected from a potentially powerful neighbour by an extensive network of British garrisons, while the Australian colonies paid for their own (admittedly limited) military needs.[23] In 1860 the costs of garrisoning British North America had been highlighted by the report of a parliamentary military committee.[24] The publication of its report coincided with an increase in the tax burden in the early 1860s: in the space of a few years, the income tax rate in Britain increased from five pence to ten pence in the pound. Although very low by modern standards, this tax rate was the source of bitter complaints. In this context, expenditure on colonial garrisons was an easy target.[25]

Given that Canada took relatively few British manufactured goods, it is not surprising that leading anti-imperialists such as Richard Cobden and John Bright were factory owners.[26] Manchester, the great manufacturing city, was a centre of Little Englander sentiment. Moreover, Manchester's mill owners knew that the raw material of chief interest to them, cotton, could never be produced in the cold climate of British North America. Of course, not every manufacturer was an advocate of separation, but this was the predominant attitude in manufacturing circles, as Alexander T. Galt, the Canadian minister of Finance who had authored the 1859 tariff, discovered when he met with the Manchester Chamber of Commerce in September 1862.[27]

The politics of social class also informed middle-class Little Englander sentiment. In the minds of many middle-class factory owners, Britain's aristocrats were drones who survived by taxing the productive classes of society. The colonies, along with the armed services, were an integral part of the old aristocratic establishment despised by middle-class radicals. In the 1850s Bright had called the British Empire "a gigantic system of outdoor relief for the aristocracy" and had declared that the colonial empire existed in order to create positions for aristocratic younger sons in the army, navy, and colonial service. According to Bright, shedding the colonies would mean that tax relief could be granted to the productive classes in British society, the businessmen and workers. Moreover, it would benefit the colonists themselves by allowing the settlement colonies to develop into great republics. The only people who would suffer, according to Bright, were the promoters of speculative ventures in the City and the parasitic aristocrats who governed the colonies at inflated salaries.[28]

The role of Cobden, Bright, and the other exponents of Manchester Liberalism in the politics of Confederation will become apparent in subsequent chapters. In articulating a Little England policy, they came into conflict with the representatives of the City, London's financial services sector. British high finance took a very different view of British America and wanted the political bond with the North American colonies preserved. The British North American

Association, formed in 1862 to represent people who had invested in the North American colonies, was strongly opposed to the doctrines of the Little Englanders and thought that preserving British sovereignty over northern North America was vitally important. The investors' commitment to the project of upholding British sovereignty in these lands was connected to a reality of international business that has recently attracted the attention of scholars, namely, that the legal regime is far more important to investors and people in the service sector than to businesses engaged in trading essentially unregulated tangible goods such as raw fish or finished cotton.[29]

The export of services is sometimes viewed as a very modern form of international trade. Nevertheless, even in the middle of the nineteenth century, the period popularly remembered as a period of British pre-eminence in manufacturing, the service sector was already making an important contribution to Britain's national accounts. Indeed, the United Kingdom ran a deficit in visible goods that was partially defrayed by income from overseas investments and from exports of services.[30] Part of this business was with the lands that later became Canada.

Shipping services were among Britain's premier exports at this time. Gauging how much of this service Britain sold to British North America is extremely difficult because colonial ships were, in the eyes of the British authorities, British. Indeed, many timber ships of British registry had been constructed in North America.[31] Before 1850 the carrying trade between Britain and her colonies had been reserved to British and colonial vessels, but the repeal of the Navigation Acts had allowed low-cost foreign competitors to engross much of the business of carrying goods to and from British North America. In particular, the timber trade between Quebec and Liverpool had suffered from the intrusion of low-cost Norwegian vessels. Foreign competition caused many British shippers to abandon the route and was a source of bitter complaint when a parliamentary committee took testimony in London in 1860. Aside from two exceptions noted below, shipowners did not become involved in the politics of Confederation in Britain. Perhaps this was because they were preoccupied with their futile campaign to reinstate the Navigation Acts.[32]

British North America was a lucrative market for British insurance companies. Although the volume of business British insurance companies did in the North American colonies varied considerably, several firms, most notably Standard Life of Edinburgh, took a particular interest in this region of the empire. The eighth earl of Elgin, best known to Canadians for signing the Rebellion Losses Bill, was a deputy governor of Standard Life from 1841 until his death in India in 1862. Elgin played an important role in the foundation of the Colonial Life Assurance Company in 1846, the subsidiary of Standard Life that handled the firm's overseas operations. Although offices were opened in Australia and elsewhere, the principal market for Colonial Life was always Canada.[33] By 1866 the company had an agent and a designated medical officer in nearly every market town in the Canadas.[34]

The life insurance business was only one of the many financial threads connecting British North America and Britain on the eve of Confederation. British North America enjoyed privileged access to London's capital market because British investors liked the idea of investing in British colonies.[35] Popular guides to investing perceived important differences between British possessions and independent countries such as the United States. The author of one handbook remarked that colonial bonds were "generally considered next to English Government securities" in terms of safety. Colonies borrowing in London paid a very modest risk premium that reflected the low probability that they would repudiate their debts.[36] Even publications with Little Englander leanings equated British colonial status with fiscal responsibility. In 1866 London's *Daily News* declared: "British provinces never repudiate their engagements."[37]

In the decades before Confederation, British North America received far more British capital than the United States in per capita terms,[38] a pattern related to both the growing aversion of British investors to the United States and the different financial needs of a newer and less-developed country. While the United States may have been popular with British investors during the brief American bond manias of the 1830s and 1840s, the tendency of American states to repudiate debts deeply distressed British investors. Especially after the famous Pennsylvania default of 1842, British investors tended to shy away from American investments in favour of domestic, imperial, and European ones.[39] The overall level of British investment in the United States fell during the middle decades of the century.[40]

John Madden estimates that in 1860 Britons held American securities with a nominal or par value of £35 million, of which there was £3 million in federal bonds, £15 million in railway bonds, £5 million in company shares, £11 million in state and municipal bonds, and the rest in miscellaneous securities. Madden cautions that these are par values and that many of these securities were severely depreciated, meaning that the real level of investment was actually lower.[41] The population of the United States in 1860 is known and can be used as a divisor: Madden's estimate suggests that there was roughly £1.2.0 of British capital invested in the country for each American in 1860.

The equivalent figures for British North America were much higher. In the North American provinces, the analogues for the federal and state debts of the United States were the provincial debentures. Amounting to £8.9 million in 1855, the Canadian provincial debt rose to £11.9 million in 1860 and £13.6 million in 1863.[42] Most of this debt was held in the United Kingdom: two-thirds of the Dominion's public debt was domiciled in London in 1874 and it is unlikely that the percentage was lower in 1860.[43] Unlike state bonds, colonial government bonds were perceived as a very safe investment. Before the Civil War, their market prices were always above par value. Even in 1863, two years after the attack on Fort Sumter, Canadian government bonds were trading at prices near their face value. Although they fell dramatically after that, it is interesting that Canadian bonds held their value during two years marked by massive bloodshed and destruction in a neighbouring country.[44]

With two and a half million people in 1860, the Province of Canada's per capita provincial debt was £4 15s 3d sterling. In that year, Nova Scotia's public debt was £1,012,536 (or £3.1.1 per capita) and New Brunswick's was £1,012,536 (precisely £4 per capita). Using the proportion of Canada's debt held in Britain in 1874 as a guide allows us to estimate the value of Canadian public securities held in London in 1860 at £3.2.10 per capita. This figure is substantially higher than the £1.2.0 that Madden estimates Britons had invested in *all* classes of American securities, public and private, per head of population. The figure of £3.2.10 does not include British investments in the colony that are more difficult to value, such as municipal bonds, railways, and other private ventures. H.C. Pentland estimates that the Province of Canada imported an astonishing $100 million in mostly British capital between 1850 and 1859.[45]

Discussing Canadian-American differences in the penetration of British investment, D.C.M. Platt and Jeremy Adelman observe that "whereas for the United States foreign capital was a luxury which permitted accelerated economic expansion on the secure base of domestic resources, for Canada (on any major scale), to borrow abroad was a virtual necessity."[46] Indeed, the preference for colonial investments displayed by wealthy Britons was so marked that it disturbed some free-market purists who worried that the empire's boundaries were distorting the worldwide allocation of British capital. In their view, only non-political factors such as the location of mineral deposits should determine where money was invested.[47] The preference on the part of investors for colonial over American projects was likely rooted in the legal and constitutional structures that Douglass North and other New Institutionalist economists rightly regard as crucial to economic growth: English or Scottish investors knew that money invested in the colonies remained under the protective umbrella of the empire and its legal system.[48]

The direction of British capital to Canada may also have been an unintended consequence of certain features of the American legal system. Madden argues that the status of the foreigner in American law repelled British investment. He observes that "the legal security of investments in American railroads was always a source of irritation to British investors" and that this was partly caused by "the federal nature of the United States and partly because of their inability to obtain legal redress when their securities failed to pay interest or dividends."[49] Moreover, many states curtailed the right of foreigners to own land[50] or to serve as corporate directors.[51] In the British colonies, laws restricting foreign participation were not an issue, at least not for fellow British subjects. Indeed, as Peter Baskerville has shown, anti-foreigner sentiment in Canada had been directed against the Americans and had worked to tighten the British hold over the colony's railway industry.[52]

While it is unlikely that significant volumes of British capital flowed into the colonies from patriotic rather than self-interested considerations on the part of investors, patriotism cannot be excluded entirely from the picture. Investing has always had a sentimental component. Moreover, the status of the provinces as British possessions may have created the (perhaps false) sense that conditions there were not as different as those in the United States. The financial sections of many British newspapers followed the semi-official *Course of the Exchange*, the official register of prices on the London Stock Exchange, in differentiating colonial stocks from foreign (including American) ones. Typically, quotations for colonial government securities from all over the British Empire were lumped together under one heading, with Indian and colonial railways in another. United States and European securities were listed separately.[53] It seems that in the mental landscape of the compilers of financial data, the world consisted of concentric circles centred on London and that the overseas British possessions fell in a zone in between Ireland and foreign countries.

British North America offered a wide variety of options for the British investor, but some of these investments were less dependent on the institutions of formal colonialism than others. For instance, Upper Canada's status as part of the British Empire was irrelevant to the operation of Edward Miall and Company, a small carpentry works in Oshawa, Upper Canada, incorporated in the United Kingdom.[54] Indeed, there was no political or legal reason why Edward Miall's business could not have been located in a town in the northern United States. On the other hand, colonial status was extremely relevant to other enterprises in the colonies. The imperial charter incorporating the Bank of British North America was legally valid in the colonies precisely because they were colonies, rather than American states.[55] Investors in British North America's railways and land development companies had a similarly strong interest in seeing British sovereignty over the colonies preserved. Moreover, these enterprises were highly politicized: their investors understood that future dividends depended on the choices made by politicians.

The Hudson's Bay Company had been created in 1670 by a royal charter granted to court favourites and politics had been its lifeblood ever since. The political fortunes of the company were about to change. The superficial stability of the company in the 1850s and early 1860s obscured the powerful historical forces that would soon threaten the very survival of the firm.[56] Demographic pressure in eastern North America was building and in Upper Canada, Reform publications such as George Brown's *Globe* began to question the legitimacy of the HBC's title to its lands.[57] In the eyes of free traders in England,[58] the company was an anachronism, a chartered monopoly in an age of free enterprise. The abolition of East India Company rule in 1858 had set a dangerous precedent.

An equally politicized and Anglocentric enterprise was the Canada Company, which controlled a million-acre tract in Upper Canada. The company had been created in the aftermath of the War of 1812 as a way of solving a number of problems peculiar to Upper Canada, including the failure of the Clergy Reserves to generate much revenue for the Anglican church.[59] John Galt, a Scottish novelist, superintended the company's Canadian operations in the 1820s. Under his leadership, the Canada Company had attracted settlers by making considerable capital expenditures on roads, inns, and harbours.[60] John's son, Alexander T. Galt, later served as manager of the similarly structured British American Land Company (BALC), which operated in the Eastern Townships. In 1858 Alexander Galt become inspector general, or minister of Finance, in the Cartier-Macdonald government, a position that brought him to London for frequent meetings with Thomas Baring, George Carr Glyn, and individuals who would later play a role in the BNAA.[61]

Although their structure was somewhat different from that of the land companies, the landed credit companies served a similar function in that they allowed colonial land to be developed with capital supplied by the gentlemanly capitalists of London. Acting under the general direction of its trustees, Thomas Baring, MP, and George Carr Glyn, MP, the Trust and Loan Company of Upper Canada lent British money to Canadians on landed security. Its clients included municipalities wanting to borrow on the security of future property tax revenues as well as individuals. The Trust and Loan Company enjoyed political clout and special legal privileges: legislation in 1858 limited the interest Canadian banks could charge to seven percent but did not touch the limit of eight percent stipulated in the company's special charter.[62] The company's Canadian operations were based in Kingston and John A. Macdonald guarded its interests in the legislature.[63] The Canada Landed Credit Company in Toronto functioned along similar lines, although it was controlled by Canadian merchants. The Toronto firm used British imperial patriotism in its appeals to British investors,[64] emphasizing the loyalty Canada had displayed during the Crimean War.[65]

The Trust and Loan Company was less bombastically patriotic when trying to raise capital, but its promotional literature also stressed that Canada was a British colony. The 1851 prospectus noted that a similar firm had existed in New York since 1830, but it claimed advantages the American firm did not possess, including the right to charge up to eight percent interest, which was then seen as sufficient latitude in rates. Another attractive feature of Canada pointed out in its prospectus was the public registries of deeds that had been established in both sections of the province. The prospectus argued that the system of registration ensured that land in Canada was excellent collateral.[66] The Canadian landed credit companies were profitable and quickly imitated by people in other British colonies. London's *Money Market Review* observed in 1863 that "the success of the Trust and Loan Company of Upper Canada has been attended with the formation of several other companies on a similar principle" operating in colonial territories from New Zealand to Natal.[67]

Another form of investment were the Canadian municipal bonds marketed in London by Glyn, Mills and Company.[68] The popularity of Canadian municipal bonds as investments was likely related to the widespread belief that the imperial government would not permit a public entity in a colony to default.[69] As one financial journal put it, colonial public borrowers enjoyed a "prestige" in the British money market not enjoyed by other overseas borrowers.[70] The 1861 default of the City of Hamilton, Upper Canada, demonstrated to a group of unlucky British investors that this assumption was not always correct. In this case, the imperial government proved unwilling to exert itself on behalf of the bondholders, politely listening to their complaints but doing nothing to pressure the municipality into resuming payments.

When the bondholders despatched an attorney to levy a property rate on their behalf, Hamilton's clerk "accidentally" misplaced the assessment roll needed to collect the outstanding bond interest. The outraged editor of the *Money Market Review* believed "that if Canada had been an independent State the bondholders would have had more attention from our Ambassador than there have met with either from Her Majesty's Viceroy or our Colonial Minister."[71] The people of Hamilton, he later declared, had borrowed money in London "under the guise of fellow-subjects," but when the British investors attempted to use the normal legal procedures to recover their money, cosubjecthood had been revealed as a "mockery, a delusion, and a snare." The British troops stationed in Hamilton had done nothing to help the bondholders recover their money.[72] Noting that France and Britain were currently working to protect the rights of the holders of Mexican bonds, the newspaper declared that "Canada being a crown colony is not to be perverted into a licence for tricking Englishmen out of their money."[73]

Because of the stance assumed by the provincial and imperial governments, the Hamilton bondholders were forced to return to their negotiations with the municipality in a position of weakness.[74] When the terms of the settlement were finally announced, the *Money Market Review* was scathing in its criticism of Canada. It declared that the institutional rot in the province extended from the "Prime Minister down to the humble functionary already referred to" and gleefully noted the higher borrowing costs now faced by Canada: "The quotations of their Government stocks in our market are the lowest of all colonial government securities."[75]

In reality, the depreciation of the provincial securities was less a function of the Hamilton debacle than the political turbulence created by the ongoing Civil War. Moreover, the bonds of other Canadian municipalities continued to sell after Hamilton's default, perhaps because investors believed that the problems of Hamilton were peculiar to that municipality.[76] Moreover, the prices of Canadian government bonds did not fall until 1863, by which point the Hamilton controversy had been underway for several years.

This fall in prices was especially unfortunate because issuing debt in London was crucially important to the political and economic systems of the colonies. The public debts of the provincial governments were extremely important both in terms of volume and because they helped to create other types of investment. In his exploration of the process by which pre-Confederation Canadian governments borrowed in the London money market, Michael Piva concludes that the state played an even greater role in Canadian economic life than earlier economic historians had believed. Not only were railways financed by huge government deficits but borrowing in London made it possible to sustain Canada's chronic trade imbalance. Rosemary Langhout's research on Nova Scotia and New Brunswick shows that government borrowing in London had a major impact on the lower provinces as well.[77]

In selling bonds in the London money market, the governments of colonies did not deal directly with individual investors. Two London bankers, George Carr Glyn of Glyn, Mills and Company and Thomas Baring of Baring Brothers, were the London financial agents of the Province of Canada. Baring Brothers alone represented New Brunswick and Nova Scotia. In choosing London agents, the provincial government had acted wisely. While Barings' annual revenues were never as large as the combined ones of the Rothschild families, some contemporaries believed the Barings were more important politically. The firm's involvement in the financing of the French reparations arranged at the Congress of Vienna led one French diplomat to quip in 1818 that there were six great powers in Europe: England, France, Prussia, Russia, Austria, and Baring Brothers.[78]

Thomas Baring was a partner in the bank from 1828 until his death in 1873. His distinguished political career extended over much of the same period. In 1843, when he stood as a protectionist candidate opposed to repeal of the Corn Laws and Navigation Acts, contemporaries described him as the most important single capitalist in the City. Benjamin Disraeli asked him to serve as Chancellor of the Exchequer in the early 1850s but Baring refused, pleading that private business took up too much of his time. In addition, Baring was chairman of the Lloyd's insurance syndicate for many years. He was an advocate for Latin American bondholders, the godfather of the Corporation of Foreign Bondholders, and an active member of Parliament. He was involved in London's 1862 International Exhibition and countless other philanthropic enterprises.[79]

The involvement of the House of Baring in North American finance had begun before Thomas's birth. In 1803 the firm financed the Louisiana Purchase. During the War of 1812, Barings' continued to service the American debt held in Britain, although they prudently refused to issue new bonds for the US government.[80] Mixing politics and business sometimes led to accusations of unpatriotic behaviour. Charges of this sort were made when Lord Ashburton, Thomas's uncle, negotiated an end to the boundary dispute between Maine and New Brunswick in 1842, a diplomatic manoeuvre denounced by Lord Palmerston and others as a sell-out.[81] While there can be no doubt that Ashburton thought that the treaty was in Britain's national interest, his American wife and extensive Maine land grants were not overlooked by his many critics.

In the 1830s Barings' helped issue American private and public securities in the London money market. The firm typically took large blocks of debt on consignment in the expectation that they could be disposed of with profit. While there was potential for gain, the risks involved were serious. If for some reason the securities could not be sold at a reasonable price, Barings' would have to hold them until circumstances improved. The bank prudently shared the risks involved with the stockbroking firms that dealt with individual investors by striking agreements whereby the subcontractors took portions of the debt on consignment from Barings'. This meant that if the bonds proved unsaleable, the bank would not be left with all the losses. Instead, it would be the centre of a phalanx of London firms able to work as a group to improve the situation.

At first, the House of Baring's North American interests were primarily in the United States, but that began to change after 1837, when colonial business became more and more important. The shift in focus was partly driven by state government defaults and partly by the war between President Andrew Jackson and the Second Bank of the United States (an entity closely tied to Barings').[82] When Pennsylvania defaulted, Barings' and another London bank, Overend, Gurney and Company, provided the funds to help unseat the politicians who had been responsible. Their campaign involved newspaper subsidies and getting local clergymen to deliver sermons on the moral aspects of the issue.[83]

A new crop of politicians was installed in office and the state resumed payments, but the episode badly damaged British confidence in American state bonds. In the eyes of the English squires and clergymen served by Barings', American securities were too risky.[84] The growing dissatisfaction with American investments coincided with the decision of the Province of Upper Canada to begin looking to the London capital market. After an unsuccessful attempt to raise money for canals through Thomas Wilson and Company, Upper Canada switched its accounts to Baring and Glyn. Officially, only Glyn was the province's agent,[85] although the close working relationship between Baring and Glyn led many contemporaries to refer to the two men as Upper Canada's financial agents. Their dual agency was formalized by the United Province of Canada after 1841 and led to their involvement in other Canadian ventures.[86]

Given the global reach and domestic stature of his bank, it is not surprising that Upper Canada would have wanted Thomas Baring to be involved in its financial affairs. George Carr Glyn was a less obvious choice because Glyn, Mills and Co. had focused on domestic business for most its history. However, Glyn's bank had taken a leading role in the building of Britain's canal network and this fit Upper Canada's borrowing requirements. In the 1840s the bank played a similarly important role in creating the British railway system. Glyn's greatest accomplishment was undoubtedly the London and North Western Railway, the main national artery from London to Birmingham.[87]

When shares and bonds of the Grand Trunk Railway of Canada were issued in London in 1853, Baring and Glyn agreed to market them. This was natural because they were the agents of the provincial government and the railway was the creation of a group of politician-businessmen, most notably Francis Hincks.[88] The Grand Trunk was not the product of a single coherent plan but the result of the fusion of a number of schemes. One of them was the Halifax-Quebec railway, a concept mentioned in Lord Durham's report of 1839, which proposed solutions to the problems that had caused the rebellions in Lower and Upper Canada. During the British railway mania of the mid-1840s, there was a brief flurry of interest in building the Halifax-Quebec line. A few years later, the concept was revived when Lord Grey, the Colonial Secretary, conceived a scheme whereby Irish peasants would be settled along the wilderness sections of the line in military-agricultural colonies. However, Britain's Board of Railway Commissioners withheld its assent to the plan on financial grounds.[89]

The focus then shifted to a railway that would connect all the major centres of Canada. The plan presented to the investing public in 1853 involved a line running from Sarnia through Toronto and Montreal before branching in two, one line running towards Quebec City, the other through the Eastern Townships to Portland, Maine. The line was promoted in London by Baring, Glyn, and two stockbrokers, William Chapman and Phillip Cazenove, who did not share the aversion to "company accoucheuring" felt by most stockbrokers.[90] If all had gone according to plan, their involvement with this railway would have ended with the sale of the securities and the collection of their commission. Indeed, there was every expectation that Cazenove and Chapman would make money from the transaction. Cazenove, a highly respected figure, provided investment advice to a distinguished client base and urged his wealthy clients to invest in the railway. Moreover, the Canadian legislature's Guarantee Act of 1849 seemed to promise a sure return on investment.[91]

Despite all these factors in their favour, the Grand Trunk shares were not popular with investors, leaving Baring, Glyn, and the brokers who had taken blocks of stock on consignment in the lurch.[92] A complicating issue was that the names of Baring and Glyn had been added to the published list of directors without their consent. Because they owned large numbers of as yet unsaleable securities, Baring and Glyn were in a vulnerable position. Rather than demanding the removal of their names from the misleading prospectus, Baring and Glyn resolved to work with the railway to make it a success so that they could eventually sell the stock and bonds at a profit.

The other Canadian railways did not perform very well as investments, but the Grand Trunk was nothing short of a financial disaster. Given the magnitude of the enterprise and the amount of British capital invested in it, its problems were bound to affect the relations between the colony and the metropole. Even as early as the mid-1850s, there were growing complaints from the shareholders about expensive building materials, corruption, incompetent management, and the presence of Canadian politicians on the company's board. The more fundamental problems with the railway, among them that it competed with the most magnificent system of water transport in the world, the Great Lakes-Laurentian system, were ignored.

Cost overruns during construction led to new issues of debt and increased subsidies from the Canadian government. The subsidies were largely paid for by raising loans in London rather than by raising taxes in Canada.[93] In the short term, Baring and Glyn benefited from this decision because it created commission income on bond sales. By 1860 around fifteen million pounds sterling had been invested in the Grand Trunk Railway and its allied works, such as the spectacular Victoria Bridge at Montreal. Contemporaries agreed that almost all of this capital had come from the British Isles rather than from local savings. Much of the money came from Baring and Glyn and a few other large investors, although there were many small investors as well. Baring and Glyn both died wealthy, escaping the fate of people like Sir Morton Peto, MP, the contractor paid in Grand Trunk bonds who declared bankruptcy in 1866.[94] Nevertheless, their losses were serious and represented a significant portion of their net worth. By 1860 the House of Baring had lost a total of £1.2 million because of the Grand Trunk fiasco.[95]

With each financial crisis, the reflex of the railway was to look to governments first. When it came to be used as a precedent for additional demands, some politicians began to regret the 1849 Guarantee Act. While the government was only legally obliged to guarantee interest on a limited number of bonds, many British investors now argued that the legislation had implied a moral guarantee to give the railway whatever was needed to break even. At the same time, grumbling in the colonies about the Grand Trunk's pervasive political influence was intensifying. Over the course of the 1850s, the Canadian government issued a massive amount of debt in order to inject fresh capital into the colony's railways, but it was never enough for the Grand Trunk. Railway subsidies were justified by pointing to positive externalities, but modern scholars argue that the social rate of return of the Grand Trunk was low.[96] This analysis helps to explain the public anger towards the subventions the railway received.

It is difficult to determine the precise number of British people who lost money by investing in the Grand Trunk.[97] In the absence of a register of share- and bondholders, we can make an educated guess as to the profile of the typical investor. Historians Lance Davis and Robert Huttenback found that imperial investments were preferred by the old landed elite and were avoided by those whose money came from manufacturing.[98] In 1864 the *Economist* believed that government-guaranteed bonds of the sort issued by railways in British possessions were chiefly popular with the "country gentry."[99] In other words, many Grand Trunk investors were members of the social class that continued to hold the reins of power in England until the 1880s.[100] They were a potentially powerful constituency.

By the late 1850s, several distinct approaches to solving the problems of the Grand Trunk had emerged. A few of the smaller British investors attempted to use guilt to get money out of Baring[101] or simply threw themselves on his mercy.[102] Aside from these individual initiatives, there were two major schools of thought within the ranks of the Grand Trunk investors about how to rectify the situation. The Liverpool faction was a constant thorn in the side of both the London board of the company and its

salaried managers in Canada. Indeed, at an 1862 shareholders'
meeting one member of this group went so far as to suggest that
Thomas Baring deserved to go to prison.[103] The leader of the group
was Henry Cleaver Chapman, a broker who came from a prominent Liverpool family and whose brother was a Montreal wine
merchant.[104] Chapman undertook fact-finding missions to Canada
aimed at uncovering waste and managerial incompetence.[105]

In their communications with Baring, Chapman and the other
Liverpool investors made detailed practical suggestions and demanded major changes in personnel. For instance, they demanded
that the grade of a particular stretch of track be reduced and that
General Manager Thomas E. Blackwell be fired for incompetence.[106]
They also advocated the depoliticization of the railway, maintaining
that the benefits accruing from the firm's close ties to the Canadian
government were outweighed by the costs. These costs included
the construction of politically necessary but commercially unviable
lines. The Liverpool shareholders thought that the railway should be
run on strictly commercial principles.[107]

In contrast, political and legal solutions were central to the London
party's plan to rescue the railway, although they agreed with the
Liverpool faction on the need to find some efficiencies. William
Newmarch's 1861 plan for the salvation of the Grand Trunk gives us
a sense of the overall approach of the London group. Among his
many recommendations, Newmarch suggested improvements in
traffic management and the more efficient use of rolling stock, but
his main emphasis was on getting more money from the provincial
legislature. In his eyes, any solution would require a substantial increase in the postal subsidy paid by the Canadian government and
the construction of the Halifax-Quebec line. He favoured the latter
measure as it would inject traffic into the massively unprofitable section that had been built east of Quebec City. Newmarch proposed a
complex financial transaction that would reorder the company's finances and reduce its borrowing costs, but any such operation
would be dependent on political decisions made in Canada.[108]

In the 1870s the loss of political power in Canada by the Grand
Trunk and its replacement by newer railway interests forced
the Grand Trunk to adopt the apolitical approach outlined by the
Liverpool party in the 1850s. A decade before, however, the
London group's approach was in the ascendant. The clash be-
tween the Liverpool and London factions was more than simply a

squabble within a firm about how best to achieve profitability. In fact, the dispute says a great deal about the nature of capitalism in Canada on the eve of Confederation.

The importance of the disagreement is illuminated by Joseph Schumpeter's concept of "pure capitalism." Schumpeter viewed all existing capitalist systems as a mixture of apolitical businesses (which he admired) and the politicized firms he linked to imperialism and nationalism. According to his typology, businessmen of the pure-capitalism variety seek to get rich by making their firms more efficient, a boring and pedestrian task compared to the political manoeuvring employed by the other sort of businessman.[109]

While the terminology is different, the concept of "crony capitalism" used by some modern development theorists also illuminates the approach of the London party. Development theorists who employ the term crony capitalism argue that its predominance over pure capitalism in developing countries has unwholesome effects on business and politics alike. In a society where businessmen get rich through political connections rather than by making better mousetraps, the political process is corrupted at the same time as firms lose the incentive to be efficient.[110]

Two very different forms of capitalism were at work in British North America on the eve of Confederation. On the one hand, there was the type of capitalism represented by the Liverpool party, which corresponds to Schumpeter's concept of pure capitalism. The carpentry shop of Edward Miall and Co. is another example of pure capitalism in the colonies. In sharp contrast were fundamentally colonial enterprises such as the Hudson's Bay Company, Canada Company, and Grand Trunk. These firms depended on the political process for the subsidies and legal privileges that were their very lifeblood.[111]

In seeking political rather than business solutions to their predicament, the London faction within the Grand Trunk faced numerous obstacles. The Colonial Office had to balance the concerns of British investors with the more important task of preserving the goodwill of the colony and eliminating grievances that could lead to separation. More important was the financial condition of the Province of Canada. The provincial government was heavily in debt and ran frequent budgetary deficits. Politicians knew that increased subsidies to the Grand Trunk would mean higher taxes, which would be unpopular with the electorate.[112]

By the 1850s Baring's name was fairly well known in Canada and some people had come to resent his involvement in their affairs. The historian F.X. Garneau, for instance, attributed the British government's forced union of the Canadas in 1841 to the influence of the Baring family.[113] George Brown also denounced Baring and attributed the collapse of the 1858 "Short Administration" to his evil sway over Sir Edmund Head.[114] Sir Edmund certainly sympathized with the plight of Baring and the other Grand Trunk investors in England and felt that the Canadian government ought to treat them with "more honour" (i.e., bestow more subsidies),[115] although it is unclear whether this attitude influenced his actions during the ministerial crisis of July-August 1858. During this crisis, an administration that included George Brown had been formed. The governor's refusal to call the election requested by this government resulted in its defeat and the return of Macdonald and Cartier to power.

While they faced many obstacles in their quest for financial salvation, the Grand Trunk investors enjoyed a number of advantages. The Cartier-Macdonald ministry was deeply concerned about the line's financial health. In fact, Cartier was the railway's solicitor and John Ross, the president of the railway, sat in the provincial cabinet. Another advantage enjoyed by the Grand Trunk was the sympathy of the *Canadian News and British American Intelligencer*, a London newspaper that specialized in business and political news from the colonies.

Like many in the broad middle of British politics, London's *Canadian News* was hostile to the anti-imperialist ideas expressed by Goldwin Smith, the London *Daily News* and the Cobdenite *Star and Dial*, also out of London. However, the *Canadian News* went further than most publications in its defence of Canada and the colonial connection. Even when the *Times*, the great bellwether of English opinion, expressed irritation at Canadian tariffs or the failure to pass a proper militia bill, the *Canadian News* viewed the Canadian situation sympathetically, counselling people in the metropolis not to overreact. The important role of the *Canadian News* in the shaping of colonial policy will become evident in subsequent chapters.[116] Baring and Glyn were lucky to enjoy the paper's support; for they were in an unenviable situation by the end of 1859 and things were about to deteriorate further. This sequence of events is the subject of the next chapter.

3

From Bad to Worse: 1860–1862

The first twenty-four months of the 1860s were a terrible time for those Britons who had invested in the North American colonies. The decade began with the festive visit of the Prince of Wales,[1] but a far more significant event in the history of British investment in the colonies occurred on the first Tuesday in November 1860 when Abraham Lincoln was elected president of the United States. The sharp downturn in the North American economy that swiftly followed Lincoln's election was only a foretaste of the tribulations that lay in store for British investors in Canada.

The Civil War was an "equal-opportunity" crisis that threatened profitable ventures (such as the Trust and Loan Company) and non-performing investments alike, but the impact of the war was most acute in the railway sector. At the Grand Trunk, the crisis dashed the hopes that had been raised by the opening in 1860 of the Victoria Bridge. Connecting Montreal Island to the south shore of the St Lawrence, the bridge made it possible to send traffic over the entire length of the line. In the late 1850s investors had been promised that once the bridge was operational, the railway would become profitable. However, the anticipated traffic receipts did not materialize due to the drastic reductions in crossborder trade that began in 1860. Everyone knew the railway was in trouble and a vicious cycle was set in motion: shippers became hesitant to send perishable and other goods on the Grand Trunk, fearing that if the railway were seized by creditors, their property would be left stranded in locked wagons. When the Grand Trunk missed interest payments on its bonds, the prospect of a bankrupt railway in default began to set the line's many classes of creditors at odds. They began arguing about priority of payment.

The visit of the Prince of Wales had thrown the province's railway system into the spotlight and the Grand Trunk seized the resulting political opportunities. Soon after the departure of the prince, the railway presented the Canadian cabinet with an ultimatum – if subsidies were not increased, all service would be suspended. The British investors had long complained of the injustice of having given Canada one of the longest railways in the world while receiving nothing in return. Now Baring and Glyn were threatening to take back the railway, having earlier obtained a lien on the rolling stock of the Grand Trunk that permitted them to seize and sell its moveable assets.

It is not clear whether Baring and Glyn would actually have carried through with this threat. Perhaps it was just a bargaining tactic; but shutting down the railway would have embarrassed the provincial government in the eyes of both the provincial electorate and the British world. Thomas Galt, the Toronto lawyer who was the brother of the minister of Finance, represented the railway in the high-stakes negotiations with the Canadian cabinet.[2] At a point when the talks were stalled, George-Étienne Cartier and John Ross, the cabinet members most closely tied to the company, submitted draft letters of resignation. Eventually, their cabinet colleagues gave in to their demands for more money, but, fearful of the electoral consequences, they insisted on secrecy.[3] Their desire to defer public knowledge of the subsidy until after the election testified to the growing unpopularity of the Grand Trunk. The relative open-handedness of the mid-1850s was a distant memory.

This measure was a stopgap and did not solve the long-term problems of the railway. The British investors continued to pressure the Canadian government for more money. However, the negotiating position of the British investors was undermined when judges in both Upper and Lower Canada decided that the railway as a public utility was too important to be shut down by any set of creditors.[4] In 1861 these judicial decisions were reinforced by provincial legislation that made it difficult for creditors to railways. In effect, the British investors were told that they were not allowed to play their trump card: closing the railway.[5]

Rescuing his Grand Trunk investment was particularly important for Thomas Baring because of the losses he had recently sustained in other parts of his portfolio. Baring's iron mill at Weardale had proved a financial disaster, its own losses only partially mitigated

by the sale of iron rails to the Grand Trunk.[6] Rescuing the money
his bank had previously lent to the Government of Mexico was
also proving very difficult, despite the French invasion of that
country beginning in 1862. The late 1850s had been relatively
good years for Baring Brothers, but the financial side-effects of the
American Civil War and the other major conflicts of the 1860s
proved very disruptive for the bank, whose capital fell from a
peak of £1.4 million at the end of 1859 to £772,000 by the end of
1863. The bank's capital reached a low point of £627,000 in 1865
and then began a difficult recovery.

It should be pointed out that Baring Brothers was still a private
bank rather than a corporation whose shareholders enjoyed limited liability. When the joint-stock bank Overend, Gurney and
Company failed in 1866, the owners had the comfort of knowing
that at least their private assets were off limits to creditors.[7] Baring
and Glyn did not have that cushion and could have lost everything. Moreover, for a banker like Thomas Baring, his reputation
was his greatest asset and it was being undermined by the Grand
Trunk affair. The fiasco made him look foolish at best and down-
right duplicitous at worst.

This period of crisis saw the introduction of a powerful new force
into the affairs of the British investors in Canada: Edward Watkin.
In 1861 Baring and Glyn hired Watkin, one of the leading railway
figures in Victorian England, to solve the problems of the Grand
Trunk. This task led to his involvement in other aspects of British
North American business and politics, including the purchase of
the Hudson's Bay Company and the promotion of colonial union.

Watkin was consistently modest in talking about his role in
bringing about Canadian Confederation and always depicted
himself as the lowly helper of the great visionary duke of Newcastle. Comparing Confederation to a Greek temple, Watkin recounted how on a visit to the Acropolis he had pulled up a tuft of
grass at the base of a column to reveal a compass mark made centuries earlier by an architect's assistant. Watkin analogized this
small scratch on history to his part in carrying out the duke's vision, but given his frequent interaction with the Fathers of Confederation, there are grounds for thinking that his assessment of
his own role was excessively self-effacing.[8]

Edward Watkin's social origins were far more humble than
those of the fifth duke of Newcastle. Edward's father had risen

from poverty to become a prosperous Manchester merchant. Absalom Watkin had been a pillar of the Anti-Corn Law League and this had led to Edward's employment by the league as a young man.[9] After the victory of free trade, Edward directed his energies into railways by joining the London and North Western Railway, the massive enterprise that George Carr Glyn had helped to create. Over the course of the 1850s, Watkin moved away from Cobden's hardline position, although as late as 1857 Cobden offered him assistance in the electoral contest at Yarmouth.[10] While Watkin remained hostile to protective tariffs, he became increasingly supportive of other forms of state intervention that were anathema to Cobden. In 1867 Watkin actually proposed that Britain's most indebted railways be nationalized. Watkin also discarded Cobden's hostility towards colonies and came to regard the overseas empire as one of Britain's glories.[11]

In the early 1850s Watkin visited North America and published a small book on his travels. One day, while travelling on one of the trains he managed, Watkin spotted Newcastle reading his book and used it as a conversational opener. His evolving relationship with Newcastle demonstrates that he had the ability to turn crisis into opportunity. When sparks from one of Watkin's locomotives damaged property belonging to the duke, for example, Watkin decided to pre-empt a lawsuit by visiting Newcastle at home. As the hours passed, the topic of conversation shifted from the fire damage to other matters of mutual interest, such as Newcastle's new colliery and the affairs of the colonies. Thereafter they met more often and by the time of the Trent Crisis, outlined below, the men were good friends.[12]

Their relationship was mutually beneficial. Newcastle was a pillar of the establishment in Britain. By the early 1860s Watkin had befriended many of the leading men in British North America. In 1861 Leonard Tilley stood next to Watkin and swore an oath that committed both men to working to build a transcontinental railway on an "all-red" route, that is, a route that did leave British colonial soil: neither Tilley nor Watkin would rest until they had seen the waters of the Pacific from the windows of a train that had come from Canada.[13]

In the early 1860s, a new element – constitutional political economy – appeared in British discussions of the problems of colonial investors.[14] Constitutional political economy refers to the belief that a country's prosperity depends on its having the right political system. Present-day disagreements about whether it is better to make long-term investments in authoritarian China or democratic India[15] have definite nineteenth-century parallels. Constitutional political economy was embedded in the writings of Lord Macaulay, the Whig historian who argued that eighteenth-century England's prosperity was based on the constitutional principles established at the Glorious Revolution of 1688.[16] That nineteenth-century British thought was imbued with the idea of constitutional political economy helps to explain why the British investors in Canada eventually turned to a constitutional solution to their problems.

Rather than focusing on the actions of any particular Canadian politician or party, British observers seemed to believe that the colony's political system was the underlying cause of the investors' problems. While the impulse to take a constitutional approach may have been prompted by British ignorance of local parties and political personalities, it also reflected a deep-seated fear of democracy. At a time when the aristocracy continued to dominate British political life, most colonial political leaders came from the social classes that supplied municipal councillors in the British Isles.[17] E.J. Herepath, editor of *Herapath's Railway and Commercial Journal* (London), suggested that Canada's system of responsible government had contributed to the problems faced by the Grand Trunk investors. He contrasted the flourishing finances of railways in "despotic" India with the deplorable condition of the Grand Trunk.[18]

Of course, Herapath was not arguing that Canada should be converted into a benevolent despotism or even that the grant of responsible government should be somehow reversed. He was merely recognizing that the rules of the political game that confronted Canadian investors were particularly complex. British people who invested in railways abroad generally agreed that constitutions mattered a great deal. Indeed, some investors preferred relatively authoritarian political systems, such as the France of Napoleon III, because it was simpler to deal with one ruler than with competing gaggles of elected legislators. One correspondent in *Herapath's* declared that railways "in democratic countries" could never be profitable, even if the railway was being promoted by "great names" in Britain. He reasoned that democratic governments were "too weak to resist the demands of speculators for rival lines," leading to dangerous competition for traffic. Because it had a strong central authority, France was a good place to invest in railways: "When we see the immense dividends paid by the French railways in consequence of the monopoly granted to them ... it makes us regret that our money was not invested under an imperial regime."[19]

This correspondent was writing to critique the proliferation of competing railways in Britain. The democratic tendencies of which he complained were even more pronounced in Canada. Canada was more democratic than Britain in the sense that a larger percentage of the male population was entitled to vote.[20] It is not surprising, therefore, that class-based concepts such as honour and the code of the gentleman crept into the analysis of Canadian politics presented in British financial publications. Several authors suggested that the excessive strength of the democratic branch of the Canadian constitution was harmful to the interests of British investors in the colony.

When the city of Hamilton, for instance, defaulted on its municipal debentures in 1861, the *Canadian News*, a weekly London newspaper specializing in British North American events, attributed such dishonourable, short-sighted, and immoral conduct to the low franchise requirements in Canada.[21] Similar ideas were expressed in London's *Bankers' Magazine*, which proposed that the "unfortunate and ill-used" Grand Trunk bondholders should seize the railway and suspend service until the Canadian government provided a comprehensive subsidy package. This package would include "an additional guarantee, a thoroughly comprehensive scheme of emigration, the providing of machinery for the carrying on of direct trade between the upper lakes and Europe" and "grants of land to the shareholders." Such drastic action was necessary because "the Canadian rabble is too unscrupulous and too powerful to listen to appeals of any kind."[22] The use of the term "rabble" to describe the Canadian electorate reveals the class bias of the paper.[23]

The use of constitutional political economy in analyzing colonial investments was probably connected to the ongoing debate on the probable economic effects of democracy that had been sparked by the abortive 1859 bill for parliamentary reform in Britain. In the aftermath of the bill, many people asked themselves what impact increasing the influence of mass opinion in Britain's system of tripartite "mixed" government would have on economic policy. Most writers thought that increasing the size of the electorate would have some effect on the role of government in the economy, but beyond that there was little agreement. Many advocates of laissez-faire saw strengthening the popular element in the constitution as a way of limiting the size of the state.[24]

Martin Daunton argues that British Radicals demanded parliamentary reform less for its own sake than as a means of limiting the power of interest groups and eliminating "militarism and waste."[25] The theoretical foundations of this line of thinking were articulated by John Stuart Mill in *Considerations on Representative Government* (1861), in which "the interest of the government" in maximizing taxation was contrasted with the interest of the broader community in being "as little taxed as the necessary expenses of good government permit." Mill believed that strong and broad-based representative institutions could limit overtaxation and the other "evils incident to monarchical and aristocratic governments."[26] The Liverpool Financial Reform Association echoed this idea, arguing that, *ceteris paribus*, franchise expansion tends to promote economy and prudence in government expenditures.[27]

The idea that democratization would tend to shrink the public sector was robustly contested by the social philosopher and railway engineer Herbert Spencer, who thought on the contrary that democracy would lead to creeping socialism. Spencer predicted that mass suffrage would inevitably bring about the confiscation of wealth and its redistribution to the poor.[28] The legal writer John Austin made a similar prediction.[29] The political economist Henry Fawcett advanced a more limited version of the same basic argument. Fawcett felt that including too large a proportion of the population in the electorate would increase the number of departures from laissez-faire made by governments. He attributed the protectionism of some of Britain's colonies of settlement to their wide electorates. Britain's more limited electorate had opted for the wiser policy of free trade.[30]

If these three thinkers worried that democracy might cause too much intervention in the economy, the third Earl Grey, a Whig aristocrat who had been the architect of colonial responsible government in the 1840s, feared the exact opposite. Grey shared Spencer's dislike of democracy but saw a link between excessive democracy and *under*interventionism. Writing in 1859, Grey conceded that the weakness of the democratic branch of the British constitution before the parliamentary reform legislation of 1832 had led to excessive expenditure and the misdirection of public funds to vested interests, but the felt that excessive democratization was now threatening to push the pendulum too far in the direction of unfettered markets and low taxes. Grey argued that Britain was now undertaxed and underserviced and that in the democratic colonies the problem was even worse, although not quite as bad as in the United States.[31]

British North American politics on the eve of Confederation provided plenty of evidence in support of Grey's thesis and tended to falsify Spencer's prediction that democratization would result in an overmighty state and ruinous socialism. At a time when British income tax was being collected even from "clerks and curates," the level of taxation in the colonies was comparatively low. Moreover, as Gladstone disapprovingly noted, Canada's political class was taking no steps towards following Britain's lead in introducing income tax.[32] The low level of taxation in Canada had a direct impact on investors in Britain because it limited the provincial government's ability to provide assistance to private companies. John Ross, the former president of the Grand Trunk, certainly felt great frustration at the level of taxation in Canada. In a letter to Baring written around 1860, he expressed his hope that the government would improve its finances by introducing direct taxation (i.e., income tax) to supplement customs duties.[33]

In the early 1860s the Grand Trunk management in London pursued three major political strategies in its search for financial viability. The disappointing provisions of the 1862 Grand Trunk Arrangements Act (a Canadian statute that provided only modest assistance to the railway) demonstrated that the first tactic, lobbying the Canadian government for more money, had played itself out. While a majority of shareholders accepted the act at an August 1862 meeting, there was considerable opposition. J.C. Conybeare, an investor, claimed that the ratification meeting had been called on short notice in order to facilitate a fraudulent transaction. He said that if the Grand Trunk management succeeded in obtaining the approval of investors in attendance, he would petition the Colonial Office to disallow the Canadian legislation. Henry Cleaver Chapman, the disruptive Liverpool shareholder, suggested that

Messrs Baring and Glyn were frauds who deserved to be "picking oakum" (i.e., in prison). For good measure, he denounced the Canadian political class as a set of "rascally rogues."[34] The use of such vitriolic language was a sign of the worsening position of the railway.[35]

Searching for an infusion of cash, the railway's management had unsuccessfully proposed that the government pay it in advance for the provision of twenty-five years' worth of postal and military services. The government had refused this proposal, instead referring matters to a board of arbitration. This action began a long and tangled political process.[36] The postal issue seems to have focused investor attention on fundamental political issues. In June 1864 Edward Watkin explained the deadlock in the Canadian legislature to the shareholders and bondholders of the Grand Trunk. In speaking of a deadlock, however, he was not referring to linguistic divisions over the issue of representation by population. Instead, he meant the stalemate over the issue of the Grand Trunk's postal subsidy that had resulted from the parties in the legislature being "so nearly balanced."[37] The parties in question were the railway's supporters and opponents.

Another solution that appealed to the Grand Trunk was amalgamation with other railways. Grand Trunk shareholders had long complained of the ruinous rivalry between their line and the two other major Canadian railways, the Great Western of Canada and the Buffalo and Lake Huron. In 1862 a merger agreement was reached, but the planned amalgamation raised fears of a railway monopoly in Canada, the Canadians noting that the Grand Trunk was proposing amalgamation with several other lines, including the Northern and the Ottawa and Prescott. When the Canadian Parliament refused to permit the amalgamation of the three lines covered by the 1862 agreement, the Grand Trunk was forced to shelve the planned amalgamation, at least temporarily.[38]

Hopes for recovery began to focus more and more on the extension of the railway. It was usually assumed that extension would bring the railway eastward, although Edward Watkin advocated the extension of the line into the far west as well. In his memoirs, Watkin revealed that he had written an 1861 article in the *Illustrated London News* promoting an interoceanic railway on British territory.[39] John Ross noted that the idea was discussed during his 1858–59 visit to England, although he had dismissed it as wildly impracticable.[40] In a letter of November 1860[41] Watkin dwelt on the importance of a transcontinental railway for Britain's trade with China and Australia, anticipating many themes that arose in subsequent debates on the imperial importance of such a line.[42] Although a line to the Pacific was a long-term possibility, extending the line into New Brunswick was the primary goal of the Grand Trunk management at the time.[43] The failure of the negotiations to build the Halifax-Quebec railway in 1858[44] did little to dent Watkin's enthusiasm for the project or his sense of its importance for the Grand Trunk. Indeed, Watkin declared in 1861 that going east was the only way the company could become viable.[45]

Given the significant financial challenges facing the existing Grand Trunk system, one is inclined to ask why a financially troubled railway would have wanted to expand instead of concentrating on improving the management of the existing assets. Watkin's motives in wanting to build an interoceanic railway are complex. Getting further subsidies was the perennial goal of the Grand Trunk, and a massive program of expansion wrapped in the Union Jack would have provided politicians with ample justification for giving the railway yet more public money. Moreover, the generally accepted rules of railway accounting made expansion especially attractive: constructing a new line would have changed the ratio of interest payments generated from fresh bond issues rather than from traffic receipts.[46] In the short term, at least, the railway would have more financial breathing room. Another strand of Watkin's reasoning is suggested by the phrase "injecting traffic"; for Watkin thought that connecting the Grand Trunk to lines in New Brunswick and Nova Scotia would generate a considerable volume of through traffic on the underutilized eastern sections.[47]

In the late autumn and early winter of 1861 delicate political negotiations took place concerning the Intercolonial. The fortuitous arrival in London of Joseph Howe and Leonard Tilley in search of imperial aid for the project coincided with the outbreak of the *Trent* crisis, a diplomatic incident that brought Britain and the United States to the brink of war. The affairs had begun when American Marines boarded a British vessel, RMS *Trent*, and removed two representations of the Confederate States of America. For several anxious weeks in December 1861, war seemed imminent and large numbers of troops were rushed to the North American colonies, a task complicated by the onset of winter and the lack of a rail link between Canada and the ice-free port of Halifax. Most of the troops destined for Canada were landed at Halifax and forced to proceed overland to Rivière-du-Loup, trudging through the snow for much of the way. The crisis concluded when the American government backed down in early January 1862 and released the Confederate envoys.

British interpretations of the Trent Crisis varied widely. Lord Palmerston used it to argue for subsidized construction of the Halifax-Quebec railway. The suffering of troops marching in the snow, he thought, justified the abandonment of what he sneeringly called "our economical mode" of government.[48] But for Little Englanders, the affair provided a powerful argument for separation from the colonies. Although Palmerston supported imperial aid to the line, any subsidy package needed the approval of a cabinet deeply divided on the issue. Gladstone, the Chancellor of the Exchequer, led the opposition to imperial assistance while the duke of Newcastle rallied supporters.[49] In late 1861 and early 1862, it was by no means certain which way the cabinet was going to lean. Major figures on each side of the debate were pessimistic about the outcome. Writing to John Bright, Richard Cobden predicted that Gladstone would lose his cabinet battle with Newcastle and that the colonial promoters would succeed "in getting their hands into our pockets"[50]: "Gladstone will be thwarted and damaged" because of a lack of "vigour or will in the Cabinet to prevent" the subsidy.[51] A few weeks later, Edward Watkin reported to the duke of Newcastle that "the gossip one hears at the clubs and elsewhere would lead me to suppose that Mr Gladstone's anti-colonial views will prevail and that no assistance will be extended to the Halifax railway."[52]

The significance of this cabinet dispute tends to be underestimated in the secondary literature.[53] Most accounts reduce it to a matter of high politics, clashing personalities and cabinet manoeuvring, ignoring the broader implications of the conflict. It would be a mistake to characterize it simply as a struggle between City and Industry, but it is possible to see it as a struggle between different form of capitalism. The distinction between industrial and financial capitalism is perhaps less relevant than the distinction outlined earlier between crony capitalism and pure capitalism.

It is highly unlikely that the disagreement between Gladstone and Newcastle was personal in origin; the two men had been friends since Oxford and were on good terms. Gladstone did have a personal enemy in the cabinet, but it was Lord John Russell,[54] who happened to agree with him on this issue. The awkward personal complications created by the dispute over North American colonial policy is suggested in a letter Newcastle sent to Gladstone in 1863, when they were arguing over imperial financial assistance for the proposed transcontinental telegraph line and postal road. Newcastle assured Gladstone that he had no intention of "appealing to the Cabinet from your objections" and that it was only "with great pain that I felt compelled to do so last year in the matter of the Intercolonial Railway." Newcastle stated that he did not like debating Gladstone on these matters, and that "nothing but a sense of duty" would induce him fight with Gladstone about "a matter forming another link in the great scheme which I confess I have very much at heart."[55]

When Joseph Howe appealed to Gladstone to change his mind on the issue of the guarantee, he reminded the chancellor of his personal friendship with Newcastle and suggested that the Intercolonial would help Newcastle to repair the mistakes of the past. Howe was probably alluding to the blame that had attached to Newcastle during the Crimean War. Howe told Gladstone that allowing the Intercolonial to go ahead would ensure that Newcastle's visit to Canada with the Prince of Wales "should bear fruits substantiated and memorable." Howe also alluded to the plight of the Grand Trunk investors, arguing that by ceasing to oppose the imperial subsidy, Gladstone would be aiding "a body of British Gentlemen to recover an enormous amount of capital which is now in great peril." If Lord Grey had succeeded in constructing the Intercolonial in the late 1840s, said Howe, "the £10,000,000 sunk by British shareholders and bondholders would not have been lost." But because he had hesitated, "the results have been patent to us all."[56]

The debate over the Intercolonial exposed deep ideological fault lines within Palmerston's coalition, revealing two radically different visions of empire. It was also an opportunity for anti-colonial figures outside the cabinet to make their voices heard.[57] Newcastle's vision of empire involved a vast scheme of imperial communications. He foresaw a network of railways, steam lines, and telegraphs connecting all parts of the empire and running exclusively on British territory and the (British-dominated) high seas. Newcastle's vision of an integrated imperial system implied that the imperial government should be involved in building infrastructure in overseas British possessions. What contemporaries in the Cobdenite wing of the Liberal party called "Free Trade in railways," a system in which lines succeeded and failed according to pure market forces, held no attraction for Newcastle.[58] Nor did he demarcate provincial from imperial interests as strictly as Gladstone and the other advocates of colonial self-sufficiency did. Newcastle argued that financial assistance to the colonies would be repaid in goodwill and colonial assistance in future conflicts.[59]

Gladstone subscribed to a very different vision of empire. He was not a Little Englander and, unlike Richard Cobden and Goldwin Smith, he believed that it was important to retain the constitutional link between the colonies and the mother country, a position made very clear in his testimony to the Committee on Colonial Military Defence.[60] But, beginning with his period at the Colonial Office in 1840s, Gladstone set forth a prescriptive vision of the empire rooted in the concept of rugged self-sufficiency. Gladstone's ideal empire was a network of autonomous, financially independent communities of Britons throughout the world united by allegiance to a common sovereign, flag, and other national symbols.

Gladstone's reasons for wanting the colonies to become financially self-sufficient were not primarily economic: colonial cost-cutting was consistent with his advocacy of frugality in domestic administration. It was the moral and ethical aspects of the issue that were paramount for him. In his eyes, subsidies to colonies injured the colonial "freemen" by causing them to become "enervated" through an unnatural and unwholesome dependence on the mother country. Gladstone's ideas regarding colonial financial self-sufficiency paralleled the widespread notion that outdoor relief for the able-bodied was injurious to the recipients. It should be noted that Gladstone's opposition to state transfers of wealth from mother country to colony did not extend to private philanthropy; he was an active supporter of efforts to raise private funds for Anglican institutions in Upper Canada such as Trinity College, Toronto.[61]

Gladstone's vision of the empire as an association of self-sufficient communities was shared by many Liberals and some Conservatives, notably Charles Bulwer Adderley. Adderley argued that anything short of colonial financial independence would be "degrading" to British colonial manhood. In his writings, Adderley dwelt on the so-called manly virtues of the seventeenth- and eighteenth-century colonial militias and inaccurately claimed that the colonial militiamen of earlier eras had never asked the imperial exchequer for funds. Adderley also discussed the various ways in which this golden age of colonial self-sufficiency could be restored, arguing that colonial federations could serve as a stepping stone to this goal.[62]

According to W.L. Morton, Gladstone's ideas rested on the belief that "money could be usefully employed only by private hands."[63] But it is simplistic to label Gladstone as a proponent of *laissez-faire*. In 1868 he supported the nationalization of Britain's telegraphy industry and as early as 1844 he had provided the legal foundation for the eventual nationalization of the British railway industry.[64] Gladstone appreciated the benefits of both competitive private enterprise and public utilities administered by civil servants but objected when private companies obtained government assistance through political connections. Writing in his diary in April 1862 on the issue of government subsidies for a new transatlantic telegraph, Gladstone stated his opposition to subventions, hoping that entrepreneurs would "cure themselves of the vicious habit ... of looking for Government money". Instead, those who wished for transatlantic telegraphy and other "novel enterprises" should wait for technical knowledge to "reach such a point as to bring capital forward freely for the purpose without the great mischief of State intervention."[65] Rather than being grounded in any animus towards Canada, Gladstone's dislike of the Grand Trunk's Intercolonial project reflected his general dislike of the concept of providing government assistance to private enterprise.

Gladstone's opposition was supported by Richard Cobden, whose dislike of the Intercolonial was rooted in a complex mixture of anti-imperialism, classical political economy, and a liberal internationalist outlook that interpreted the strategic arguments in favour of the railway as militarist. Cobden detested military spending and believed that some of Britain's recent wars had been instigated by profit-seeking colonists.[66] The colonies, with their large garrisons, logical connection to the fleet, and aristocratic governors drawing inflated salaries, were an integral part of the aristocratic system Cobden wanted to abolish.[67]

During the Trent affair, Cobden said that he was uncertain whether Palmerston's cabinet would choose peace, noting that the government contained people from both the pacific middle classes and the warmongering aristocracy.[68] Cobden certainly did not think that Canada was worth fighting for, a conclusion he based on two visits to the colony. He regarded the French Canadians as a reactionary race and thought that the English-speaking colonists aped British ways too closely for people living on the practical and egalitarian continent of North America. His attitude to Canada was also informed by the Grand Trunk debacle. Writing in his diary in Montreal, Cobden censured Thomas Baring and George Carr Glyn for having misled the investing public and denounced the Victoria Bridge as "a splendid monument of engineering skill and wasted capital."[69]

John Bright, Cobden's close associate, was convinced that Watkin, Howe, and Tilley actually wanted war between Britain and the United States and were lobbying the British government to that end. Bright considered the activities of this evil triad especially despicable because of its pecuniary motives and expressed disgust that men would spark bloodshed "all for a railroad speculation and to get money from this Government to make a line from Halifax to join the Grand Trunk Line in Canada."[70]

Similarly inflammatory language was used in public by the Liverpool Financial Reform Association (LFRA), a group of businessmen that promoted deep retrenchments in public, especially military and colonial, expenditure. Headed by Robertson Gladstone,[71] the brother of the Chancellor of the Exchequer, the LFRA included many entrepreneurs who had been active in the fight against the Corn Laws, including Henry Ashworth, president of the Manchester Chamber of Commerce.[72] When a parliamentary select committee examined colonial military expenditures in 1861, the LFRA was one of the loudest voices for retrenchment.[73] Its organ, the *Financial Reformer*, was highly sympathetic to Gladstone. It defended him against the Tory financial press and went so far as to compare the historical importance of his life mission to that of Jesus Christ.[74]

During the Trent Crisis, the *Financial Reformer* condemned the government for sending troops to British North America; it was a provocative act, the paper claimed, and the taxes spent on colonial garrisons were "one of the penalties we pay for the barren glory of extended territory." The paper informed its readers that American independence in 1783 had benefited Britain and that the arguments in favour of American independence now applied "with equal force to Nova Scotia, New Brunswick, Canada, fog banks, and hunting grounds." The paper maintained that the real reason for colonialism was "to keep up certain stations for what Mr Bright calls our 'out-door system of relief for the aristocracy.'"[75] Referring to Britain's costly fleets and colonial garrisons, the *Financial Reformer* declared: "The fact is that John Bull, who, from his simplicity and gullibility, ought rather to be called Jack Ass, the universal pecuniary scapegoat."[76]

Cobden was convinced that the old aristocratic politico-economic order of high taxes, big armies, and extensive colonies could be abolished if the middle classes remained united. By themselves, he argued, the aristocracy and the remnants of the old colonial system, such as the Hudson's Bay Company, would be unable to withstand the Radical challenge. The willingness of ambitious men from the middle classes to accommodate themselves to the existing order deeply disturbed Cobden. In an 1840 letter to Edward Watkin, he had denounced those industrialists who were "wanting in self-respect and do not stand by their order."[77] Although this comment appears to have been directed at Sir Robert Peel and other manufacturing Tories, Watkin's subsequent career exemplified the very social trend of which Cobden complained.[78]

In 1861–62, the battle between Gladstone and Newcastle over the Intercolonial subsidy was fought with lengthy memoranda and copious facts and figures. Watkin and the visiting colonial politicians actively assisted Newcastle in crafting his rebuttal to Gladstone's argument. Working in conjunction with Watkin, Premier Tilley of New Brunswick, Premier Howe of Nova Scotia, and, to a lesser extent, P.M. Vankoughnet, the Canadian commissioner of Crown lands, Newcastle scoured the available papers to find counterarguments. Watkin played an important role in facilitating dealings between the Colonial Secretary and the colonists. Thus, when Howe expressed reluctance to visit the duke's seat at Clumber, Watkin intervened, urging him to seize the opportunity. Howe then travelled to Clumber and worked with Watkin, Newcastle, and Newcastle's houseguest, Sir Allan MacNab of Hamilton, on a lengthy countermemorandum to Gladstone's arguments.[79]

In their campaign for imperial assistance, the promoters of the Intercolonial faced a number of impediments, including the lack of a political organization representing British American interests in London. The Canada Club, a venerable dining society open to Britons who had passed at least one winter in Canada, was primarily a social rather than a political organization and thus could not be used as a vehicle for pro-Intercolonial lobbying.

Moreover, Edward Ellice, Sr, a fierce opponent of the proposed railway, was a member of the club. Ellice was a powerful figure in his own right, with investments stretching from Van Dieman's Land to New York's Erie Canal. Ellice is today principally remembered for orchestrating the merger of the HBC with the North-West Company in the 1820s. But while Ellice had once played a massive role in Canadian economic life he had subsequently sold most of his assets in Canada.[80] Ellice's disengagement from Canadian enterprises such as the Canada Company and the Beauharnois seigneury paralleled his drift to a Little Englander political stance. In November 1861 Ellice stated that since Canada had become "ten times as democratic as the United States," maintenance of its colonial status was "fast becoming impossible."[81]

Ellice denounced the proponents of the Intercolonial to Gladstone in the strongest possible terms. Gladstone inclined to the view that they were thieves out to rob the public purse, noting that "many persons in England are interested in Canadian Railways, and have suffered by them. They may be counted upon, perhaps, as allies in the attempt now made."[82] Although he had the ear of Gladstone, Ellice believed that he had little influence at the Colonial Office, where he was "considered poorly," and feared that "the Government must fall into the hands of jobbing lawyers" and "unscrupulous and clever adventurers like Messrs Galt and Hincks, who make their own fortune and ruin the public."[83] His final letters on Canadian affairs were bitterly critical, characterizing Newcastle as "the dupe of Mr Watkin" who was trying to fill "his pockets at the expense of a foolish public" through the construction of "impracticable works, telegraphs and roads across the desert from Lake Superior to Columbia."[84] Ellice's hostility was reciprocated by the promoters of the Intercolonial, with Watkin declaring that Ellice looked "Jewish."[85]

Ellice and the other obstacles to success were counterbalanced by certain advantages enjoyed by the supporters of the Intercolonial. The Colonial Secretary was sympathetic, as was the *Canadian News*. Moreover, the widespread hostility towards the United States aroused by the Trent affair appears to have led many Britons unconnected with railway investments to believe that building the Intercolonial was necessary for British honour, the defence of the colonies, and even the comfort of the British soldier.

The supporters of imperial aid to the Intercolonial had an inside man in the citadel of Little Englandism, since Edward Watkin was a member of Manchester's municipal council. Indeed, Watkin managed to get a committee of the council to endorse imperial aid for the Intercolonial in a memorial sent to the British government.[86] The existence of allies in Britain's manufacturing towns would prove important to the gentlemanly capitalists of the City in the coming years. Cain and Hopkins argue that while the gentlemanly capitalists were the driving force behind imperial policy, they sometimes made strategic alliances with manufacturers and other non-City interest groups in the British Isles. The formation of a political body capable of coordinating such a political alliance is discussed in the next chapter.

4

The British North American Association
and Its Campaign

The BNAA represented some of the most important investors in British North America, yet references to it in histories of Confederation are usually cursory.[1] The one historian to do more than briefly mention the organization was Don Roman. Roman's suggestion that the association served the interests of British manufacturers and exporters reflected Robinson and Gallagher's general theory of economic imperialism rather than any in-depth research into the composition of the organization.[2] Closely examining the BNAA has implications for both the Robinson-Gallagher thesis and the newer finance-centric interpretation of British imperialism supplied by Cain and Hopkins. The BNAA certainly enlisted the support of people in British manufacturing towns in its campaign in favour of British aid to the Intercolonial, but the manufacturers played only a supporting role designed to lend credibility to the demands of the financiers of the City.

The formation of the BNAA in January 1862 was an important step towards Canadian Confederation. In 1858–59, the Colonial Office had been cool and indifferent to the federation proposal made by the Canadian government, effectively killing the plan. The creation of an organization in London that contained a large number of wealthy and influential people supportive of colonial unification altered the dynamic. Writing to Howe in February 1862, Edward Watkin noted a change in the atmosphere, remarking that the BNAA "had given all provincial questions a shove which they have not had for years."[3] In the summer of 1862, the Colonial Office reversed its earlier attitude towards Confederation and began actively encouraging the concept with a circular despatch to the colonies from the Colonial Secretary.[4]

Ged Martin argues persuasively that Newcastle's July 1862 circular was important because it gave a green light to the supporters of colonial union in the colonies.[5] Newcastle made it clear that while the initiative for any colonial federation would have to arise from a meeting of the colonists themselves, the British government would "heartily" support the plan and lend it encouragement.[6] This expression of support was crucial because Colonial politicians would not have initiated discussions leading to colonial union without reasonable assurances that they would receive a warm welcome in London.[7]

Given the importance of this dispatch, it is worth examining the lobbying that went on in the months before it was composed. The BNAA was in a position to influence policy because its membership included wealthy and influential people, including a number of MPs. Moreover, it enjoyed the warm support of Frederic Algar, owner of the *Canadian News*, the main supplier of British North American intelligence to Londoners. Algar also published the *Australian Mail and New Zealand Express*, a digest of commercial and political news from the Antipodes. Although Algar's publications were specialist ones with limited circulation, they were important resources for Londoners interested in the colonies.

The creation of the BNAA was suggested by Joseph Howe in a letter sent to Thomas Baring on 31 December 1861. Howe said that having reflected on the "position of the British capitalists who have placed their money in Canadian Companies which do not pay," he had "come to the conclusion that we ought to have some Association that will form a Common centre for the collection and diffusion of information about the Colonies." Forming an association would allow these capitalists to "appeal for justice and fair consideration either to the Government or to the people of England." Howe proposed that the organization be based in London "with a working committee not formed exclusively of Grand Trunk people but combining all the B[ritish] North American interests." Such a diverse body "could do a vast deal for the Provinces and for themselves." He also mentioned that he had "talked the matter over with Mr Watkins [sic] who agrees in the main with me. A few thousand expended in this way would be returned back hundreds of thousands." Howe closed his letter by asking Baring to promote the idea of forming an association: "If you think my opinion of any value, show this note to Mr Glyn, who I know but slightly."[8]

The British North American Association was formed in January 1862, immediately after the dénouement of the Trent Crisis. While it shared the name of a group that had existed in Halifax in the early 1850s, its actual mode of operation was more akin to that of the Australian General Association, a London body that had been established in the late 1850s to promote higher subsidies for antipodean steamships and that discussed the confederation of the Australian colonies.[9]

The aims of the BNAA listed in its printed articles of association included such blameless objectives as opening a permanent office in London that would house a library and serve as a place where visiting colonists could collect their mail.[10] These functions fitted with the association's goals of promoting emigration and investment in British North America. More controversially, the articles stated that the association wished to promote "colonial union," although they did not specify what type of union, whether legislative, federal, or something else. Howe had not proposed that the organization deal with the subject of colonial union; that goal appears to have been added afterwards by the other organizers.[11]

The BNAA met at the London Tavern on Bishopsgate Street, a venerable institution that was the location of countless shareholder meetings as well as many political gatherings connected with City financial interests. The location underscores the business orientation of the BNAA. Indeed, there was much overlap between the association membership and the syndicate that had just been formed to construct the Intercolonial. The BNAA and the syndicate worked in conjunction with each other and on one occasion held meetings at different rooms at the tavern on the same day.[12]

While the overwhelming majority of BNAA members were permanent residents of the British Isles, a few were colonists. Joseph Howe and Thomas Chandler Haliburton, the Nova Scotian novelist then sitting in the imperial Parliament,[13] were members, as were two Grand Trunk contractors resident in Canada, D.L. Macpherson and Casimir S. Gzowski. The ranks of the BNAA also included the commissioners responsible for the Canadian display at the 1862 international exhibition in London. The exhibition commissioners were, in turn, linked to Thomas Baring, a fellow exhibition commissioner.[14]

Sir Samuel Cunard had been born in Nova Scotia but now lived in Britain. His association with the BNAA is particularly noteworthy because of the size of his fleet of transatlantic steamships and the extent of his political connections.[15] Cunard's line was subsidized by the British Post Office and enjoyed the political support of the Admiralty.[16] The London agents of Sir Hugh Allan's Montreal Ocean Steamship Company were also members of the BNAA.[17] Cunard's ships competed with the Allan line for business on the North Atlantic, but the association of both firms with the BNAA suggests that they had interests in common.

The BNAA included some of the most illustrious figures in the City and no less than seventeen of the founding members of the BNAA sat in the House of Commons.[18] *Bradshaw's Railway Directory* reveals that many of these men were directors of English or Irish railways. Thomas Baring and George Carr Glyn were, of course, founding members of the BNAA as were several of their business partners and male relatives.[19] Of these business partners, Kirkman Daniel Hodgson, MP, was probably the most important politically. He served as governor of the Bank of England from 1855 until 1859 and then again from 1863 to 1865. Hodgson was a major holder of Grand Trunk securities and in the 1860s his bank, Finlay Hodgson and Company, came under severe strain. Its 1867 merger with Baring Brothers shocked the financial world, which had been oblivious to the strains both firms faced. The merger helped to restore Barings' capital from £760,000 to £1.39 million, a level approaching its 1858 high-water mark.[20]

The Canada Company was represented in the BNAA by Charles Franks, its governor, and three other directors.[21] Robert Benson and Henry Paull, MP, were members of the BNAA because of their connection to the International Financial Society (IFS), a syndicate then in the planning stages that involved a number of other BNAA members.[22] The leading light of the IFS, Edward Watkin, had announced in 1861 the creation of a transcontinental postal and telegraph company. Although the scheme collapsed in February 1863 when Gladstone thwarted an IFS application to the British cabinet for a subsidy, Watkin's interest in Rupert's Land persisted.[23] The IFS purchased the Hudson's Bay Company in June 1863.

Watkin had begun negotiations to buy the HBC in the expectation that Thomas Baring and George Carr Glyn would join the IFS, but when they proved financially unable to participate, several junior members of the Glyn family took up shares.[24] The IFS was an unorthodox financial institution; for while most English banks attempted to keep their assets as liquid as possible by putting money into short-term commercial loans, the IFS was conceived as a vehicle for long-term investment. Purchasing an immense tract of land in the expectation that immigration would eventually fill it with farms and cities was entirely consistent with the investment philosophy of the IFS.

Two firms of "parliamentary solicitors" were represented in the BNAA: Bischoff, Coxe, Bompas; and Baxter, Rose, and Company. Parliamentary solicitors were essentially lobbyists and these two firms specialized in getting railway bills passed.[25] Because private railway bills were the legal foundation of railway enterprise, parliamentary solicitors were of vital importance for what contemporaries called "the railway interest in Parliament."[26] Phillip Rose, a partner in the second firm, was a particularly influential figure, not least because he had been Benjamin Disraeli's "business manager" since 1846. Disraeli trusted Rose to handle his personal financial affairs and sometimes turned to him for advice on matters of state. In the 1870s, for example, Disraeli listened to Rose's advice and purchased all of the Egyptian government's shares in the Suez Canal, a decision regarded by many historians as an important turning point in British imperial history.[27]

Rose's business partner, Robert Baxter, also joined the BNAA in January 1862. Baxter is an intriguing figure because he was one of the outstanding lobbyists of the nineteenth century. Indeed, he is described by the legal historian Rande Kostal as a major figure in the development of the British railway system.[28] After the collapse of the railway mania in 1845, Baxter had been called to testify about his activities before a parliamentary investigation. The inquiry does not seem to have damaged his trade irreparably, however, and by the 1850s his lobbying business was flourishing once again. While he cheerfully worked with MPs of all persuasions, Baxter was closely tied to Disraeli's Conservatives.[29]

The membership roll of the BNAA also contained the names of three stockbrokers, two of whom had been involved in the ill-fated initial public offering of Grand Trunk stock in 1853.[30] The third stockbroker, James Capel, had not been involved in the initial offering but had helped to retail Grand Trunk Second Preference debentures in 1860.[31] Capel had experience in political efforts to recoup bad investments. He was chairman of the Committee of Spanish Bondholders, an organization that exerted pressure on the Spanish government to honour its obligations. One technique used by nineteenth-century creditors was to deny private borrowers who were in a defaulted country access to British capital markets until payments on the sovereign debt were resumed. As chairman of the stock exchange's board of managers for an extended period, Capel was in a perfect position to coordinate credit boycotts of this type.[32]

Included among the members of the BNAA were individuals connected with Sir Hugh Allan's shipping line. The firm of Montgomerie and Greenhorne, the London agent for the Montreal Ocean Steamship Company, was represented by two partners. Sir Samuel Cunard's decision to join the BNAA was likely connected to his experiences during the Crimean War, a conflict that convinced him of the military necessity of the Intercolonial.[33] The Atlantic Royal Mail Steam Navigation Company (the so-called Galway Company) was represented in the association by its deputy chairman and by a director.[34] Negotiations for the merger of troubled Galway Company with the Allan line were underway at the time of the formation of the BNAA.[35]

Several BNAA members had no business relationship with Canada but were connected to other regions of the British Empire. Among there were Robert W. Crawford, MP, an investor in Indian railways,[36] and Hugh Childers, whose colonial experience lay in Australia rather than North America. In 1858 Childers had travelled to the colony of Victoria on a mission for Baring Brothers connected with the proposed purchase of the colony's troubled railways by its government. The Colonial Office was so impressed with Childers's efforts in the Australian colony that he was later asked to meet the delegates from Nova Scotia and New Brunswick when they came to London on railway business. Childers was a strong proponent of Australian colonial federation and later spoke in the 1867 parliamentary debates on the British North America Bill.[37]

BNAA member J.A. Roebuck, MP, is interesting because of his long association with Canada. Born in Madras in 1807, Roebuck had moved with his mother to Upper Canada in 1815. He returned to England nine years later to study at the Inns of Court. As a law student, he became a disciple of Jeremy Bentham, advocating democratic reforms such as householder suffrage and the secret ballot. Elected to the first reformed Parliament in 1832, he quickly took up the cause of Papineau and the Lower Canadian

Reformers, acting as their parliamentary agent until 1837 when he lost his seat. Over the course of the 1840s, Roebuck's views became increasingly conservative. He had also come to support the union, federal or otherwise, of the British North American colonies. Roebuck served as MP for the metal-trades town of Sheffield from 1849 onwards.[38]

Sir Edmund Head, the recently retired Governor General of Canada, also joined the BNAA. Head had served as lieutenant-governor of New Brunswick from 1848 to 1854 and had witnessed the first round of negotiations for the construction of the Halifax-Quebec railway, a project he had favoured. In 1854 he had become Governor General of Canada, a position that he held until his retirement from the colonial service in October 1861. Head had long sympathized with the plight of Baring and Glyn and had expressed regret at his inability to persuade the Canadian Parliament "to fulfill – not the letter – but the spirit of its moral obligations."[39] Head had also used his position to promote colonial union, although in the 1850s he had vacillated between wanting a legislative union of the Maritimes and a broader colonial federation.[40] After his return to Britain, Head continued to take a lively interest in the future of British America. In June 1863 the IFS syndicate appointed Head as governor of the Hudson's Bay Company. He remained in this position until his death in 1868.[41]

The formation of the British North American Association received largely favourable attention in the British press. While it did not comment on the separate issue of colonial union, *Herapath's Railway and Commercial Journal* endorsed the Intercolonial scheme on the grounds it would solve the problems of the Grand Trunk. The paper characterized the Quebec-Halifax railway as "vastly more important to this country" than "many a line in India now rapidly progressing" and asked why it should be starved of the capital it deserved.[42] It was well known that the heaviest losses on the Grand Trunk were on the eastern sections that had been built for essentially political reasons. *Herapath's* predicted that the Intercolonial would make these divisions commercially viable, arguing that "the Grand Trunk Railway could not be extended through New Brunswick and Nova Scotia to Halifax without deriving a large additional stream of traffic." It was glad that political support for the project was being organized by an association that included many men "rating A1 in the City."[43]

The *Canadian News* saw the creation of the BNAA as a sign of the renewed interest in London in British North American federation. The paper reported optimistically in March 1862 that the present session of the Canadian Parliament might see a major step towards federal union. The paper felt that British North American federation was the best way to preserve the political connection between Britain and the colonies, a political bond that was under threat from foreign powers and from the teachings of Goldwin Smith. Conceding that the Civil War was not an auspicious time to be creating new federations, the paper thought the British North American union would benefit from observing the mistakes of the United States.

The paper drew two main lessons from the lamentable experience of the republic to the south. First, a loose confederation or an intercolonial *zollverein* should be out of the question; a strong central state was essential.[44] Second, democracy needed to be limited. The paper approvingly quoted a Canadian contemporary: "God forbid that, in the face of the melancholy example which is being held up before us, all power should be vested in the *hoi polloi*. We do not believe that *vox populi* is *vox dei* – rather *vox diaboli*." Centralization could temper democracy in British North America: "Let there be a central and a permanent power, not subject to the whim of a mob which may be led away by a popular cry."[45]

Soon after its formation, the BNAA occupied office space near London's Guildhall. Other expenditures connected with the launch of its campaign included hiring space for sponsored lectures, subsidizing pamphlets, and buying stationary with BNAA letterhead. Although two hundred pounds came from the governments of Nova Scotia and New Brunswick,[46] most of the costs of running the BNAA were met by donations from businesses in the City. The donors included Baring Brothers and Glyn Mills and Company, each of which gave fifty-two pounds. Similar levels of support came from the Canada Company, Bank of British North America, Gillespies Bank, Trust and Loan Company of Upper Canada, and Finlay Hodgson and Company.[47]

Soon after its formation, the BNAA began a national campaign to push for imperial assistance to the Halifax-Quebec railway.[48] This effort extended far beyond London and into manufacturing towns throughout the three kingdoms. The decision to engage the support of the manufacturing towns was a response to Gladstone's pointed observation of the absence of supportive memorials "from the trading towns and Chambers of Commerce."[49] Joseph Nelson, the secretary of the BNAA, undertook the task of getting the trading towns to send petitions in favour of imperial aid to the Board of Trade. Nelson later recalled in a letter to Sir John A. Macdonald that the thick stack of memorials he managed to obtain had brought great satisfaction to the duke of Newcastle and had helped grind down the opposition of Gladstone.[50] Nelson's campaign is important, for the extent of the support it received shows that a diverse range of British businessmen were engaged with British North American issues on the eve of Confederation. Moreover, even the opponents of assistance were remarkably well informed on British North American matters.

Nelson appears to have begun the campaign with the expectation that he would be paid a salary. Because the money was not forthcoming, Nelson became a bitter enemy of Watkin and in later years mercilessly attacked him and the Hudson's Bay Company in spiteful pamphlets.[51] After Confederation, Nelson's enemies portrayed him as a mercenary lobbyist willing to campaign for anything.[52] This was unfair, for his interest in the colonies significantly predated the foundation of the BNAA. Nelson was involved in a scheme to mine for copper in New Brunswick[53] and was a shareholder in the Canada Landed Credit Company.[54] Nelson had also been a small shareholder in the short-lived Halifax and Quebec Railway, incorporated in 1858,[55] and had written a pamphlet to bolster the syndicate's political case.[56]

Nelson had a very high opinion of his own historical importance and described himself as the prime mover behind Confederation: "The construction of the Intercolonial Railway, therefore, having been secured by me, all other questions of Confederation were simply matters of detail."[57] Nelson later claimed that Gladstone had said that his efforts had been crucial in getting the imperial government to support the Intercolonial. Coming from Gladstone, this comment was doubtless an expression of condemnation rather than praise, but it does underscore Nelson's importance.[58]

While there were precursors to Nelson's efforts, such as Joseph Howe's December 1861 address to the Bristol Chamber of Commerce,[59] Nelson's 1862 campaign was vastly more extensive and elaborate. The degree of coordination is suggested by the great similarity in the wording of the memorials received by the Lords of Trade in February 1862. All of these memorials called on the British government to guarantee interest payments on railway bonds issued by the colonial governments and explained that without this guarantee, the colonies would find it too difficult to raise the money need to build the railway. The covering letter accompanying the petition from London explained that the "merchants, bankers, and others of the City" favoured the railway's construction because it would help in "reviving the identity of interest with her [Canada] which has been too long engrossed by the United States."[60]

The signatures on the London petition represented an impressive amount of capital. The presence of such firms as the Canada Company, Glyn Mills, Finlay Hodgson, James Capel Norburry Trotter, Crawford Colvin, and Gillespies Moffat is hardly surprising Aim each had partners who were members of the BNAA. Shareholders in the Canada Company and the Trust and Loan Company of Upper Canada also signed the petition and gave their company affiliations. No less than ten signatories were connected to the Electric and International Telegraph Company.

Nineteen members of the Lloyd's Committee identified themselves as such on the petition. It should be remembered that Thomas Baring was chairman of the Lloyd's insurance syndicate. Morrison Dillon and Company,[61] a dry-goods firm with investments in the Trust and Loan Company and other ties to Canada, endorsed the memorial.[62] Alfred Charles Bridge of the General Mining Association supported the petition, as did John Gladstone, brother of the Chancellor of the Exchequer and an investor in the English and Canadian Mining Company.[63]

Similar petitions were circulated in other cities. By 22 March 1862 the British government's Board of Trade had received memorials from merchant bankers in London, Liverpool, Manchester, Glasgow, Belfast, and Bristol. Other memorials represented broad cross-sections of the economy in various localities. The corporations of Manchester, Chester, and Gloucester sent memorials as did the Cutlers of Sheffield. Chambers of Commerce in Glasgow, Belfast, Bristol, Leith, and other centres also decided to support the measure.[64]

Support for the Intercolonial, however, was far from uniform and many towns failed to petition the Colonial Secretary despite Nelson's efforts. The debates over the railway in two centres, Sheffield and Belfast, deserve detailed consideration. Although only partially successful, Nelson's efforts to obtain support in the steel-making town of Sheffield are particularly important in evaluating the distinction between industry and high finance drawn by Cain and Hopkins.

In Sheffield, the supporters of imperial aid to the Intercolonial managed to obtain the support of the Corporation of Cutlers in Hallamshire. Originally a guild governing the precision metals trades, the corporation had come under the control of the large producers of iron and steel by the 1860s.[65] The largest ironworks in Sheffield, such as the plants owned by John Brown and the Vickers Brothers, had grown by then into mammoth enterprises employing thousands of hands[66] and consuming vast amounts of raw material. The British North American colonies did not yet export considerable quantities of iron, but it was well known at this time that Canada contained vast deposits of iron ore as well as of precious metals.[67] Moreover, Sheffield's large steelmakers were increasingly worried about their dependence on Swedish ore.[68]

On 30 January 1862 a public meeting on the Intercolonial was held at Sheffield's Temperance Hall. Watkin and Howe were not present, disappointing at least one Sheffield steelmaker who had hoped to hear the famous Nova Scotian.[69] Instead, the audience listened to the Canadian Commissioner of Crown Lands, P.M. VanKoughnet, who informed them that while English capital was constantly being "swallowed up by American railways, American canals, and American schemes" the British colonies had been utterly starved for lack of investment. J.A. Roebuck spoke next, asserting that if Lord Derby had remained in power after 1859 the line would already have been built. At that time, the railway had been delayed by "party spirit," but it now looked as if the necessary bipartisan cooperation could be achieved. Roebuck declared that Sheffield needed to do its duty by indicating its support.[70]

The question was laid to rest for two weeks, when Sheffield's Chamber of Commerce asked Mayor John Brown to raise the subject of the Intercolonial at the next council meeting.[71] At the meeting, Brown moved a resolution in favour of granting imperial aid to the Intercolonial. Alderman Vickers, a fellow steelmaker, seconded it. Vickers described the arduous overland journey from Halifax to Quebec made by the troops during the *Trent* crisis, providing a patriotic and humanitarian reason for building the Intercolonial. He then recounted a lengthy anecdote about "a quantity

of manufactured pig iron from Nova Scotia [that] had very recently been sent to this country."

Other aldermen opposed the resolution on the grounds "that
the mother country ought not to be taxed for the benefit of the colony without getting the slightest return for it." One councillor demanded to know why public money should be invested in
Canada when the colony's independence was both imminent and
highly desirable: "If we gave up the colony we should get just as
much advantage from it as we did now, without the enormous expenditure." Another pointed to the inconsistency of asking the
government to reduce income tax while voting for the resolution.
In the end the resolution failed, with eighteen members in favour
and twenty-three against.[72]

The defeat in Sheffield's town council of a motion to support the
Intercolonial is striking in light of the support shown by the city's
largest employers, and given that the city was represented in Parliament by J.A. Roebuck, a BNAA member. Even more strangely,
the council's vote came at a time when Goldwin Smith's proposals
for colonial independence were being denounced by Sheffield
newspapers of both political persuasions. The Liberal *Sheffield
Daily Telegraph* strongly opposed Smith and printed articles on the
necessity of building the Intercolonial.[73] The Conservative *Sheffield
and Rotherham Independent* also attacked Smith's doctrines.[74]

The Sheffield Council's refusal to endorse imperial aid to the Intercolonial highlights a tension within Britain's manufacturing
community. While some felt that spending tax money to cement
the connection with the colony was worthwhile, others believed
that reducing their tax burdens was more important than helping
a protectionist colony. Henry Ashworth, the Manchester manufacturer who had founded the Anti-Corn Law League, felt that British businessmen who supported the Intercolonial did not fully
understand the consequences of their actions. He estimated that
the recent expedition in Canada would "involve about 3d [in the
pound]" in additional income tax and that if "our tax paying
mfrs" understood this, they would revolt over the issue of the Intercolonial. Ashworth felt it was necessary to inform British manufacturers that Canadians enjoyed full control over "the Crown
Lands or Clergy Reserves" and had been relieved of "the expense
of their own defence." They should also be reminded of Canada's
protectionist tendencies, he said.[75]

In sharp contrast with Sheffield, support for the Intercolonial was widespread in Belfast, a port city with strong ties to British North America. Some British port towns, most notably the ones on the North Sea, failed to support Nelson's campaign, but Belfast was in a very different situation in that thirty-five percent of her overseas trade went to British North America.[76] Belfast's trade with North America was peculiar in that it was heavily weighted towards British North America rather than to the more populous United States. For instance, while Liverpool did twenty-six tons of trade with British North America for every one hundred tons with the United States, the ratio in Belfast was 681 to one hundred in British North America's favour.[77]

In view of the city's trading ties, it is not surprising that the coverage of British North American issues in the Belfast newspapers was unusually extensive relative to other British provincial newspapers in this period. In the weeks surrounding the presentation of the memorial in Belfast, for example, the *Belfast News-Letter* carried stories on British Columbian goldfields, aboriginal protection, and the social importance of Anglican bishoprics in new societies.[78] British North American issues were especially important in Belfast and the BNAA campaigners were able to exploit this level of interest.

The memorial from the Belfast Chamber of Commerce dated 10 February 1862 contained the signatures of a long list of "merchants, bankers, and other of the Borough and vicinity of Belfast." The memorialists supported the project of connecting Canada with an ice-free port on the grounds that it "would render us perfectly independent of the United States." The Belfast Harbour Commission also voted unanimously to write in favour of imperial aid to the railway.[79]

In Belfast, religious and cultural issues existed alongside the commercial reasons for supporting the Intercolonial, for the town's Protestant-dominated press was extremely hostile to the anti-imperialist ideas of Goldwin Smith. The *Belfast News-Letter* declared that British taxpayers should not begrudge defending Canada and attacked the "movement being made to compel the colonists to defend themselves or to pay the English nation to defend them." It asked whether "three millions of loyal men, the majority of whom are true Protestants, [were] to be put into the scale against a paltry monetary consideration?" The paper concluded by reminding its readers that "Canada is the gate to a vast dominion, stretching grandly from the Atlantic to the Pacific, every foot of which is the property of the British people."[80]

While the promoters of the Intercolonial were able to obtain the support of Chambers of Commerce in many British towns, they failed to gain the support of the national umbrella organization, the Association of British Chambers of Commerce (ABCC). The minutes of the Standing Committee of the ABCC indicate that the organization was deeply divided by Nelson's request for support. On 19 February 1862 Nelson and a deputation from Canada were invited by J. Jobson Smith of the Sheffield Chamber of Commerce to address the national executive in London. After a debate, the committee resolved that the controversial question of lobbying the government to assist the railway "should be left to the consideration of the separate Chambers."[81]

Joseph Nelson's lobbying effort continued into the summer of 1862. The *Times* condemned the BNAA's campaign as one aimed at rescuing the fortunes of the very people responsible for "the calamitous failure of the Grand Trunk Railway of Canada,"[82] but its denunciation could not derail the success of Nelson's operation.[83] Gladstone was forced to abandon his opposition to the scheme. Just as importantly, the supporters of the Intercolonial had succeeded in conflating the railway with the broader issue of Confederation, and by July 1862 the duke of Newcastle had come to see the two projects as one and the same.[84]

Ged Martin has pointed out that the several elements of the Confederation settlement achieved in 1866–67 were not, in logical terms, mutually dependent. The Halifax-Quebec railway could have been constructed without political unification, and neither a colonial federation nor a simple *zollverein* really required building a railway.[85] But by the middle of 1862 these distinct questions had become fused.

Conflation of the issue of colonial federation with the railway was important; for it gave British policy makers an additional reason to interest themselves in the constitutional future of the colonies. Vague ideas of British North American federation had been discussed for decades, but it only became practical politics after a powerful interest group, the investors in the Grand Trunk, came to favour it. The Confederation settlement that emerged in 1864 was a package deal that embraced colonial federation, specific constitutional reforms aimed at resolving Canadian disputes, a constitutionally entrenched promise to build the Intercolonial, and other resolutions.

As Phillip Buckner has shown, many colonists were torn by the package deal offered in 1864.[86] They liked the general idea of colonial union but disliked the particular version that emerged out of the Quebec Conference. Financial themes loomed large in the Confederation debates and, as the next chapter makes clear, British North Americans in the 1860s were divided over important issues of political economy. There was no consensus on whether the costly Intercolonial railway and other state-subsidized routes to economic development were desirable. In the period 1862–64, the debate over economic policy threatened to derail the move towards Confederation. This crucial period is discussed in the next chapter.

5

Attempted Economic Decolonization: The Short Premiership of John Sandfield Macdonald

The year 1862 saw progress towards an imperial loan guarantee for the Halifax-Quebec railway. But just as Gladstone's resistance was being overcome in Britain, a new impediment emerged in the Province of Canada. While the governments of New Brunswick and Nova Scotia continued to act in ways congruent with the aims of the gentlemanly capitalists of the City, Canada's new government adopted a very different stance on the question of the Intercolonial and on more fundamental issues of political economy. Because Canadian political history after 1841 is often viewed as a world of dull moderates, the word "radical" is infrequently applied to colonial politicians in the 1860s.[1] There was indeed something subversive, however, about the efforts of the governments under Sandfield Macdonald to loosen the grip of British gentlemanly capitalists over the provincial economy.

A number of factors allowed Sandfield Macdonald and his allies to gain power after their years in the political wilderness. One of these was the militia bill that the Bleu-Conservative government had attempted to pass in the interests of making the colony more self-sufficient in terms of defence. The defeat of this bill on 20 May 1862 resulted in the resignation of the government and the formation of a ministry led by Sandfield Macdonald and L.V. Sicotte.[2] The militia bill had failed partly because the threat of conscription, however remote, was disliked and because the Macdonald-Cartier regime was itself increasingly unpopular.[3] Many Upper Canadian Conservatives who were disaffected over the failure to introduce some measure of representation by population had deserted the ministry. Moreover, the massive cost overruns on the Parliament buildings in Ottawa were perceived as a symptom of general financial mismanagement. Galt's budget, introduced in May 1862, offended all sides by increasing taxes, including those on tea and sugar, while leaving a deficit of about three million dollars to be met by further borrowing in London.[4]

Peter Baskerville suggests that Luther Hamilton Holton, Sandfield Macdonald's second minister of Finance, was motivated by Canadian economic nationalism. As evidence, he quotes Holton's observation that an immediate reduction of the tariff would be politically imprudent because it would create opposition from "special interests."[5] Baskerville extrapolates from this statement that Holton was a protectionist and therefore a nationalist. It is far more plausible, however, to ascribe his decision to leave the customs duties at the existing levels to a mixture of political expediency and the state of the provincial treasury. One has to work very hard to read economic nationalism into Holton's actions. In fact, mid-Victorian Radicalism, a quintessentially British ideology, was the force that animated the economic decolonization agenda of the government under Sandfield Macdonald.

Holton had a long-standing commitment to free trade and his ideas were undoubtedly influenced by the Gladstonian emphasis on "liberty, retrenchment and reform."[6] In 1846 Holton had taken a leading role in establishing both the Free Trade Association of Montreal and the *Canadian Economist*, a paper modelled after the English *Economist*, an anti-Corn Law publication. These actions set him apart from the bulk of the Montreal mercantile community, whose members regretted the end of mercantilism, and connected him with the much larger movement of classical liberals in Britain.[7] In the 1860s Holton's agenda was applauded by important figures in British liberalism: Robert Lowe, M P, regarded the Sandfield Macdonald governments as far preferable to those led by Cartier and Macdonald, which he characterized as "the impersonation of evil." Lowe remarked that the Macdonald-Cartier regime had been a highly destructive force in Canadian life and condemned its "great servility to the moneyed interests in England."[8]

By servility to the moneyed interests, Lowe was probably referring to the willingness of successive Canadian governments to subsidize enterprises controlled by Thomas Baring and George Carr Glyn, namely, the Grand Trunk and the Bank of Upper Canada. Sandfield Macdonald was unusual in that he attempted to cut off the supply of money to these companies. He also embarked on other policies aimed at gradually freeing Canada from the grip of the City of London. For instance, his government sought to reduce dependency on the London money market through retrenchment in public spending and by borrowing money in Canada. It should be noted that neither Macdonald nor his ministers believed that Canada should repudiate its existing external debts. Indeed, George Brown was highly critical of the treatment of the bondholders by the City of Hamilton.[9] But while Holton, Brown, and other proponents of economic decolonization held that current obligations must be honoured, they also wanted to curtail and eventually eliminate future debt issues in London.

Lord Monck, the Governor General during Sandfield Macdonald's premiership, was unpopular with British investors because of his passivity and leanings towards separatism. Edward Watkin expressed outrage upon hearing of Monck's repeated declarations that he would be Canada's "last Governor-General." Watkin was alarmed by the implication that Canadian independence was just around the corner. He was also offended when Monck declared that railways and canals should not seek government handouts. Monck's belief that the colony's infrastructure should be built by unaided "private enterprise"[10] had obvious implications for the subsidy-dependent Grand Trunk. Given Monck's leanings in the direction of classical liberalism, it is not surprising that George Brown came to see himself as an "amicus curiae," or friend of the Governor General's court.[11]

Although responsible government had reduced their power, Monck and other Governors General in this era were still able to exercise their discretion in proroguing legislatures and in forming ministries. This residual power had been demonstrated during the 1858 ministerial crisis when Sir Edmund Head refused to call the election requested by the short-lived Brown-Dorion administration. The result of Head's actions had been the return of Cartier and Macdonald to office. Brown and other Reformers attributed Head's actions during the 1858 ministerial crisis to the malign influence of Baring and other London financiers. They had charged that Head's support for Cartier and Macdonald stemmed from a desire to please London bankers anxious to keep the conservatives in power.[12] In contrast, Monck seemed to be a quite different governor. Robert Lowe praised Monck for supporting Sandfield

Macdonald. Lowe was refering to Monck's May 1863 decision to call an election at the request of the premier, who improved his position in the legislature as a result.[13]

One of the inaugural acts of the Macdonald-Sicotte ministry was to cancel the board of arbitration established to deal with the Grand Trunk's claims for a higher postal subsidy on the grounds that the board was filled with Grand Trunk sympathizers.[14] This decision led to howls of protest from Galt, who claimed that it, along with the failure of the militia bill, had ruined Canada's reputation in the London capital market.[15] The Macdonald-Sicotte ministry remained in office until May 1863 when the government was reconstituted in a more radical form. A cabinet reorganization saw the replacement of W.P. Howland, the middle-of-the-road minister of Finance, by Luther Hamilton Holton. Holton agreed to take over the Finance portfolio on condition that Sicotte, a moderate, be replaced by the more radical *rouge* A.A. Dorion. George Brown, who had left politics in 1861, returned to the legislature in 1863,[16] reinforcing the movement towards a more liberal political landscape. Brown did not join the Sandfield Macdonald ministries but lent them independent support.[17]

As minister of Finance, Holton introduced an austerity budget that received the warm approval of the *Economist* of London[18] and the *Globe* of Toronto.[19] The Canadian deficit had been escalating rapidly and even the most enthusiastic advocates of deficit financing recognized that something needed to be done. In his budget speech, Holton identified himself with Sir Robert Peel, whose free trade policy and adoption of direct taxation had, in his eyes, brought about the "regeneration" of Britain.[20] The *Globe* lauded Holton for his determination to cut government spending, reduce the deficit, and move Canada "into accord with the Free Trade policy of the mother country." The borrow-and-spend policy of the previous ministries, it declared, had placed "the Province at the mercy of Lombard Street."[21] The *Globe* contrasted Holton's honest and self-reliant approach with that taken by Galt, whose policy as minister of Finance had been to solve all problems by borrowing in London.[22]

Luther Holton's main goal was eliminating the deficit. However, he was also convinced that if the government had to borrow the evil should be minimized by doing so locally and he negotiated a major loan with the Bank of Montreal. At the same time, he removed the government's lucrative account from the Bank of Upper Canada, a firm tied to Baring, Glyn, and the Grand Trunk, and transferred it to the Bank of Montreal, an enterprise outside their control. This decision inflicted a wound on the Bank of Upper Canada that proved fatal within a few years.[23]

The government's agenda of economic decolonization was supported by George Brown's *Globe,* which saw no contradiction in upholding the British political connection while supporting efforts to free the colony from the influence of City. The *Globe* felt that Canadians should be tied to the mother country through the Governor General and the Colonial Secretary, not through a web of credit. The paper's arguments in favour of Canadian financial self-sufficiency worked on a number of levels, economic and moral. It maintained that the "purity" of public administration had suffered in the years since Canadian governments had begun borrowing in London[24] and thought that it would be a "happy day" when the Canadian government could meet all its borrowing requirements within the colony's own cities. The newspaper maintained that ending dependence on external sources of capital would mean that Canadian politicians would no longer "tremble at the frown of a Lombard Street banker" and would instead be subject to the will of the people.[25] At present, it said, "Messrs Baring and Glyn" enjoyed "tremendous power" over the Canadian government.[26]

The *Globe's* attitude to the BNAA was closely connected to its general suspicion of British financiers. The paper attacked the BNAA on the populist-democratic grounds that it was controlled by the large holders of colonial government securities.[27] George Brown had attended a meeting of the BNAA in 1862 but had come away unimpressed, concluding that it was simply a facade for the interests of the eight hundred or so Grand Trunk investors in Britain.[28] These investors, he thought, were trying to force Canada to spend money on a host of railway and military projects that few Canadians desired.[29]

It is not surprising that London's gentlemanly capitalists strongly disliked the Sandfield Macdonald ministry. In June 1862 George Carr Glyn conveyed his regret at the fall of the Macdonald-Cartier ministry and the departure of Galt from Finance, expressing his appreciation of Galt's efforts on behalf of the Grand Trunk and hoping that even in opposition, his "hard exertions" would continue. Although he was no longer minister of Finance, the relationship between Galt and Glyn Mills during the Sandfield Macdonald era appears to have continued on an informal level. Additionally, the bank retained Galt as a private customer,[30] perhaps in the expectation that he would soon be in a position to influence government policy.

John Ross, one of Thomas Baring's Canadian informants, described Sandfield Macdonald's government as "ungracified Radical" in its agenda.[31] John Rose chose a different epithet, claiming that Luther Holton's plan to end dependence on British sources of capital was "Utopian."[32] In January 1864 C.J. Brydges of the Grand Trunk told John A. Macdonald that he feared Holton was about to introduce an anti-Grand Trunk budget.[33] By the fall of 1863 the relationship between the Canadian government and the British investors had deteriorated into open hostility. On 6 October 1863 Holton he informed the legislative assembly that the Grand Trunk was conspiring with the opposition to bring down the government.[34] A few days later, he said that "large capitalists" in London were working with the opposition to depreciate the price of the Province's securities in an effort to remove him from office, and he implicated Watkin and Brydges, as the leaders of the Canadian arm of this effort. John A. Macdonald denied the accusation and defended Brydges, who watched the entire exchange from the gallery.[35] The Toronto *Globe* kept its readers well informed about the Grand Trunk "conspiracy" to overthrow the Macdonald-Sicotte government.[36]

The Sandfield Macdonald era witnessed the first major divergence in railway policy between Canada and the lower provinces of Nova Scotia and New Brunswick. Under Cartier and Macdonald, railway policy in the three provinces had been broadly similar in that their governments had agreed that railways should be financed through government borrowing in London. Nova Scotia was superficially different from the other colonies, having decided to build and operate its railways as a public enterprise rather than by chartering a private company analogous to the Grand Trunk.[37] But from the standpoint of a London banking operation, there was little practical difference between a colonial government that borrowed in London to build its own line and a government borrowing in London to subsidize a private company. Indeed, the headaches created for Baring and Glyn by the Grand Trunk suggest that public ownership might well have been in their interest.[38]

In Nova Scotia and New Brunswick, opposition to this system of subsidizing railways by borrowing in London was limited to a few individuals on the margins of political power. In Nova Scotia, Thomas Killam of Yarmouth denounced railway subsidies and upheld laissez-faire, but he was unable to influence policy significantly.[39] There were bitter partisan disputes in Nova Scotia over the location of routes and the confessional composition of the railway workforce,[40] but both parties accepted the City of London's role in the province's railways. When leadership of the Conservatives passed from J.W. Johnstone to Charles Tupper in the early 1860s, Nova Scotia's place in the gentlemanly capitalist system became even more secure.[41] Albert J. Smith in New Brunswick denounced the Intercolonial as yet another measure designed to benefit elites at the expense of the common man, who would be left to pay the taxes.[42] But Smith was a figure on the margins of power and his ejection from the Tilley cabinet can be interpreted as evidence that the political foundations of the collaborationist economic order were more secure in New Brunswick than in Canada.[43]

For people wishing to rescue the Grand Trunk through the construction of the Intercolonial, the timing of the Canadian political developments could not have been worse. On 10 April 1862 Gladstone recorded in his diary that there had been a cabinet vote on the resolution that "sufficient cause has been shewn for the interposition of the British government in the affairs of the Canadian Intercolonial Railway." There were eight supporters of the motion and seven dissenters. Needless to say, the duke of Newcastle voted in the affirmative. Lord Palmerston, an old Whig and leader of the more conservative side of the Liberal party, was in agreement with him as were Edward Cardwell, a future Colonial Secretary, and Lord Grey, a former Colonial Secretary. The opponents of the measure included Gladstone, Earl Russell, Sir George Cornewall Lewis, secretary of war, and Sir Charles Wood, secretary of state for India and a personal friend of Edward Ellice of the Canada Club.[44]

Although the motion for British assistance had been carried, the nature of the involvement of the British government in the railway remained to be determined. In an effort to achieve a measure of consensus, Palmerston proposed that the imperial assistance to the railway take the form of a loan guarantee rather than a direct subsidy and that the nature of the guarantee be determined after the receipt of further information.[45] This motion was carried, becoming the basis of the offer of assistance eventually made to the colonies. Imperial backing allowed the colonies to borrow at a lower rate than they could have obtained had they acted independently. There were strings attached, however, the offer stipulated that in addition to making annual interest payments, the colonies had to contribute regularly to a sinking fund, the monies to be invested in interest-bearing securities. When it came time to repay the principal of the Intercolonial loan at the end of its term, the sinking fund would be on hand, eliminating any temptation to repudiate the debt. The imperial government also specified that the sinking fund would be invested in Bank of England Consols. These bonds, while eminently secure, paid only three percent interest. The colonies had five years in which to accept or reject the offer.[46]

In April 1862, shortly after receiving a despatch from Newcastle specifying the terms of the offer, the Macdonald-Cartier government had invited the other colonies to meet at Quebec to discuss the offer. A conference was scheduled for September. When Sandfield Macdonald and his ministers took over in May, they did not cancel the meeting, but they approached it with a distinct lack of enthusiasm. Nor were they terribly excited about the topic of colonial federation, which the government of Nova Scotia had succeeded in tacking onto the agenda. At the Quebec meeting, the question of colonial federation was shelved.[47] The Canadian ministry assented to the Intercolonial proposal in principle, promising to send delegates to London to work out the details of a scheme for a joint imperial-colonial subsidy to the line.

It was only at the London meetings that Tilley and Howe realized how far the Canadians were prepared to go to obstruct the building of the line. They sabotaged the negotiations on the pretext that the British government had failed to comply with the colonists' proposals in every particular.[48] In general, the British Treasury officials had proved remarkably flexible in negotiating the details of the loan. For instance, the British government agreed to borrow on its own account and then turn the money over to the provinces "without any charge for brokerage or commission other than the ordinary expenses which the British Government are required to pay." Furthermore, the Treasury, in what Howe described as "a spirit so liberal as to leave nothing to desire," proposed a schedule of repayment that extended over forty years with the heaviest repayments of the principal being pushed to distant decades.[49] For Treasury officials strongly committed to the principle of colonial financial self-sufficiency, this was a major concession.[50]

The one minor sticking point was the issue of the sinking fund. At the start of the negotiations, the colonial delegates had maintained that a sinking fund was unnecessary; the Treasury, on the other hand, wanted a sinking fund governed by strict rules. The compromise eventually agreed by Gladstone favoured the colonies: instead of being placed in three percent British Consols, the moneys for the sinking fund should be invested in higher-yielding colonial government securities. This change in the investment rules would allow the colonial governments to borrow from themselves and would mean that the sinking fund would grow at a faster rate. The colonists had been given almost everything they asked for.

Tilley and Howe readily agreed to the terms conceded by Gladstone. Tilley returned home, confident that the Canadian representatives would also concur. But as Howe informed him, this was not to be the case. Howe spent half a day trying to get the Canadians into line, but Sicotte was determined not to be satisfied. Howe became convinced that the Canadians had been opposed to the Intercolonial from the outset and had attempted to use the issue of the sinking fund to derail the discussions. That Sicotte and Howland had taken a trip to Paris in the middle of the discussions strongly suggested that they had never seriously wanted the railway built.[51] After their return to Canada, the Canadian delegates sent Newcastle a lengthy memorandum ostensibly favouring the railway, but as Edward Watkin saw it, the memo was really "a laboured argument constructed to persuade the Canadian government and Parliament not to make the Intercolonial Railroad."[52]

Describing the situation to Lieutenant-Governor Arthur Hamilton Gordon, Tilley attributed the actions of the Canadian government to the weight of popular opinion in the Canadas. He argued that the Intercolonial was opposed by French Canadians who feared that it would lead to colonial union and by Upper Canadians who thought that New York and Portland were sufficient seaboard outlets for their grain. Tilley felt that Sicotte should have been open as to his true motives for opposing the Intercolonial: "Greater frankness was due by Mr Sicotte to Mr Gladstone and to his co-delegates upon this point."[53] Sicotte's behaviour alienated the duke of Newcastle, who regarded him as a "very small-minded jobbing Canadian Lawyer of little ability and less direction."[54]

Faced with Canadian obstructionism, Howe, Watkin, and Newcastle devised a plan during the Christmas season to obtain Canada's consent through the lure of a postal and telegraph route to the Pacific. Under this scheme, the imperial government would have subsidized a transcontinental route, but only if Canada accepted the Treasury's terms regarding the Intercolonial loan. In return for this concession by Canada, Watkin's International Financial Society would lend the colonies £500,000 at four percent to cover the costs of the route to the Pacific. Canada and British Columbia would then jointly guarantee the interest on the telegraph bonds.

Howe believed that they were facing the last possible chance to build the Intercolonial, informing Tilley that "the Duke and Watkin are both determined that the Intercolonial shall be accepted or that the North-West may go to the devil. But for this path, which we have on the rascals, we should all be solid again." It was probably with an eye to appealing to the Reformers of Upper Canada that Watkin and Newcastle conceived the idea of coupling western expansion with the Intercolonial. Although George Brown opposed the Intercolonial on cost grounds, he was interested in expansion into Rupert's Land.

Watkin, Howe, and Newcastle spent a great of deal of time together in December and a sense of their increasing familiarity is given by Howe's account of the Christmas season, which included carol-singing with Newcastle at Clumber and Watkin's "charming" birthday party in Sheffield.[55] The role of the BNAA in its corporate capacity appears to have been limited to social events honouring the visiting colonial delegates.[56] These gatherings served an important function, however, in that they raised the visibility of the project in Britain. At about this time, the promoters succeeded in enlisting the support of the earl of Shaftesbury, a widely respected philanthropist and advocate of colonial emigration.[57]

During the period between the departure of Howland and Sicotte in December 1862 and the formation in June 1864 of the so-called Great Coalition embracing George-Étienne Cartier, John A. Macdonald, and their long-time enemy George Brown, the BNAA undertook little political action. There were several reasons for the group's quiescence. Watkin, for one, was very busy at the time with the negotiations that led to the purchase of the Hudson's Bay Company by the International Financial Society. Thomas Baring and George Carr Glyn were also distracted by more pressing matters, such as repelling an attempt to corner Grand Trunk shares in British stock markets undertaken by an obscure stockbroker named Alexander McEwen.[58] Someone with the same name later made an absurd offer to buy Rupert's Land.[59] In both cases, Baring and Glyn were confronted a minor figure who had the capacity to be an exasperating, if temporary, nuisance.

Another reason for the low profile of the BNAA during this period was internal strife, one factor in which was the hostility of the old Canada Club. BNAA secretary Joseph Nelson believed that the Australian Association had folded because of the malevolence of the Canada Club and feared the same fate lay in store for his organization.[60] Nelson's salary demands were a divisive issue in themselves. Some members objected to them on the grounds they would divert money away from food, drink, and elegant premises. Nelson later recounted that his demands were resisted by those BNAA members, such as Hugh Childers, who wanted to turn the association into "a purely social institution" that would "possess all the advantages of a first class West End club."[61] The original intention had been to establish a club without a "refectory department,"[62] but a key faction within the BNAA now wanted it to become a recreational organization. The BNAA's move from an office building in the City to a townhouse near Pall Mall, the location of many gentlemen's clubs, reflected the agenda of this element within the BNAA.

When Nelson renewed his claims for payment, he was deposed as secretary at a meeting where "the only parties present were Kinnaird, Bischoff, and B[aring]."[63] Nelson appears to have survived in the position for somewhat longer: a month later he wrote from the association's new premises to request Howe's help in incorporating a bank and mortgage company in Nova Scotia.[64] Eventually, however, his association with the BNAA was terminated.

While the BNAA was relatively quiet, the *Canadian News* remained active in its advocacy of colonial federation. It did so in terms designed to appeal to the conservative instincts of Britain's propertied classes.[65] For instance, the paper connected the end of adult male suffrage in Nova Scotia to the proposed federation by asserting that those who had reintroduced a property qualification for voters also supported a wider union as a way of controlling "the tide of democratic influence." According to the paper, strengthening "monarchical principles" would help to "rescue

Canada and the whole group of British provinces from the influences" of the democratic element that was "frightfully, ungovernably rampant in the capitals of the Northern States."[66]

Rebutting the anti-colonial arguments of the Little England school was another of the paper's preoccupations. Goldwin Smith had articulated a case for colonial separation in a series of articles in the *Daily News* and the *Canadian News* responded[67] by reprinting Thomas D'Arcy McGee's reply to Smith. The paper also printed numerous small articles stressing the loyalty to the Crown of the people of the colonies. These included a story dispelling rumours of a treasonous plot in Toronto,[68] Cartier's speech on the monarchism and loyalty of the French Canadians,[69] and an account of the toasts drunk to the memory of General Isaac Brock, hero of the war of 1812, at the annual dinner of the Loyal Canadian Society at Grimsby, Upper Canada.[70] The *Canadian News* also presented good-news stories related to Canadian securities. Its readers learned, for instance, that the City of Hamilton had adopted a property rate of twenty cents in the dollar, with seventeen cents going to the payment of coupon interest and just three cents allocated for general municipal purposes.[71]

Just in case anyone continued have lingering doubts about the wisdom of retaining Canada, the paper emphasized the utility of a transcontinental railway through British territory connecting Britain to Asian markets. When the BNAA sponsored a lecture by Captain Millington Henry Synge on the proposed wagon road to the Pacific, the *Canadian News* provided sympathetic coverage of this worthy project.[72] The paper quoted the parts of Synge's speech in which the possession of extensive colonies was extolled as the source of England's greatness. Synge conceded that getting rid of the colonies might save the taxpayer some money but argued that "a Britain shorn of its colonies," navy, and army would eventually fall prey to foreign aggression: "War contributions levied by a conqueror are heavier than any domestic tax." If the Cobdenite proposal for colonial independence was adopted, "no one [would] rejoice more than the enemies of England, for assuredly it paves the way for her destruction."[73]

Although the eventual collapse of Sandfield Macdonald's government in March 1864 was due to domestic sectarian politics rather than outside influence, few tears were shed in either the Colonial Office or the London headquarters of the Grand Trunk. Newcastle was quite pleased with Macdonald's loss of power,

remarking that he did "not favour him personally." Perhaps Newcastle was also happy because he thought it marked a return to
stability that had been provided by the long-lived and cooperative
Macdonald-Cartier ministries.[74] However, this was not to be the
case and parliamentary volatility in Canada continued: the coalition ministries formed in the first half of 1864 proved unable to
carry on the business of government.

C.J. Brydges, the general manager of the Grand Trunk, wrote that
it had become evident "to every reflecting person" that there must
be "entire change in the constitution of the country" if Canada was
to avoid "a state of anarchy and confusion which may eventuate a
similar misfortune to those which now afflict the States."[75] It was
probably such concerns that drove Brydges to swallow his pride
and approach the Grand Trunk's great enemy about participating
in an "omnibus arrangement" that would solve many of the constitutional and infrastructural problems facing the colony. Although
George Brown did not accede to Brydges's request right away, a dialogue had been opened.[76]

At a meeting in London of Grand Trunk bondholders on 9 June
1864, Watkin touched on the possibility that a British North American union might be arranged; he analogized such a federation to the
Grand Trunk's pending amalgamation with the Buffalo and Lake
Huron Railway. Watkin mentioned that at a recent meeting with the
Colonial Secretary, a group of Grand Trunk gentlemen had been told
that the imperial government would arrange financing for the Intercolonial the moment Canada had a government willing to do its part
for the scheme. Confederation, he said, would benefit the provinces
just as much as the construction of the Intercolonial would benefit
the Grand Trunk. Watkin told the assembled bondholders that people in the United States were beginning to recognize the growing
commercial importance of the united provinces. He even suggested
that the merger with the Buffalo and Lake Huron might somehow
encourage the Americans to continue the Reciprocity Treaty, which
provided for free trade in natural products between British North
America and the United States.[77]

Before dissolving Parliament and calling fresh elections, Lord
Monck wanted to exhaust the options provided by the current legislature, strongly encouraging the formation of a broader coalition
in the hope that it might prove more stable. It was with this guber-
natorial support that the Great Coalition was formed. Brydges

approved of the coalition's federation union initiative, thinking that if it were "carried out as I hope it will be," it would end a long period of strife while simultaneously serving as a "means of consolidating British interests upon this continent."[78] Brydges also saw in the plan for a broad colonial federation a chance to persuade Brown and other people to accept government assistance to the Intercolonial. This could be done, he said, by using an "omnibus" agreement that would make western expansion politically dependent on spending money on improving communications with the lower provinces.[79]

With the formation of the coalition, the stage was now set for a critical moment in the history of British investment in the colonies: the movement for colonial union. British businessmen played a minor role in the formation of the Great Coalition and had nothing to do with the deliberations at Charlottetown and Quebec, but their reactions to the constitutional proposal that emerged from these meetings were important. While it would be overstating the case to say that the City had a "blackball," or absolute veto, over colonial policy, its opinion mattered. If the City had reacted negatively to the scheme and had made it clear that it was opposed to it, pushing the required measures through the British Parliament would have been extremely difficult, if not impossible. As it was, a favourable reaction facilitated the carrying of Confederation.

The Province of Canada had passed an important fork in the road without deviating from its course of borrowing and spending. Had Holton been able to implement his plans for the curtailment of public borrowing in London, Canadian economic history might have been very different. But instead, Canadian representatives of the gentlemanly capitalist tradition of deficit financing and corporate subsidization were able to regain power, albeit in a coalition with George Brown. Although they were constrained, at first, by their partner in government, Macdonald and Cartier were able to cooperate with like-minded people in the other provinces in crafting a constitution and in setting the direction of the new country. Gentlemanly capitalism in Canada had lived to see another day.

6

Reconciling Britishness and Federalism: British Reactions to the Quebec Resolutions

In organizing the Charlottetown and Quebec conferences and drawing up resolutions outlining a constitution, colonial politicians took orders from nobody, least of all a group of bankers in London. The constitutional vision contained in the resolutions was entirely the work of the delegates. Moreover, the decision to hold the conference in camera[1] meant that outsiders, including the investors, had limited knowledge of the intentions of the constitutional architects. It was extremely difficult for people in London to predict what sort of constitution would emerge from the Quebec Conference. They knew that some sort of union of the colonies, perhaps a federal one, was under discussion, but the rest of the details were hazy.

The British North American press were not much help on this score. The constitutional plan published by the Canadian government on the eve of the Quebec conference had been noticeably vague on details aside from two basic points: the new constitution would involve representation by population and would not threaten Lower Canada's distinctive legal system.[2] Indeed, Canadian newspapers that were united in their support of the Great Coalition disagreed about what sort of union was on offer: the *Montreal Gazette*'s prediction that something close to a legislative union would be blueprinted was rebutted by *La Minerve* of Montreal, which insisted that the union being sought was a truly federal one in which Lower Canada's language, religious institutions, and system of law would be protected.[3]

British investors were isolated from the conference proceedings by an ocean and a wall of secrecy. Even those investors who had close connections to senior Canadian politicians were left in the dark.

Charles Bischoff, the chairman of the British American Land Company, complained of this in a letter to Galt, the former head of the firm's Canadian operations. Bischoff thought that since he was on "terms of personal intimacy" with many of the delegates, he should have been informed directly about the contents of the Quebec Resolutions before they appeared in the press. He said that being left out of the loop on such matters would tend to undermine his "position in the City as being the Individual best up in Canadian Affairs."

Bishcoff reported that he was "daily applied to by Individuals for information" regarding the details of the proposed union and that "many enquirers" were "men of large property and deeply interested in Canadian securities." He argued that it was important to curry favour with these men, for they could "restore full confidence in Canada if they can but once be satisfied." According to Bischoff, the secretive attitude adopted by the Quebec Conference in regard to their friends in London might even undermine the chances for "the success of the measure."[4]

British investors had good reasons for wanting to know what was going on at the conferences at Charlottetown and Quebec; for the proposed constitution would affect business in many ways. From the investors' point of view, perhaps the most important thing about these conferences was that Luther Holton, L.V. Sicotte, and other individuals who had driven the economic decolonization program were absent. Indeed, Holton and Sicotte went on to become anti-confederates. But while most of the delegates at the Quebec Conference approved of the gentlemanly capitalist order of borrowing and subsidizing, Canada's Great Coalition also contained George Brown, who had supported the economic-decolonization agenda of the Sandfield Macdonald ministries from the sidelines. Moreover, Brown had dangerous ideas regarding provincial autonomy within the new federation. Brown's involvement helps to explain the note of ambivalence that ran through the British debate on Confederation in 1864 and 1865. After Brown left the Great Coalition in December 1865, the British financial press became far less uncertain about the scheme.[5]

Monck sent an official copy of the Quebec Resolutions to London on 7 November 1864. It arrived in Britain at about the same time as the leaked or unofficial version.[6] Many of the precise details of the resolutions need not be discussed here as they would have been deeply uninteresting to British investors in the colonies. Thomas

Baring and Edward Watkin probably did not care whether auction-
eer licences were a matter of federal or provincial regulation. On the
other hand, the financial details and the overall contours of the
scheme were of interest. Informing Galt of the state of City opinion,
Charles Bischoff remarked that Baring and Glyn would not take the
"requisite time" to read the text of the Quebec Resolutions and
would rely on others to get the gist of the proposed constitution.[7]

For British investors, probably the most important thing about
the resolutions was the delegates' evident desire to remain part of
the British Empire. Far from having anything like separation in
mind, the third resolution stated that their guiding principles "in
framing a Constitution" had been a desire to perpetuate the connection with the mother country and replicate her political institutions
"so far as our circumstances will permit." The first resolution declared that the "present and future prosperity" of the provinces depended on remaining under the Crown of Great Britain. There can
be little doubt that the gentlemanly capitalists of the City were of
the same sentiment.

The subordinate details of the scheme were similarly reassuring.
Given the problems British investors had encountered as a result of
the federal nature of the United States,[8] the British investment community must have felt some trepidation upon hearing that a federal
union had been outlined. A close reading of the Quebec Resolutions
would have helped lessen these fears; for while the colonial political leaders had designed a federal state, they had committed the
main levers of economic policy to the general government rather
than to the provinces. The federal government was to assume the
existing public debts and the regulation of trade and commerce,
shipping, financial services, bankruptcy, and all lines of communication save for enterprises lying entirely in one province. The taxation powers of the provincial governments would be restricted,
while the general government would be entitled to impose all
forms of taxation, direct and indirect. The resolutions also committed the general government to constructing "without delay" the Intercolonial and to improving communications with the Great West.
They also provided for the admission of the North-West Territory
and the colonies of Vancouver Island and British Columbia.[9]

The reaction of British financial markets to the Quebec Resolutions was debated by contemporaries and has been commented on
by historians. On 9 December 1864, a pro-Confederation speaker in

Halifax claimed that the price of Nova Scotia's bonds had jumped ten percent when word of the Confederation scheme had arrived in London. Canada's bonds, he reported, had increased by fifteen percent.[10] For historian Tom Naylor the increase in the price of Canadian government securities reflects the true motives of the British supporters of colonial union; he refers sarcastically to Baring Brothers as the true Fathers of Confederation.[11] Naylor's remark contains an element of truth, although the reality was more complex than his cursory analysis of bond prices would suggest.

Participants in the legislative debates on Confederation in Canada and Nova Scotia hotly disputed the effect of the Quebec resolutions on the London price of each province's respective securities, with proponents of colonial union suggesting that the arrival of the resolutions had made the provinces more attractive to investors. When David L. Macpherson, a Canadian supporter of Confederation, advanced this argument,[12] the anti-confederate Benjamin Seymour was able to respond with devastating force. Clutching the financial pages of the London *Times* from November 1864, he refuted the argument by providing a more complete series of quotations showing that Macpherson had been misrepresenting the numbers.[13] A similar exchange occurred during the debate in the Nova Scotia legislature when pro-confederates claimed that the Quebec Resolutions had raised the price of the province's debentures in London. William Annand, an anti-confederate, replied that the change in price was actually due to a coincidental increase in interest rates by the Bank of England. Annand argued that the price of the bonds issued by British colonies in all parts of the world had increased simultaneously because of the bank's actions and that it was therefore fallacious to praise the Quebec scheme for having improved the creditworthiness of the provinces in London.[14]

Like most contemporaries, Macpherson, Seymour, Tupper, and Annand did not discuss bond yield spreads, which are a more accurate indication of political instability than price alone. Bond prices reflect many factors (such as the monetary policy adjustments referenced by Annand). Calculating current bond yield spreads in the 1860s would, however, have undermined the anti-confederate view that the receipt of the Quebec Resolutions did little to improve the creditworthiness of the colonies: the greater the likelihood of Confederation's being implemented, the lower the borrowing costs faced by Canada in the London capital market. Between June 1864 and October 1864, the yield spread between Canadian bonds and the eminently secure British Consols widened from 2.4 percent to a peak of 3.3 percent on 18 October. Thereafter the yield spread narrowed, falling to 2.8 percent in early November, where it hovered until January 1865.

The narrowing yield spread indicates that financial markets approved of the general thrust of the Quebec Conference, especially since the yield spread widened in January 1865 after an election was announced in New Brunswick on the issue of Confederation. After the defeat of Tilley's pro-Confederation government, the yield spread did not fall below three percent for the rest of 1865. The securities of New Brunswick and Nova Scotia exhibited a broadly similar pattern, the yield spread versus Consols remaining above three percent as long as the anti-confederate government of Albert J. Smith remained in power in New Brunswick. Only once Tilley was back in office and Confederation was back on track did the yield spread narrow.[15]

The analysis of the resolutions that appeared in London's financial press provides some clues as to why markets approved of Confederation. The papers were supportive of the general concept of colonial union but were wary lest a plan for a weak federation should emerge from the Quebec Conference. In general, the financial journalists saw a legislative union of the colonies as the best option and a federation just of the Canadas as the worst possible outcome. It should be remembered that the Great Coalition had been formed on the understanding that it would work to achieve a British North American federation, but that if this goal became impossible to attain, it would federalize the Province of Canada. Thus, for British people supportive of British North American federation, the Great Coalition's platform was a double-edged sword. That Victorian definitions of the words "federation" and "confederation" were very flexible further added to the confusion: it took time to realize that the so-called confederation outlined at the Quebec conference was actually a quite centralized union.

George Brown's association with the Great Coalition informed the *Economist's* initially ambivalent attitude towards the scheme. In August 1864 the paper's editor, Walter Bagehot, criticized Brown's federation proposal because it would lead to an excessively decentralized government and a weakened state at a time when an "Absolute Parliament" was required. As late as October, the paper was predicting the emergence of a spineless decentralized federation instead of one with a strong central authority. There was a palpable sense of relief in the article on Confederation that appeared on 26 November 1864. It reassured readers that the authors of the union scheme desired a strong central government and did not envision independence. The *Economist* congratulated the colonial delegates for having moved in the right direction and thought that further progress could be achieved at their forthcoming meetings with Edward Cardwell. The paper expected that Cardwell would insist on including clauses to increase the central power further and hoped that the British North American delegates would have the good sense to submit.[16]

While it took the arrival of the full text of the Quebec Resolutions to soothe the *Economist's* concerns that the new federation would be too decentralized, *Herapath's Railway and Commercial Journal* was sanguine from the outset, reporting soon after the formation of the Great Coalition that the proposed federal constitution would give the provinces control over only "purely local matters" and would leave important things such as canals, the public debt, and the ocean mail service to the federal legislative body. The benefits of Confederation were a topic to which the paper returned in subsequent months: British North America was at last going to get the strong central government it needed.[17]

The attitude of the *Canadian News* towards the Great Coalition lay between the optimism of *Herapath's* and the *Economist's* initial dread of what sort of constitution a conference involving George Brown might produce. The first edition of *Canadian News* issued after the arrival of the program of the Great Coalition included copious extracts from Canadian papers favourable to its program. In subsequent months, the pages of the *Canadian News* were filled with praise for the scheme. The paper emphasized the monarchical motives of the scheme's projectors and the fact that the new federation would remain part of the British Empire.[18] However, the paper's praise of the Confederation initiative was frequently tempered with the criticism that the proposed federation would not be centralized enough.

The basic message of the *Canadian News* was that if a federal union was a good thing, a legislative union would be even better. The paper's editor, Frederic Algar, reprinted articles from colonial newspapers that shared his premise that a legislative union would be ideal. These ranged from an editorial from the *Montreal Gazette* that reassured readers that the proposed confederation would actually be very close to a legislative union,[19] to a piece from the *Halifax Citizen* expressing a preference for legislative union[20] instead of federation.

Correspondents in the *Canadian News* also thought it was very important that the new union should remain under the suzerainty of a hereditary monarch. One letter writer, an Anglican minister in Lancashire named A.A. Bridgeman, favoured a legislative union of British North America on the grounds that federations were essentially incompatible with the spirit of monarchy: legitimate authority, in his eyes, flowed downward from the Crown rather than upwards from the people. Bridgeman also proposed that the federation's upper house be made a hereditary chamber, suggesting that at the very least a sort of colonial life peerage could be instituted.[21] Bridgeman alluded to the eighteenth-century struggle between Parliament and the Crown but said that in the nineteenth century, the democratic element was the main threat to the constitutional balance: "The danger which now menaces constitutional and responsible government arises either from the Legislature itself or the people that elect it."[22]

In October 1864 the *Canadian News* printed a letter from "A Backwoodsman," a correspondent claiming to be in Upper Canada but who was really Thomas D'Arcy McGee of Montreal.[23] McGee stressed the need for monarchy and a strong, active government. Reversing a famous eighteenth-century resolution on the dangerous growth of the power of the Crown,[24] a "Backwoodsman" argued that nowadays the main danger came from having a weak executive and weak monarch: "Formerly, it was found necessary to move in the British House of Commons that 'the power of the Crown had increased, was increasing, and ought to be diminished.' With us, for many years, the exact converse is true – the power of the Crown is diminishing, has diminished, and in my mind ought to be increased."[25]

The letters of Bridgeman and McGee reveal a deep distrust of popular authority that was doubtless shared by many readers of the *Canadian News* and other propertied Englishmen in an era when manhood suffrage was still a radical idea. They also reflected the idea that decentralization and plebeian power often went hand in hand. This belief, and the corollary notion that centralization promoted a more elitist mode of government, sometimes crept into official British discussions of the North American colonies. For instance, in 1860 Lord Mulgrave, the lieutenant-governor of Nova Scotia, had discerned a tendency for the legislatures of small jurisdictions to be filled with untalented men who lacked social standing and "private means." Mulgrave had speculated that unifying the colonies would produce legislatures composed of wealthier men.[26] While ostensibly based on his own experiences, Mulgrave's thinking may have been influenced by C.B. Adderley, who had published a similar argument in 1853.[27]

Frederic Algar also believed that devolving power to local legislature had the effect of encouraging "all ranks" of society to participate in politics. This comment helps to explain why Algar was so keen on centralization.[28] Indeed, one could argue that the Quebec Resolutions were well received in London precisely because they embodied values so similar to those of mainstream British politics: a belief in deference, hierarchy, and the need to limit the political power of the unwashed multitude. These anti-democratic values would also have been shared by the vast majority of investors and financiers in this era.

Charles Bischoff of the British American Land Company summed up the largely positive attitude in the City of London towards the proposed constitution in a private letter to Alexander Tilloch Galt, the Canadian minister of Finance and former head of the firm's Canadian operations: "I consider that you have accomplished wonders, but having accomplished so much, I would hope you may still go a little further." Bischoff elaborated, explaining that "to create a Kingdom, the Local Legislatures must be reduced to the position of Municipalities. You have made great progress towards this but in carrying out details pray let this be your aim."

The details that caught Bischoff's eye in the Quebec Resolutions included provincial jurisdiction over property and civil rights, which Bischoff thought unfortunate because it would prevent the central legislature from rendering uniform the property and commercial laws of the country. He observed to Galt that in Britain "we daily see the difficulty of having one law, or rather one practice, for Scotland and another for England." Bischoff also declared that the resolution giving the provinces jurisdiction over "loans of money on the credit of the Province" was dangerously vague. He argued that the provincial credit must be subordinate to the federal, which "must take priority so as to preserve the National or Federal Credit as in our Counties in England."

The holdings of the British American Land Company were in Lower Canada and the interest that Bischoff took in the place of that province in the new constitutional order was natural. In his letter to Galt Bischoff advocated increasing Lower Canada's weight in the future federal Parliament and disliked the fact that the delegates had adopted the principle of representation by population in the allocation of seats in the lower house, arguing that in Lower Canada "the probability is you will find the great centre of commerce and wealth as Intellect—other portions increase in population, not in knowledge." Bishcoff also suggested that Lower Canada's distinctive legal system be replaced with a common British American legal code that would facilitate interprovincial commerce.

Notwithstanding these criticisms, Bischoff told Galt that he was generally pleased with the outcome of the Quebec Conference, recognizing that the immediate introduction of a unitary state was impossible and that it had been prudent to "concede nominal privileges" to the local legislatures "for the moment." He reported that "the plan is universally well spoken of" in England and asked Galt to show his letter to Macdonald, Cartier, and Brown.[29] In another letter, he mentioned an interview with Edward Cardwell on the subject: "The Federation is universally approved here — the only fear is that you may give each State or Province too much authority."[30] Galt gave a speech in Sherbrooke on the financial aspects of the scheme, and when the particulars of the speech arrived in England, Bischoff was even more supportive of the proposed constitution, praising the speech and suggesting that it was the object of interest in the City.[31]

Writing in the *Edinburgh Review*, Arthur Mills, a Conservative MP,[32] endorsed the Quebec Resolutions as a truly "Conservative" document; he found it ironic that the Quebec Conference had been called in response to the grievances of a Canadian political party that "we in England have regarded as a democratic movement" for demanding "representation by population." Remarking on this political alchemy, Mills said that "in adopting the image and superscription of Her Majesty as the frontispiece of their first edition, the authors of this Constitution prove themselves to be wise in their generation." He explained that while the original principles on which the Great Coalition had been founded were susceptible to a democratic interpretation, the passage of time had moved things in the more conservative direction suggested by the Quebec Resolutions.

Mills informed his readers that "nearly all" of the changes to the Canadian constitution proposed by the Quebec Resolutions were "of a distinctly 'Conservative' character." He suggested that by uniting with other provinces, Canada would be limiting the excesses of democracy. For instance, the Quebec scheme would entrench the property qualification of legislative councillors in the constitution, while at present they were dependent on a mere statute. Moreover, while legislative councillors in Canada were presently elected, the Quebec scheme would bring the province into line with the healthier practice of the other provinces by creating an upper house whose members were "nominated for life."

Mills admitted that while the Quebec scheme did not contain any "specific proposition respecting the franchise, it is understood that the tendency in Canada is rather towards raising than lowering the qualification of electors." Reassuringly, "we do not hear a whisper of vote by ballot" in the resolutions, "nor is it proposed to shorten the duration of the Federal Parliaments." Another "Conservative" feature Mills identified was centralization, writing that in "order to centralize authority, and to reduce as far as may be to a municipal level the local Legislatures," the statesmen assembled at Quebec had given all residual powers to the central government, rather than to the state governments, as in the United States.

Linking the movement towards Confederation to a movement away from decentralization and individualism, Mills observed that "amalgamation is the order of the day" in all spheres of life. In the business world, it was the process by which "capitalists of all classes are doubling their profits and defying their competitors." Following the precedent set by "our railways companies and millionaires the co-operative infection has spread to our mechanics and artisans," who were forming trade unions. Moreover, the tendency for consolidation was not merely a British trend, as "men of all sorts and conditions, at home and abroad (theologians excepted) are seeking in union that strength with which it is proverbially identical."[33] In Mills's eyes, Confederation was consistent with a global tendency represented by the unification of Italy and much of Germany.

The harshest critic of the proposed Confederation was the liberal anti-imperialist Goldwin Smith, who condemned the Quebec Resolutions as bad for both Britain and the colonies. The evident desire of those who had framed the resolutions to perpetuate their colonial status irked him, for colonial independence would be in everyone's interests, according to Smith. In his view, the passage of this constitution that would see the colonial bond "ratified anew" would result in heavier burdens for Britain and increased risks for the colonists.

Moreover, the implications of the proposed constitution for the internal life of the colony went entirely against the grain of Smith's thinking. He denounced the resolutions for providing a unitary state in disguise: "They intend to create not a federation but a kingdom." He was convinced that the overcentralized nature of the proposed constitution would lead to friction between the two levels of government and the possible triumph of the Celtic principle of authority over the spirit of liberty that ran in the blood of the Teutonic part of the Canadian population. Smith viewed the Quebec Resolutions as a reactionary document, out of keeping with the liberal spirit of the age and the genius of the New World. He did not doubt that British America was on its way to becoming a great and prosperous community, but he thought that the colonists had choices about what sort of prosperity they enjoyed. He argued that if the colonists choose to base their prosperity on the political connection with Britain, they would be limiting their future freedom of action.

Suggesting that the Galway Company's notorious transatlantic mail contract was an example of what might be in store for British America, Smith argued that the tendency of the proposed constitution would be to promote the politics of corruption, diverting the colonists away from the honest pursuit of riches and into the making of grandiose schemes in Ottawa hotels. In any event, by adopting the interventionist economic philosophy of Alexander Hamilton, the framers of this constitution were forgetting that as civilization advances, the importance of state initiatives decreases while the importance of "voluntary action and spontaneous action" increases. Laissez-faire and a constrained central government, rather than statist schemes, were the true path to economic progress.

Smith saw the real property qualification for the proposed senate as "an attempt on the part of the framers to create a hereditary aristocracy, as far as circumstances permit." According to him, the colonists needed to build their civilization on the basis of the "principle of social and political equality," rather than on the "traces of feudalism."[34] Writing to a friend in New York, he called Confederation an attempt by the British aristocracy "to plant an offset" in North America, expressing the hope that the "Canadian monarchy" would go the way of the recently toppled Mexican Empire.[35]

In the period 1865-66, the greatest obstacles to Confederation were the attitudes of swing voters in New Brunswick. Even before the defeat of the Tilley government in the 1865 general election, the *Canadian News* was monitoring the situation closely, attributing anti-Confederation sentiment to the fears of the urban workers, "a cry having been got up by the opponents of confederation in New Brunswick that the union of the provinces would be injurious to the interests of the working classes engaged in mechanical and handicraft trades." The paper confidently predicted that the "master mechanics and manufacturers" of Saint John would be able to persuade their less enlightened employees of the advantages of colonial union.[36] The paper's vision of the colonial polity was clearly one in which manual workers deferred to the wisdom of the property-owning classes.

The optimism of the *Canadian News* was only barely dented by the victory of an anti-Confederation coalition in the election of February-March 1865; for it cheerfully reported in April 1865 that there had been "gratifying intelligence that the confederation of British North America is progressing in a most satisfactory manner" and that "the check which was given by the New Brunswick elections is proving to be of much less importance than was at first supposed."[37] While historians consider that the Confederation process was entirely stalled during A.J. Smith's anti-confederate ministry in New Brunswick, the organized efforts of the BNAA continued unabated. In June 1865, for instance, BNAA members hosted an unusual noon-hour speech by Thomas D'Arcy McGee on the advantages of British North American union. Held in the London Tavern, just steps from the premises of Barings', the lecture was attended by numerous City businessmen. Many BNAA members were also present at a banquet for visiting colonial delegates held that month, including Thomas Baring, Edward Watkin, Robert Benson, and Gisborne Molineux.[38]

The complications created for the British government by New Brunswick's lieutenant-governor, Arthur Hamilton Gordon, are well known. Gordon disliked the idea of Confederation, favouring instead a legislative union or at least a highly centralized federation on the New Zealand model.[39] Less well understood is the influence of British business interests on British policy at this juncture. However, it is clear that metropolitan economic interests continued to agitate for Confederation after its apparent rejection by New Brunswick voters.

Writing from London to console Tilley on his defeat, Watkin stated that "every one here, especially in official circles, give you full credit for having made a gallant and patriotic fight for a great measure for the general advantage of the British Empire." As Watkin's comment indicates, the Quebec Conference was being followed by a number of groups in London that included the Colonial Office and investors such as himself. Watkin informed Tilley that he had written to Howe "to say what a grievous mistake has been made in NB and how much securities will be damaged." He explained that because the "British heart" had been cooled by the New Brunswick vote, much more than the price of New Brunswick bonds was at stake: "Upon the back of the great Confederation idea we might just now have carried in Parliament" rode "almost any assistance the Provinces might reasonably want for the Intercolonial, fortifications, etc." However, "as matters now stand" these proposals "will be chilled" and "every shilling" of Imperial money would have to be fought for.[40] Watkin wanted it known that access to British capital depended on acceptance of the scheme.

Premier A.J. Smith's attempts to persuade the British government to reconsider the question of Confederation went nowhere. Joseph Nelson informed Tilley that Smith's mission to London had been a dismal failure: "I have learnt that the New Brnsk [sic] delegates have not only failed in making any influence with the Govt but have more confirmed them that Confederation is most desirable and that the objections to it are quite unworthy of a moment's serious consideration." Nelson also mentioned that Watkin was planning to meet with Smith in order to give him the opportunity to turn a necessity into a virtue by becoming a supporter of Confederation.[41] If this meeting ever took place, Smith rejected Watkin's suggestion.

In the face of New Brunswick's opposition, Edward Cardwell published a statement proclaiming the "determination of Her Majesty's Government to use every proper means of influence to carry into effect without delay the proposed Confederation."[42] Cardwell instructed Gordon to use his influence to get Confederation approved by the New Brunswick legislature.[43] Cardwell informed Gordon that while he wished "to avoid all appearance of *undue* pressure or of dictation," he wanted it to be "thoroughly understood that this question of Confederation is one in which the Home Govt is quite in earnest" and that it was proper for the opinion of the imperial government to "have great weight in the province." Subtly hinting that continued British protection was dependent on the acceptance of Confederation, Cardwell stated that a colony so dependent militarily on Britain as New Brunswick "cannot assume to be independent of the wishes and the opinion of G[reat] B[ritian]." He also believed that Gordon, acting as the queen's representative in the province, could produce a massive change in the composition of the assembly by using moral suasion on swing voters.[44]

The Grand Trunk's role in the 1866 New Brunswick election has been a matter of historiographical controversy.[45] Writing in the 1920s, G.E. Wilson argued that the war chest delivered in person by C.J. Brydges, the Canadian head of the Grand Trunk, was a factor in the victory of Tilley's forces. This viewpoint has been rejected by other historians, most notably A.W. Currie who said that it smacked of the "Marxist interpretation of history."[46] Given the paucity of archival evidence, the controversy will never be settled. What is clear is that the pro-Confederate forces sought outside money to topple Smith's government: Tilley estimated the electoral expenses required to carry Confederation in New Brunswick at "$40 000 or $50 000."[47] It is also clear that Tilley's well-funded campaign worked in conjunction with pressure from the Colonial Office, the Fenian scare, a supportive Catholic hierarchy, and even public statements to the effect that the queen herself was in favour of Confederation.[48]

Tilley's success in the 1866 New Brunswick election reactivated the push for Confederation. The implications of his victory were immediately recognized by the gentlemanly capitalists in London. At the June 1866 annual general meeting of the shareholders of the Trust and Loan Company of Upper Canada, reference was made to the probable imminence of Confederation during a discussion of the laws regulating interest rates in the Province of Canada and the impact of recent rate hikes by the Bank of England. Faced with the rising cost of money in London, the company had become dissatisfied with the legal eight percent limit on what it could charge borrowers.[49] When a shareholder asked what progress had been made in lobbying the Canadian government to change this law, one of the directors, William Chapman, replied: "There was reason to expect that a modification of those laws would take place on the meeting of the Legislature, and that as soon as the Confederation came into operation they would be entirely abrogated."[50] Chapman was a member of the BNAA and his comments suggest that he thought Confederation would bring about free trade in money. His comments also show that the British businessmen who supported Confederation appreciated the significance of the New Brunswick elections.

At first glance, it is hard to see why Canada's union with the lower provinces would have made the legal environment in Upper Canada more hospitable to lenders, as the usury laws of Nova Scotia and New Brunswick were even more stringent: the maximum rate on interest in the lower provinces was six percent rather than the eight percent allowed in Upper Canada. In fact, just a year earlier Charles Dickinson Archibald, a Nova Scotia businessman living in London, had favourably compared the Canadian law to the usury statutes of the other provinces in a letter to Tilley. Archibald had urged Tilley to abolish his province's restrictions on interest, arguing that usury laws were obsolete in an age in which most countries allowed the price of money to be regulated by "the laws of supply and demand" just like "any other commodity." He pointed out that while "Upper Canada, where the legal rate of interest is 8 percent is flooded with English capital," nobody in London would consider lending money in the lower provinces. Until the New Brunswick usury laws were repealed, the province would "remain a terra incognita to capitalists. I could at this moment divert large sums to the lower provinces if there was free trade in money."[51]

Archibald's comment suggests that the assimilation of the various provincial laws towards a national compromise rate would have been unfavourable rather than beneficial to lenders in Upper Canada, however welcome it would have been to people who supplied capital in the east. Why then did William Chapman, the director of a company operating in Upper Canada, believe that Confederation would lead to "free trade in money"?[52]

The answer probably relates to issues of democracy and social class. During the Confederation debates in the Parliament of Canada, several speakers had objected to the allocation of power over interest to the general government. John Sandfield Macdonald, an opponent of the Quebec scheme, declared his opposition "to what is called free-trade in money," stating that he would always support restrictions on the legal rate of interest. Macdonald argued that "moneyed corporations" such as the "Trust and Loan Company" were harming the province by draining profits back to Britain. He felt that something should be done to protect Canadian farmers from this menace and that usury laws were the answer.[53]

J.B.E. Dorion, a *rouge* opponent of colonial union, stated that regardless of his personal opinion on the wisdom of laws limiting interest rates, if "nine-tenths" of the population of Lower Canada desired such laws, he, as a democrat, was obliged to vote for them. Dorion also argued that a truly democratic constitution would allocate jurisdiction over this issue to the legislative body best able to reflect the popular will in each community, observing that in the neighbouring republic, the laws regarding interest varied widely from state to state. Dorion thought that the decision to give the exclusive power to regulate usury to the central government was yet another illustration that the proposed union was not a "real Federal system."[54]

These populist attacks on the Trust and Loan Company underscored the necessity of centralizing political power as much as possible. After all, if politicians of democratic principle were attacking the creation of a strong federal government because it would lead to unfettered lending, there was an additional reason to support a scheme in which banking, insurance, and all other financial matters would be placed under the firm control of the central government. By removing decisions over interest from the provinces to a more remote level of government, the influence of popular, lower-class prejudice on the business environment could be limited.[55]

Tilley's victory in the New Brunswick election of 1866 paved the way for a final conference in London to work out the details of the proposed constitution. Preparations for the conference were begun by Colonial Secretary Edward Cardwell and were finalized by his Conservative successor, Lord Carnarvon, after the Liberals went out of office in July 1866. Indeed, Cardwell helped Carnarvon to make many of the arrangements. They recognized that this bipartisan cooperation was unusual but justified by the subject's "great importance in an imperial point of view." Both men knew that time was of the essence, for an election likely to result in an anti-Confederation majority was imminent in Nova Scotia.[56] The colony needed to be legislated into Confederation during the life of its current legislature.

The two men also saw eye to eye on the need to modify the Quebec Resolutions and move the future federal system in the direction of centralization. Like Cardwell, Carnarvon thought it would be a good thing to obtain "the acquiescence of the Delegates" in the reduction of the list of provincial powers in the bill.[57] The few disagreements between Carnarvon and Cardwell were about means rather than ends. For instance, Carnarvon disliked the draft constitutional bill for the North American confederation that had been prepared by Cardwell. This bill stated that there were to be no areas of exclusive provincial jurisdiction and that all the areas in which the provincial "councils" would have been permitted to issue "Ordinances" were subject to paramount federal jurisdiction. Moreover, rather than providing for elected provincial councils, Cardwell's draft bill would have left the mode of "selection" to be determined by the British government at a later time. Carnarvon objected to this bill not because of its centralizing thrust (which he admired) but because it left many important details, including the list of provincial powers and electoral qualifications, to be decided by the imperial cabinet rather than by the imperial Parliament.[58]

Cardwell's draft bill remained a centralizing daydream. Nevertheless, while such drastic departures from the Quebec scheme were not made at the London Conference, Cardwell's successor attempted to make more modest reductions in provincial power. At Quebec, the local legislatures had been given jurisdiction over "property and civil rights excepting portions thereof assigned to the General Parliament," and it was left to the London Conference to make the actual assignment. The limitations on provincial jurisdiction over property and civil rights proposed by Carnarvon on 22 January 1867 were fiercely resisted by Langevin and Cartier, just as John A. Macdonald had predicted to Monck.[59] Eventually, a compromise was achieved, and the British North America Act gave the provinces power over "property and civil rights in the province." This formula protected the federal government's control over forms of property with an interprovincial aspect, such as insurance policies and bills of exchange, while assuring the French Canadians that matters relating to farm, family, and Church estates would be under provincial control.

Carnarvon worked to limit the autonomy of the future provinces in other ways.[60] In a move that would have important long-term consequences, he obtained the consent of the delegates for the expansion of federal jurisdiction over fisheries and penitentiaries. When the text of the British North America bill was finally published, the Toronto *Globe* was quick to note these departures from the plan embodied in the Quebec Resolutions. The paper remarked that "the more carefully we consider the effect of the changes made on the Quebec scheme by the gentlemen now in London, the more deeply we regret" the move in the direction of greater federal power. The paper predicted that these last-minute changes to the Quebec scheme would probably result in "increasing budgets, annual deficits, and fresh taxation," all of which were anathema to the paper's classical-liberal ideology.[61]

While the major British investors in Canada probably would have preferred a legislative union, they approved of the essential features of the Quebec scheme, namely, the preservation of a constitutional link with Britain, the creation of a strong central government, and construction of the Intercolonial Railway. While there are no signs of investor involvement in the London Conference or in the modifications to the Quebec scheme subsequently achieved by Carnarvon, the last-minute constitutional changes were entirely congruent with the known preferences of Bishcoff and the *Canadian News*. We do know that in the making of policy concerning British North America, Carnarvon was anxious to gain the approval of the investment community. For instance, when Walter Bagehot told him over lunch that people "in the City" had liked Carnarvon's dispatch to the colonies on the Fenian threat, Carnarvon recorded his pleasure at their reaction in his diary.[62]

Of course, not all representatives of the British business classes thought that Confederation was in Britain's national interest. While the gentlemanly capitalists of the City had been convinced of the merits of Confederation, dissent came from the social groups most closely associated with classical liberalism. There was considerable opposition to the Confederation settlement by those who saw themselves as the representatives of the progressive and industrial part of the British nation. In 1867 the struggle between these two politico-economic visions played out on the floor of the House of Commons.

7

The British Parliamentary Debates on Confederation

Canadian historians have traditionally viewed the British parliamentary debate on Confederation as something of a non-event, maintaining that the bipartisan consensus in favour of the main elements of the Confederation settlement precluded any clashes of ideas or interests on the floor of the House of Commons. Donald Creighton claimed that the British were essentially indifferent to Confederation and that the associated parliamentary proceedings were a pro forma exercise. He famously declared that the British MPs regarded the British North America bill as less important than the dog tax they subsequently debated.[1]

The belief that British politicians were not interested in Confederation is erroneous. It is true that the remarks of the moderate Liberals and the Conservatives on the issue had a bipartisan tone of mutual congratulation.[2] However, the speeches of important backbenchers show that Confederation was a contested policy. After all, it raised questions of democracy and self-determination that were central to Britain's struggle for parliamentary reform. In 1867 Britain was in turmoil over the issue. Not long before Confederation came before Parliament, a protest in Hyde Park by working men seeking the vote had turned violent, raising fears that the franchise question would cause social disorder.[3] British Radicals condemned the undemocratic way in which the free trade bastion of Nova Scotia was being forced into the Canadian federation. The decision-making elite, however, had little time for such democratic niceties: they ignored the opinions of Nova Scotia and pushed ahead with Confederation. To have supported Nova Scotia's right to democratic self-determination might have opened a philosophical Pandora's box for the British Isles.

As Catherine Hall has recently pointed out, the struggle in the 1860s over parliamentary reform was a forcing ground for political theory and a major step towards white manhood democracy in Britain and its empire.[4] Although it was generally accepted that at least some of Britain's skilled workers would have to be given the vote, many aristocrats feared that parliamentary reform might result in something approaching manhood suffrage, a deplorable arrangement that might well lead to communism, anarchy, Irish home rule, or at the very least the disestablishment of the Church of England. Democracy, the "government by the people" of which the much-loathed Abraham Lincoln had spoken, was anathema to most propertied Britons, as was its corollary, the plebiscite.

Given the centrality of social class to British politics in 1867, it is not surprising that ideologies of class shaped British views of colonies inhabited mainly by lower-class Britons and their descendents. The democratic peril was even more of a threat, in the eyes of some Britons, to those subjects of the queen who lived hard by the border of the American republic. Discussing Confederation in the *Westminster Review* in 1865, the historian J.A. Froude observed that the question whether democratic colonies could remain permanently connected to an aristocratic mother country was regarded by many Britons as central to the future of the empire.[5]

Confederation was important to the British because it raised the question whether the British Empire in North America should have a future. The parliamentarians who debated the British North America bill generally saw Confederation as a means of cementing the ties between the British North Americans and the mother country. They were, however, deeply divided over the desirability of preserving these ties. As we shall see, Edward Watkin and other members of the BNAA celebrated Confederation for its tendency to strengthen the bond linking the people of British North America to the British Crown. Some classical liberals disliked Confederation because they thought it would prolong Canada's constitutional association with Britain. They favoured colonial independence.

Intertwined with these great issues of constitutional principle was the more prosaic dynamic of interest group politics. In the years before 1867, the BNAA had helped get Canadian Confederation onto the British agenda. Now the issue was before Parliament. Several important members of the BNAA sat in the British House of Commons and for these men, getting the British North

America bill passed was a matter of pounds, shillings, and pence. A railway was at stake and they had every reason to try to ensure that Confederation survived the political storms of 1867 and made it to the terra firma of royal assent.

The intervening seas were rough indeed, for the ongoing crisis related to parliamentary reform had destabilized the British House of Commons and made the task of governing difficult. The issue of reform exposed ideological fault lines within Britain's nascent Liberal party: in July 1866 the conservative "Adullamite" wing of the party defeated the Liberal ministry's own reform bill, allowing the Conservatives to form a government under the leadership of Lord Derby. Schisms over reform also threatened the Conservatives. For a period in early 1867 it seemed possible that a group of diehard Conservatives led by Lord Cranborne[6] would block Disraeli's reform bill, a measure even its creator admitted was "a leap in the dark." Had Derby's Conservative government been unable to pass a measure of parliamentary reform, a general election might have been called before the British North America bill had been put to a vote.

The turbulence created by the parliamentary reform debate in Britain made the passage of the British North America bill uncertain despite the pledges of support from the leadership of both major parties. In an article published in February 1867, the Toronto *Globe* reflected on how the "inner life" of Westminster, the negotiations carried on "*sub rosa*", made it difficult to trust the British government's pronouncements regarding its legislative program. The *Globe* feared that Britain's Conservative ministry might fall before the bill was passed. The paper remained hopeful that Confederation would make it through the imperial parliament but recognized that backstairs manoeuvring and an unsettled House of Commons might dash the plans to achieve federation in 1867.[7]

The *Globe*'s fears were not entirely without foundation. After all, Lord Carnarvon, the minister responsible for getting Confederation passed, resigned as Colonial Secretary on 8 March 1867 because he could not accept Disraeli's reform bill. A somewhat old-fashioned Conservative, Carnarvon feared that enfranchising the working classes in Britain would have terrible consequences. Luckily for the supporters of Confederation, the duke of Buckingham was able to step smoothly into his shoes and the British North America bill remained on track.[8]

The cause of Confederation was aided by two powerful factors, the first being the determination of both Carnarvon and his Liberal shadow, Edward Cardwell, to carry the bill. Carnarvon and Cardwell knew that the clock was ticking: an election would soon be held in Nova Scotia and the result would almost certainly be a massive anti-Confederation majority.[9] The imperial parliament needed to lock the province into Confederation before that election. A firm believer in hierarchy and stability, Carnarvon was alarmed by the popular unrest that Howe's anti-Confederation crusade was generating in the colony. After a meeting with the Catholic archbishop of Halifax in December 1866, Carnarvon noted in his diary that the prelate was concerned about the impact the agitation was having on the Catholic laity. Although Carnarvon did not mention it, many Catholic laymen were of Irish extraction.[10]

The second factor increasing the chances that Confederation would pass in the imperial parliament was the presence of BNAA members on both sides of the House of Commons who strongly supported the British North America bill and its associated measures. In 1867 the BNAA included nine Liberal MPs, most notably George Carr Glyn, Edward Watkin, Hugh Childers, the banker E.P. Bouverie, and the Irish landlord Danby Seymour. The Conservative MPs who were members of the BNAA were of similar stature and background and included Thomas Baring and Danby Seymour. All of these men had friends and relatives in the Commons.[11] One possible objection to the thesis of business influence presented here is that neither Thomas nor George Carr Glyn, the two largest individual investors in the North American colonies, made any public pronouncements on Confederation in or outside of the Commons. Their status as the financial agents of the provincial governments is the most obvious explanation for their public silence, but they may also have been worried that their intervention would do more harm than good. After all, by 1867 the argument that sinister British business interests were behind the plans to federate the British North American colonies was a familiar feature of the anti-Confederate arsenal.[12]

Given the hostility directed towards them in the colonial press, it would have been extremely unwise for Baring and Glyn to have endorsed Confederation publicly. There are, however, suggestions that they played a role behind the scenes in assisting its passage through Parliament. Charles Bischoff of the British American

Land Company told A.T. Galt that he was planning to ask Baring and Glyn to cover the costs of printing a short statement on the benefits of Confederation that would be distributed to other MPs on the eve of the vote.[13] It is uncertain whether such a handbill was ever printed, but it is implied in Bischoff's letter that Baring and Glyn supported Confederation in a quiet way.

In *Confederation Considered in Relation to the Interests of the Empire*, a pamphlet written to convince British people of the foolishness of Confederation, Joseph Howe identified the three British interests that were cooperating with ambitious Canadian politicians to bring about colonial union: Little Englanders in the manufacturing towns who saw Confederation as a step towards getting rid of the empire; the wicked and monstrous Hudson's Bay Company monopoly; and the misguided holders of undervalued Canadian securities.[14]

Howe was without sympathy for the HBC, arguing that it had reduced the Indians to "a state of subjection akin to slavery" and was a barrier to the "advancing civilizations of Europe and America." He was somewhat more understanding of the anti-colonial manufacturers and their disgust "with the high duties which Canada had imposed on British productions," but he argued that "if Canada was in error the Maritime Provinces ought not to have been punished for her fault, seeing that they had never followed her example." The most respectable group of Confederation supporters, in Howe's eyes, were the politically influential "persons who have invested £10,000,000 or £15,000,000 in certain enterprises connected with Canada." Here, Howe was alluding to the Grand Trunk. According to Howe, the bondholders of this enterprise, "despairing of relief from other quarters," have "assumed that if the productive revenues of the Maritime Provinces could be flung into the empty treasury of Canada … and that if the British Government would throw three or four millions into the country … their prospect of dividends might be improved."

While Howe was correct in identifying the Grand Trunk interest as an important supporter of Confederation, he misread British politics when he suggested that the Little Englanders supported Confederation. Nobody in Britain appears to have taken seriously his claim that Confederation would lead to colonial independence and the dismemberment of the empire. London's *Star and Dial*, a leading organ of classical liberalism, mocked this aspect of Howe's argument, noting in November 1866 that Howe had supported Confederation until quite recently.[15]

Indeed, Howe and the other Nova Scotians who came to London to fight Confederation often misread the situation. For instance, Howe's assistant, William Garvie, asserted on 15 March 1867 that the Conservative minority government had struck a bargain with the Grand Trunk investors to pass Confederation in return for support of the forthcoming parliamentary reform bill.[16] This scenario seems implausible for several reasons. Watkin, a strong Liberal, probably would have voted in favour of the reform bill anyway.[17] Moreover, just three days after Garvie alleged that a corrupt bargain between Disraeli and the Grand Trunk interest had been made, Thomas Baring delivered a speech expressing scepticism about the necessity of parliamentary reform and urging that there should be more "safeguards" than Disraeli had envisioned. Baring ultimately overcame his aversion to expanding Britain's electorate and voted in favour of Disraeli's reform bill, but the timing of his speech strongly suggests that there was no "logrolling" agreement with Disraeli.[18]

Howe's argument in 1866 that anti-colonial manufacturers were promoting Confederation is especially curious in light of his subsequent strategic alliance with John Bright, a manufacturer who sympathized with Nova Scotia's desire to remain distinct from Canada. Indeed, Bright's decision to champion Howe's cause in 1867 and 1868 is remarkable given Howe's earlier use of his name to frighten more conservative Britons into opposing Confederation. In November 1866 Howe told one landed aristocrat that Confederation might eventually lead to the redistribution of land in Ireland and England and a British government controlled by Bright.[19] It took Howe a fair bit of time to get his story straight.

The attitudes of Radical newspapers towards Confederation further undermine Howe's notion that Little Englanders and Manchester Liberals were the people driving the British government's support for Confederation. In an article on Confederation in July 1866, the *Financial Reformer*, a classical liberal publication, expressed the hope that the North American colonies would shift from seeking internal free trade by means of federation to pursuing free trade with the world as a whole.[20] The *Daily News*, the "advanced Liberal" paper in which Goldwin Smith had published his anti-colonial ideas, attacked Confederation in November 1866, calling the scheme "a device for establishing a yet firmer hold on the imperial treasury." The paper also raised the issue of Lombard

Street's involvement in Canadian politics, snidely remarking that while constitutional change in Britain could be undertaken without the aid of financiers, "in Canada there is a capitalist in every conceivable scheme."

In November 1866, the *Daily News* warmly endorsed the criticisms of Confederation that had been offered by the *Montreal Herald*, a pro-free trade newspaper that was concerned that the proposed union would increase the costs of government.[21] But after Howe's pamphlet attacking the Little Englanders appeared in December 1866,[22] the *Daily News* ceased publishing anything in support of his cause: in February and March 1867, when the British North America bill was before Parliament, the *Daily News* fell silent on the issue of Confederation. This was hardly surprising, given that the manufacturers Howe had unwisely attacked were allies of the publication.

Howe's attacks on the anti-colonialist manufacturers appear to have alienated potential allies. Moreover, the issue of the Nova Scotia franchise cost him support. A few years earlier, Howe had supported the reintroduction of a property qualification for voters in Nova Scotia. Unfortunately for Howe, many of the Radical Liberals in Britain who might have supported his cause were also keen advocates of manhood suffrage. In a brilliant political move, Charles Tupper told as many British people as possible about Howe's role in ending Nova Scotia's experiment with manhood suffrage. This tactic probably contributed to the shift in Radical attitudes to Confederation from hostility to a mixture of indifference and even support. Howe's earlier support for a property franchise in Nova Scotia discredited him in the eyes of many Radicals in Britain.[23]

Howe compounded the situation by enlisting the support of Lord (Stratheden) Campbell, a peer known to dislike the idea of giving working men the vote.[24] In arguing against Confederation in February 1867, Campbell reasoned that the Nova Scotia legislature that had approved Confederation lacked the moral authority to do so because it had been elected on the basis of manhood suffrage. Campbell declared that the question of Nova Scotia's union with Canada needed to be deferred until an assembly could be elected on a more restricted franchise. With friends like Lord Campbell, Howe hardly needed enemies: by February 1867, Howe had alienated many of his natural allies on the left of the British political spectrum.

The British North America bill enjoyed relatively easy sailing in the House of Lords because it was perceived as an essentially conservative document. When Lord Carnarvon, the Colonial Secretary, moved second reading of the bill on 19 February 1867, fifty-two peers were present. There were a large number of British North American politicians in the gallery and the general atmosphere was convivial.[25] The central theme of Carnarvon's speech was that the bill was a truly conservative measure. He praised the landed property qualification for members of the senate,[26] arguing that it was the nearest approximation to the House of Lords that could be created in the different "social conditions" of the colonies.

Carnarvon also argued that the proposed constitution would prevent pretensions to state's rights from destroying national cohesion and encroaching on the "effective vigour of the central power." The bill would allow the provinces a degree of "municipal liberty" and would "compel" the provincial legislatures to exercise their "local powers." Carnarvon appears to have been worried that the future provincial governments would adopt a lazy attitude of laissez-faire that would keep them from legislating in their areas of jurisdiction. Moreover, he said, the bill fulfilled Britain's treaty obligations to preserve the distinctive institutions of French Canada.[27]

Several peers offered criticisms on points of detail, such as the educational rights of Lower Canadian Protestants,[28] but the general attitude in the Lords to the bill was sympathetic. Earl Russell tempered his praise for the British North America bill with regret that the union was to take the form of a federation rather than a unitary state.[29] Lord Campbell's proposal for an appeal to the people proved very unpopular with his colleagues. Lord Monck, the current Governor General, thought the demand "betrayed a great ignorance" of "the principles of the British constitution." He noted that Pitt had opposed holding a general election in Ireland on the issue of Anglo-Irish union in 1801.[30] Carnarvon also attacked the idea of holding an election to decide the question of union as being against constitutional tradition, noting that the Anglo-Scottish union of 1707 had been accomplished without an appeal to the voting public in either country.[31]

With the exception of the idiosyncratic Lord Campbell, the peers were unanimous in their support of the bill. The situation proved very different in the Commons where there was sustained criticism by radical members sympathetic to Nova Scotia. The debate on Confederation was more than a clash between industry and the City, or between the landed aristocracy and Manchester manufacturers, but recognizing the existence of these two social cleavages is central to understanding how the issue of Canadian Confederation unfolded in the Commons. Opposition to Confederation came from manufacturers who saw themselves as spokesmen for the industrial sections of the nation and from those of varied social backgrounds who adhered to ideas of classical political economy as laid down by Smith, Ricardo, and Mill.[32] In December 1866 the Colonial Secretary, Lord Carnarvon, had predicted that there would be opposition from members sympathetic to Nova Scotia. In his diary, Carnarvon recorded that the Foreign Secretary, Lord Stanley had stated that the government was willing "to force the bill on this point" if necessary.[33]

In earlier chapters, the role of Richard Cobden and John Bright in the debate over North American colonial policy has been explored in relation to their overall world views. By 1867 Cobden was dead, but Bright was alive to carry on the fight and rally supporters to the standard of Manchester liberalism. At about that time, Lord Derby was reputed to have said that Bright was the "real leader of the Opposition."[34] The parliamentary history of the various components of the Confederation policy (the federation of the colonies, the building of the Intercolonial, and the rejection of Nova Scotia's demands for repeal) lends credence to this observation, for Bright was a thorn in the side of the leaders of both parties on all of these points.

In introducing the bill, C.B. Adderley, the under-secretary for the colonies, was on the defensive, seeking to counter Radical attacks in advance. The fact that the Quebec scheme had originated in the desire of Canadian politicians to escape from a constitutional crisis was a liability he addressed by stressing that proposals for Confederation had been around for decades. Colonial union had merely been precipitated by the deadlock in the Canadian legislature, but the deadlock was "no more the cause of the proposal for the Union of the Provinces than the divorce of Henry VIII was the cause of the Reformation." He also argued that Confederation was in the interests of Britain as it would prepare the colonies for a greater degree of self-sufficiency.[35]

John Bright's opposition to the Confederation scheme would hardly have come as a surprise to anyone following British politics for it went against everything in which he believed. Confederation was a centralizing measure that involved proposals for government intervention in the economy and that was informed by a deep-seated hostility to the United States. "Bright admired the United States, favoured the night-watchman state (i.e., believed that the government's involvement in the economy should be confined to protecting property rights and enforcing contracts), and was on record as supporting decentralization in colonial government.[36] In January 1865 Bright had praised the inclusion of the principle of representation by population in the Quebec Resolutions,[37] but in his eyes, this redeeming feature was outweighed by the other aspects of the scheme.

During the debate in March 1865 on whether to expend British tax monies on building fortresses around Montreal, Bright had commented on the relationship between Canada and the gentlemanly capitalists of the City and had pulled no punches at that time. In responding to the argument that the fortifications were necessary to protect the £43 million invested in the colony, he launched into a passionate denunciation of the City's influence over public policy:

> We know what "the City" means – the right hon. Gentleman alluded to it to-night. It means that the people who deal in shares – though that does not describe the whole of them – 'the moneyed interest' of the City, are alarmed [by the United States]. Well, I never knew the City to be right. Men who are deep in great monetary transactions, and who are steeped to the lips sometimes in perilous speculations, are not able to take broad and dispassionate views of political questions of this nature.[38]

In the 1867 debate on Confederation,[39] Bright focused on the undemocratic way in which the union of the colonies was being implemented. Nova Scotia's shabby treatment was not, however, his only grounds for opposing the British North America bill: the proposed upper house also offended him. Bright stated that while he did not object to any people imitating British institutions if they truly desired them, the people of Canada did not want an unelected upper chamber. Bright also attacked the bill on the grounds that it would increase Britain's military expenditure in the colonies. He saw a contradiction between Gladstone's present support of the bill and his previous, and in Bright's eyes entirely laudable, efforts to reduce the colonial liabilities of the British taxpayer.

Of all the things Bright said in the debate on Confederation, none generated more controversy than his suggestion that the Canadians' loyalty was motivated by British military expenditures. Supporters of the bill immediately attacked Bright for his affront to the colonists and their criticism was echoed in subsequent days by the press. In its coverage of the debate, the *Bullionist*, a London financial paper, regretted that an unnamed MP representing Birmingham had cast "unworthy" doubts on the loyalty of his fellow subjects in the colonies. The paper reported that the individual had opposed every other measure "to enhance the strength, the greatness, the security, the dignity of England." While this person was not guilty of "conscious disloyalty," the paper continued, he was skirting on the borders of treason in voicing his pro-American ideas. Particularly objectionable was his infatuation with the un-English idea of the plebiscite: "a wilder, less constitutional, more American doctrine was never yet ventured into the House of Commons." According to the *Bullionist*, England had always repudiated the plebiscite and now was not the time to begin introducing such nostrums. [40]

Edward Watkin was, of course, involved in the debate on Confederation, speaking to both the British North America bill and the Intercolonial loan guarantee. In the debate on the former, he attacked Bright's separatist ideas. Watkin stated that he "supported Confederation ... not because it was the establishment of a new nation" but because it would keep the colonies British. For him, Confederation meant that the "colonies were to remain under the British Crown, or it meant nothing." In deciding whether to support or to oppose Confederation, the colonists had faced the simple choice of living under "the Crown" or "the Stars and Stripes." Britain had a choice of its own to make: whether to be a great empire or a "small country like Holland."[41]

Watkin's speech in favour of Confederation attracted the notice of the *Morning Star and Dial*, a paper associated with the late Richard Cobden that had, as noted earlier, a strong classical liberal, or limited-government, orientation. The *Star and Dial* said that while it was not opposed to Parliament's federating the North America colonies *if* that was the will of its inhabitants, the projectors of this particular scheme of federation seemed to envision lavish expenditure. The paper wondered why Watkin, hitherto a good radical Liberal, had endorsed a plan whose failings had been so ably pointed out by Bright and that had been lauded by the Tories. It declared that while "Mr Watkin has a right to his own opinions" his speech, which had generated "a Tory cheer" would displease many of his constituents.[42]

Baillie Cochrane, a Conservative, was particularly pointed in his criticisms of Bright and struck close to home when he stated that Britain's possession of colonies was the main source of her manufacturing greatness. Everyone knew that Bright was a factory owner, and Cochrane's statement drew cries of protest from several members opposite, presumably from liberals who did not see how overseas colonies benefited manufacturers.[43] Others who spoke in favour of the bill on that day included the Adullamite Chichester Fortescue,[44] and Sir John Pakington, a Conservative who had been responsible for the 1852 New Zealand constitution. Pakington said he found Bright's remarks on Canadian loyalty "painful" because the Canadian public had shown generosity in contributing to various patriotic funds including the one established to aid Crimean War widows.[45]

Because it provided for a clause-by-clause reading, the committee stage on 4 March 1867 allowed the question of imperial aid to the Intercolonial to be discussed in isolation from the bill's other aspects. The previous summer, Lord John Russell had anticipated that the clauses relating to the Intercolonial would create substantial difficulties and had asked Carnarvon whether dropping them would increase the bill's overall chances of passing.[46] Disraeli had made a similar suggestion in January 1867.[47] Both men appear to have thought that many members would be neutral or supportive on the subject of colonial federation but would be firmly against the guarantee. While there were some people in this category, there were others, such as the Liberal Roger Sinclair Aytoun,[48] who opposed the Intercolonial on cost grounds and had strong opinions on the broader constitutional questions.

Perhaps the most prominent individual to share this viewpoint was Robert Lowe, a future Chancellor of the Exchequer. Lowe opposed imperial aid to the Intercolonial and questioned whether the necessary threshold of support for union had been achieved in Nova Scotia.[49] When speaking in Parliament, he affected lofty indifference on the issue of colonial federation, claiming that it was a matter for the colonies to decide among themselves. In private, he opposed the union of the colonies, fearing that it would perpetuate "rather than diminish" their connection with Britain.[50] Although he was not an open advocate of colonial independence, Lowe definitely leaned in that direction.

The decisions of particular MPs to remain silent are almost as interesting as the speeches against Confederation. When George Hadfield, an "advanced liberal" from the manufacturing town of Sheffield,[51] was preparing to move for a delay that would permit an election in Nova Scotia, Cardwell met and somehow "dissuaded" him. Hadfield did not inform Howe of his change of mind directly but instead relayed a message through a third party.[52] The behaviour of the Adullamite MP Edward Horsman is even more difficult to explain. At one point, Horsman promised Howe that he would present an anti-Confederation petition from Nova Scotia to the Commons. For unknown reasons, Horsman changed his mind on the issue of Nova Scotia going into Confederation and did not table the petition. Howe would likely have given the petition to another member to present had it been returned promptly. Unfortunately, Horsman was slow in sending it back to Howe, and the document did not reach him until after the second reading of the bill.[53]

Because Howe invoked free trade principles in vilifying Canada, the political economist John Stuart Mill was a natural ally. However, when William Garvie asked Mill to deliver a speech opposing Nova Scotia's forced inclusion in the Confederation, Mill replied that he simply could not spare the energy to speak on the issue. Although Mill expressed sympathy for Howe's position and declared that Nova Scotia was being treated in a "disgraceful" manner, he said that campaigning for parliamentary reform in Britain was of overriding importance.[54] Garvie felt that Mill's priorities were misplaced, noting that they included the idea – clearly ridiculous to him – of enfranchising women. Another point of disagreement between Mill and the Nova Scotian anti-confederates was that Mill was firmly against any imperial aid to the Intercolonial. Howe, of course, favoured this project and regarded it as distinct from Confederation.[55]

The clauses of the British North America bill relating to the Intercolonial were given force by the Canada Railway Loan bill, which was introduced by Adderley on 28 March 1867. This legislation provided for an imperial interest guarantee of four percent on a loan of three million pounds.[56] Adderley, an advocate of colonial financial self-sufficiency, said that not "one word would fall from him approving in the abstract of guarantees of colonial loans." Indeed, he felt that imperial guarantees for colonial loans represented "the worst possible relations between this country and the colonies, bad enough for this country, but still worse for the interests of the colonies."

After expressing his sincere hope that this undertaking would be the last of its kind ever proposed to Parliament, Adderley said that "this particular guarantee was an exceptional case." He explained that the guarantee was absolutely necessary because "the two schemes of the Confederation and the construction of the railway were bound up together ... one could not stand without the other." He said that it was very unlikely that the imperial government would ever be called upon to fulfil the interest guarantee because Canada's population was increasing "not at an arithmetical, but at a geometrical rate." Adderley concluded by stating that if "England desired that Canada should remain with her – and he, for his part, hoped that the two should long be connected – the way to bind their interests was by taking a liberal view of any common enterprise."

R.S. Aytoun found it curious that Adderley supported the bill while professing to have "the greatest possible dislike of guarantees." He said that his principal "objection to the motion was that guarantees were diametrically opposed to principles of political economy," but he also alluded to current interest rates, arguing that if railway subsidies were to be given, English railways suffering from the high price of money would be worthier recipients.[57] Aytoun was not alone in using the plight of British railways as an argument against the guarantee, the *Daily News* having earlier asked why aid should be given to a colonial line at a time "when money for an English, Scottish, or Irish railway cannot be had upon any but ruinous terms."[58] 1867 was a hard year for British railways, with many struggling in the wake of the spectacular collapse of the London, Chatham, and Dover Railway and the bankruptcy of Sir Morton Peto, a former Grand Trunk contractor.[59]

Aytoun's comments were echoed by Thomas Cave, who said that "he had enjoyed considerable experience with reference to the costs of railways." As for the Intercolonial, Cave "believed that most of the stations led from nowhere to nowhere." It was nothing but a massive "job." Cave supported colonial political union but viewed the railway as a separate matter. Cave used the supporters' observation that the Canadian government could not borrow money under six percent as "proof to any man's mind" that it was a poor credit risk. Moreover, he thought that the goal of making Canada independent of the United States and its ports was a bad one, for the safety of Canada depended on "friendly communication with the United States."

Having dealt with the strategic aspects of the scheme, Cave then discussed how he had once been tricked into investing in an unnamed railway because of a misleading prospectus. The anonymous railway had subsequently incurred massive cost overruns and had been forced to issue more and more bonds. After many years, it remained unprofitable. Cave recounted that he had not realised the truly fraudulent nature of the railway until he encountered one of its directors in a state of intoxication and thus willing to speak with unusual candour.[60] The Grand Trunk's misleading prospectus was famous, and given that subsequent speakers assumed that he was discussing a North American railway, it is extremely probable that Cave was alluding to the Grand Trunk. The extent of Cave's original investment is uncertain, but his speech suggests that by 1867 he had written off this money and was now seeking to prevent the promoters from getting at his other pocket through a loan guaranteed by the British taxpayer.

Gladstone, a former opponent of the Intercolonial who now supported it because of its connection to Confederation,[61] responded to Cave, stating that the member had used the authority of his undoubted "American experience" to discredit the guarantee unfairly. Gladstone countered the charge of jobbery by stating that the railway was not the contrivance of a few private individuals but "a scheme that has had the sanction of a series of free Governments for a long period of years, who, representing a population of our own birth and race, have adopted it." He also maintained that the commercial worth of the railway was irrelevant to the question at hand, for the line was essentially a political and military matter. In any case, far from auguring an increase in British military expenditure in the colony, he thought the railway would make the colonists more self-reliant in defence.

Gladstone believed that there should be "no bounds to the efforts which this country would make for the purpose of aiding and supporting" the colonists in their energetic efforts to maintain the imperial tie. At the same time, he made it clear that this was "a totally different thing from saying that this connection is to be maintained by the expenditure" of British tax money on "pomp or display in the colony or by way of attracting favour there by lavish charge." He thought that purchased loyalty was useless and that "the connection of this country with the British colonies [ought] to be maintained on totally opposite principles." In his eyes, the empire should become a federation of self-sufficient and self-governing communities tied to the mother country by sentiment and feeling.[62]

Perhaps because he had opposed the Intercolonial until he had been outvoted in the cabinet, Gladstone's speech blended principles averse to the guarantee with arguments in its favour: his conversion, unlike the apostle Paul's, was half-hearted. The opponents of the measure seized on these contradictions, arguing that Gladstone had provided a good argument against his own position. Robert Lowe criticized the line on both commercial and military grounds, asserting that the loan guarantee was nothing more than a bribe to enter into Confederation. In any event, the proposed Confederation was a foolish attempt to set up a rival to the United States. In guaranteeing this sum, Britain was assuming responsibilities it "shall one day deeply rue." Lowe predicted that while the thirteen colonies had "separated from England because she insisted on taxing them," England would probably "separate from her colonies because they insisted on taxing her."[63]

Watkin spoke next, doing so at the request of Adderley.[64] Watkin described how a few years earlier he had been "requested by the late Duke of Newcastle to make inquiries" into the matter of the Intercolonial and had found that the "hobgoblin fears" raised by "the construction of this 375 miles of railway" were utterly without foundation. Moreover, his research on behalf of Newcastle had led him to conclude that the line was essential for the preservation of the Queen's dominion over territories that extended "over an area equal to one-eighth of the habitable globe." It would give Britain "communication not only with Canada and with 10,000 miles of American railways, but with the vast tracts of British territory extending to the Pacific," opening a vast territory to British commerce.[65] Watkin presented himself as a disinterested supporter of the Intercolonial and omitted any reference to his employment by the Grand Trunk.

When the issue of imperial aid to the Intercolonial came to a vote, the motion carried easily, two hundred and forty-seven to

sixty-seven. Many of the opponents were "advanced" Liberals
who represented manufacturing and commercial centres that had
memorialized the government in support of aid to the Halifax-
Quebec railway. The *Canadian News* sought to penalize these
members by publishing a list of those who had voted against the
guarantee as a sort of dishonour roll. It was accompanied by a letter from Joseph Nelson who pointed out that many of the members had contradicted the wishes of their respective Chambers of
Commerce, which was apparently a grave if not mortal sin.[66] One
particular target was Thomas Bazley, a staunch Liberal and cotton-
spinner who had been president of the Manchester Chamber of
Commerce for fourteen years.[67]

The significance of the vote to aid the Intercolonial was considerable. Historians such as A.G. Bailey, Donald Roman, and A.A. Den
Otter make it clear that the railway was a *sine qua non* of Confederation and that without it the Maritimes would not have accepted
colonial union. Roman goes so far as to say that the railway loan
guarantees were the locomotive of Confederation.[68] Moreover, the
British decision to assist the construction of the Intercolonial helped
to promote a vision of Canadian economic development that was
both statist and tied to external suppliers of capital. The commitment
to build the Intercolonial embedded in the constitution a vision of
state-led development based on public works that set a precedent for
other ventures, most notably the Canadian Pacific. From the viewpoint of classical liberalism, Confederation moved British North
America in the wrong direction: away from laissez-faire and towards greater state intervention in the economy. This tendency was
sensed by Confederation's classical liberal opponents in Britain.

In 1867 Nova Scotia elected an anti-Confederation government, a
victory some people in Britain attributed to the corrupting influence
of American money.[69] Flushed with this victory, Howe returned to
Britain in February 1868 to demand the repeal of Confederation or at
the very least a parliamentary inquiry into Nova Scotia's claims.
Some in Nova Scotia argued that the imperial Parliament had ex-
ceeded its legal authority in passing the British North America Act,[70]
but Howe's focus was on changing the opinion of Parliament rather
than on questioning the doctrine of parliamentary sovereignty in a
British court.[71]

Howe's major ally in this campaign was John Bright, who
moved for a commission of inquiry to investigate the complaints

of Nova Scotia on 16 June 1868. Bright drew an analogy between the settlement colonies and British municipalities when he argued that Parliament would not change the boundaries of a town in England without ascertaining the opinion of the people in the affected area. But while Bright underscored Nova Scotia's close ties to England, he also stated that the Nova Scotians "have ideas which Englishmen have not. The tie that binds them to this House, though strong, is very much less strong than the ties which bind our English counties." He scorned Buckingham's proposed remedy for the grievances of Nova Scotia, which consisted of instructing the new Governor General to investigate its concerns upon his arrival in North America. Bright predicted that nothing would come of this and that after "stopping a day or two" in Halifax, the good governor would arrive in Ottawa and come under the malign influence of the Canadian ministry.

To provide those of his colleagues who had voted in favour of Confederation with a face-saving justification for changing their minds, Bright declared that those who had supported Confederation in 1867 had acted on the bona fide assumption that union had enjoyed widespread support in the province, a false notion that had been fostered by the Colonial Secretary of the day. Nova Scotia's actual opinion, Bright said, had been revealed by the September 1867 election. He reasoned that since the degree of opposition was now apparent, an investigation into the whole matter should be held. Bright underscored that he was merely for an inquiry, not immediate repeal, and suggested that Maritime union or a modified general Confederation might be enough to address the concerns of the Nova Scotians.[72]

In responding to the motion, Adderley conceded that there was dissatisfaction in Nova Scotia but argued that the Scottish and Irish unions were precedents that justified the government's decision to proceed with union in the face of popular opposition. Bright had spoken of the noble constitution that Nova Scotia had lost at Confederation, but Adderley reminded his listeners that this constitution had been a "gift of the Crown," revocable at any time.[73] Adderley also said that while Nova Scotians had formerly feared that union would lead to protectionism and "undue taxation," the first Dominion budget had shown that these concerns had been unfounded. He said that the united colony was adopting the free trade policy of Nova Scotia and would soon shift the fiscal burden to direct taxation (i.e., income tax). In any event, the National Debt of Nova Scotia had already been merged with that of the Dominion and the united credit was now pledged to various public works. Bright's actions were creating uncertainty and harming the securities of the very colonies about which he claimed to care. Adderley concluded on a strong note, reminding the house of Bright's "great liking for the institutions of the United States."[74]

The repeal cause won some sympathy in radical circles because Howe had depicted Nova Scotia as a progressive free trade country that was about to disappear into the maw of protectionist Canada. The eighty-three votes in favour of Bright's motion included those of the classical economists John Stuart Mill and Henry Fawcett. The motion was also supported, said Howe, by "many of the leading Scotch and Irish members." This observation suggests that many MPs from the Celtic fringe had found his comparison with the unions of 1707 and 1801 plausible.[75]

In the Lords, Campbell presented a similar motion on 6 July 1868.[76] Lord Granville, the Colonial Secretary, snubbed the debate, but Buckingham spoke, arguing that there was considerable support for Confederation in Nova Scotia, that taxes in the province would have gone up anyway without the union, and that the policy of the new central government had been quite favourable to Nova Scotia's commercial interests. He pointed out that Ottawa had provided money for lighthouses and had reduced import duties on many ship components.[77] In a somewhat curious move, Carnarvon replied to Campbell's motion by denouncing John Bright's doctrines as unconstitutional.[78] The motion was resoundingly defeated; it was opposed even by Lord Lyttelton, who was sympathetic to the anti-Confederate position and who suspected that there had been "secret" proceedings in the Nova Scotia assembly analogous to the distribution of bribes witnessed when the last Irish Parliament voted itself out of existence in 1800. Lyttleton was alluding to the idea that bribes had been used to persuade Ireland's parliamentarians to authorize the legislative union with Great Britain. Lyttelton's attitude was summed up by the phrase *stare decisis.*[79]

The bipartisan character and strength of the opposition to Howe's 1868 campaign helps to explain why there is little evidence of British investors or any other group rousing themselves to rebut his claims: the investors probably knew that Howe's efforts were doomed to fail anyway. In February 1868 the *Economist* assumed a dismissive attitude to the Nova Scotian troublemakers then in London, preferring to focus on positive developments such as the successful sale of £300,000 in debentures by the new Dominion government.[80] In June 1868 the *Economist* declared that Nova Scotia's inclusion in the Dominion would have a good influence on its tariff policy: Nova Scotia's free trade ideas would eventually triumph over the protectionist tendencies of the Canadians.[81]

The British parliamentary debate on Confederation was important to its British participants. The debate witnessed a clash of interest groups largely consistent with the gentlemanly capitalist theory of empire advanced by Cain and Hopkins. Although important features of the Confederation scheme were opposed by tax-averse manufacturers, classical liberals, and others who inclined towards the Little England view that the colonies should be cut adrift, the British North America Act and its associated financial guarantees were passed easily. When speaking in the Commons, Edward Watkin assumed the pose of a disinterested student of Canadian railway affairs, but that could not obscure the fact that the passage of the BNA Act was a victory for the investors with whom he was associated.

Of course, it would be foolish to argue that interest group pressure was the sole factor shaping the British government's decision to ignore the Nova Scotian grumbling and persist in its efforts to federate the North American colonies. One can point to other factors, such as Lord Carnarvon's enthusiasm for the creation of federations in all parts of the British Empire.[82] But Carnarvon's complete failure to make any headway with his projected Australian and South African federations suggests the importance of interest groups such as the BNAA in converting proposed colonial federations into reality. Put simply, there was a group of financiers who wanted British North America federated, but there were no equivalent groups pushing for the other federations Carnarvon supported. As a result, these schemes did not leave the drawing board, at least not in the 1860s.

At this point, it would be well to summarize the argument of this work so far. In the early 1860s there was a crisis in British investment in Canada. As a result, the major British investors came to favour the political union of theß British North American colonies. The investors associated this idea with the long-awaited

Halifax-Quebec railway. In early 1862 the investors formed an organization based in London, the British North American Association. It lobbied the British government and enlisted the support of other business groups in the British Isles. Following a campaign organized by the BNAA, Britain's Colonial Office came out in favour of a union of the British North American colonies, a concept it had previously opposed.

A key player in this drama was Edward Watkin, railway executive, member of the BNAA, and friend of the duke of Newcastle, who was Colonial Secretary between 1859 and 1864. In July 1862 Newcastle issued a circular to the North American colonies inviting the colonial governments to propose a federal constitution. He promised that the British government would assist the colonies in effecting a union. The famous conferences at Charlottetown and Quebec were the result of Newcastle's invitation. Although illness forced his retirement in 1864, Britain was by then firmly committed to Canadian Confederation. Newcastle's successors continued his efforts to realize the dream of a united British North America.

The British financiers who supported Confederation did so because they thought that the union of the colonies would solidify their connection to Britain. They did not see Confederation as some sort of stepping stone to Canadian independence, an option favoured by some classical liberals in Britain. The financiers who supported Confederation valued the constitutional bond linking them to their fellow subjects in North America because colonial status made Canadian securities easier to sell to individual investors in Britain. Many British investors distinguished investments in self-governing colonies from those in sovereign countries such as the United States. Because the distinction was widespread, those who marketed Canadian investments in Britain had a compelling reason to dislike the proposal for colonial independence that had recently been advanced by Goldwin Smith.

The commitment of the Fathers of Confederation to remaining British subjects can, of course, be related to the strongly monarchical political culture of the North American colonies. But there is a more prosaic explanation for the Fathers' desire to preserve their status as British colonists: many of them were involved in projects that were dependent on the continued inflow of British investment.

Like the Fathers of Confederation, the British parliamentarians who debated the British North America bill generally saw

Confederation as a means of cementing the ties between British North America and the mother country. This widespread assumption was quite plausible, for British North American legislators did not gain any new powers at the expense of the imperial government in 1867. The subjects of legislation covered under sections 91, 92, and 93 of the British North America Act had already passed under the control of the legislatures of the responsible government colonies. Indeed, Confederation involved the partial reversal of this earlier measure of devolution, with important matters being reassigned upwards to the new federal government.

Moreover, Confederation was in keeping with the notion that larger political units were the wave of the future. The Fathers of Confederation rejected the idea of a mere *zollverein* or other forms of loose intercolonial association and insisted that a robust central government was needed. The central government they created had unlimited authority over all forms of taxation, a veto over provincial legislation, and jurisdiction over all matters not explicitly given to the provinces.

Confederation was largely but not purely an exercise in centralization. The Fathers of Confederation did nothing to reverse the earlier devolution of authority to the municipalities of Upper Canada.[83] The redivision of the United Province of Canada in 1867 involved a modest degree of devolution, albeit to two polities with populations that numbered in the millions. As Paul Romney has shown, the Fathers of Confederation differed on whether the federal constitution outlined in the Quebec Resolutions should be a permanent arrangement (George Brown's view)[84] or whether the Dominion should ultimately become a unitary state resembling the mother country itself (John A. Macdonald's view).[85] But the Fathers were united by a common desire to centralize authority relative to the status quo of 1864.

The British investors and bankers connected to Canada saw eye to eye with the Fathers of Confederation on many issues. For instance, they shared the belief that the British North American colonies should remain British. The British investors and the Fathers also agreed that colonial democracy needed to be tempered by a stiff dose of aristocracy and monarchy.[86] Yankee democracy, with its (white) manhood suffrage, elected judges, and debt repudiations, was a terrible evil that needed to be avoided. Most of the Fathers shared the investors' belief that the new federation should have a strong central government and weak provinces. In the 1860s a community of like-minded individuals on both sides of the Atlantic worked together to produce a constitutional settlement that was mutually satisfactory.

It would be inaccurate to suggest that the specific terms of Confederation, such as the property requirement to sit in the unelected senate or the precise line of demarcation between federal and provincial powers, were dictated by iron-fisted London bankers. In any capitalist society the owners of capital have power, but their power is limited by the relative autonomy enjoyed by the state and by the influence of competing interests. This is especially the case when the owners of capital are overseas. The financiers of the City of London, however, did play a role in Confederation that is largely ignored in the existing literature.

The establishment of a four-province British North American Dominion in 1867 capped the political efforts of the BNAA. The next few years would see important changes in the affairs of the colonies in which the City was deeply interested. As the following chapter will show, British colonial policy towards North America in the years following 1867 would continue to be shaped by interest-group pressure. However, 1867 was also a turning point. In 1864-67, British investors had cooperated with the Colonial Office, but the years after 1867 would be ones of conflict. The harmonious period before 1867 lends credence to the gentlemanly capitalism thesis, but the events of the Dominion's early years suggest the limits of Cain and Hopkin's paradigm for understanding the making of colonial policy.

8

Gentlemanly Capitalism
after the British North America Act

The previous chapters have shown that the major British investors in Canada played a role in Confederation that is largely ignored in the existing secondary literature. They influenced both the timing of Confederation and the character of the new polity. In the 1860s a community of like-minded individuals on both sides of the Atlantic worked together to produce a constitutional settlement that advanced the interests of both the investors and the Fathers of Confederation. Whether they supported or opposed Confederation, most contemporaries saw it as a measure that would solidify the constitutional bond between Britain and the North American colonies. Because it was an exercise in centralization, Confederation was consistent with the widespread notion that larger political units were the wave of the future.

This chapter seeks to answer the question "Who benefited from Confederation?" In 1881 the historian John Charles Dent observed: "It cannot be maintained that Confederation has accomplished all that was expected from it by its projectors."[1] Dent's observation is especially applicable to the British financiers who supported Confederation. Confederation did not result in any plump windfalls for the major British enterprises in Canada. Indeed, the problems that had induced the investors to support Confederation remained essentially unresolved. In the midst of the great depression of the 1870s, it would have been logical to view Confederation as an abject failure: the Grand Trunk was still unprofitable, British Columbia was talking about secession, Macdonald's Conservatives had been disgraced by scandal, and Canada's emigration rate was one of the highest in the western world.[2]

In other ways, however, Confederation did advance the interests of British capital in Canada. The ways in which Confederation benefited British investors become very clear once we expand our focus from the years immediately after 1867 and begin to think about the longer term. Until the twentieth century, London was Canada's financial capital, not New York. The fact that Canada was a British Dominion, albeit a self-governing one, helped to redirect Canada's business away from Wall Street and towards Lombard Street. Thus, while particular financiers or firms in London might have been disappointed by Confederation, the Canadian constitutional settlement of 1867 would prove to be of vital importance for the City as a whole in subsequent decades. Seen from the vantage point of 1874, the results of Confederation might appear somewhat mixed. Viewed from the standpoint of, say, 1910, Confederation would appear a brilliant success, a statesmanlike move that had brought massive dividends to generations of British financiers.

In 1866 a director had informed a meeting in London of the shareholders in the Trust and Loan Company of Upper Canada that the imminent union of the colonies would lead the end of the legal limitations on the interest rates it could charge. For those who had expected that Confederation would bring about "free trade in money" in the colonies, the years after 1867 must have been disappointing. Although the British North America Act had assigned the power to regulate interest to the federal Parliament, Ottawa was slow to tackle this sensitive issue. As a result, the existing laws were left in place for several years.

In 1870 Sir Francis Hincks, the Canadian minister of Finance, finally introduced a bill to establish a uniform law regulating usury. The legislation would have limited interest to eight percent, the precise level the Trust and Loan Company had found so objectionable in 1866.[3] However, even this modest step towards free trade in money was unsuccessful and the bill failed because of the opposition of Premier Sandfield Macdonald of Ontario[4] and MPs from Nova Scotia, where the existing maximum was six percent.[5] Thereafter, the Dominion passed province-specific legislation that perpetuated the diversity of laws that confronted the chartered banks, trust companies, and private lenders of money.[6]

Confederation did little to help the long-suffering investors in the Grand Trunk, at least in the short term. Indeed, the company failed to capture any substantial benefits from Confederation or the Intercolonial for over a decade. Before Confederation, many observers had assumed that the Halifax-Quebec railway would be constructed as a division of the Grand Trunk. After 1867 it was decided to build the Intercolonial as a public enterprise. Moreover, the commission responsible for building the railway was structured so as to limit the influence of the Grand Trunk. At an 1869 shareholders' meeting, President Richard Potter had attempted to put a positive spin on this situation by predicting that the Intercolonial would increase traffic on the loss-making divisions east of Quebec.[7] However, when the Rivière-du-Loup division was finally connected with Halifax in 1876 the amount of additional business it created turned out to be quite limited.[8]

The only major benefit the Grand Trunk derived from the building of the Intercolonial was the government's eventual purchase of the Rivière-du-Loup division. Even this modest boon was delayed. In 1873 the Grand Trunk had proposed that Ottawa nationalize the division and incorporate it into the Intercolonial. Macdonald had refused to include this suggestion in the Grand Trunk Arrangements Act passed that year and the company had to wait until 1879 to sell this section to the government.[9] The proceeds of the sale were applied to the construction of a line running through Michigan to Chicago: trading the Rivière-du-Loup division for a line running to a great commercial metropolis was an unusually astute business decision for the Grand Trunk.[10]

In the early 1860s Watkin and other Grand Trunk officials had mused about constructing a railway to the Pacific. But by the 1870s the Grand Trunk was financially exhausted and unable to engage in any grand nation-building schemes. Although the firm did not end up participating in the construction of the Canadian Pacific, the Allan Line, another interest that had been represented in the BNAA, did join in the syndicate in the middle of the 1873 Pacific Scandal.[11] Relations between Sir Hugh Allan and the Grand Trunk deteriorated after Confederation because Allan was a supporter of the North Shore Railway, a firm that rivalled the Grand Trunk.[12]

Under the leadership of Richard Potter in the 1870s,[13] the Grand Trunk focused on building up traffic between Ontario and the Midwestern states and in finding internal efficiencies, thereby adopting a policy similar to that advocated in the late 1850s by the so-called Liverpool Party. The Grand Trunk also pursued a policy of amalgamation, merging with the Great Western and buying up many of the other lines in southern Ontario including the Buffalo and Lake Huron, the Welland, the Northern, the Port Hope, Lindsay and Beaverton, and several others.[14] The result was that by the end of the century, much of the province's dense network of railways was in the hands of a single firm.[15]

Only in the Laurier era did the Grand Trunk achieve Watkin's dream of building a line to the Pacific. The dream turned into a nightmare. Because it created three competing transcontinental routes, Laurier's railway policy ultimately harmed the Grand Trunk and brought it to the edge of bankruptcy. The company was nationalized at the end of the First World War[16] and soon became something of a by-word for the export of British capital gone wrong. John Maynard Keynes used it as a cautionary tale in arguing for restrictions on the international mobility of capital in 1924: "If the Grand Trunk Railway of Canada fails its shareholders by reason of legal restrictions on the rates chargeable or any other cause, we have nothing. If the underground system of London fails its shareholders, Londoners still have their underground system."[17]

Edward Watkin left the Grand Trunk board in 1868, but he continued to be involved in the affairs of Canada long after Confederation. Recommendations of Canadians for honours were of particular interest to him. In 1867 and 1868, Watkin played an important role in the struggle for Cartier's baronetcy.[18] In 1887 Watkin urged Macdonald to nominate Joseph Hickson of the Grand Trunk for a knighthood.[19] Watkin travelled across Canada on the new Canadian Pacific Railway, and while he doubtless regretted the fact the Grand Trunk had not built it, he was gratified that his vision had been achieved by someone else.[20]

Knighted for his services in bringing about Confederation, Watkin's Canadian activities in the 1860s were the springboard to greater prominence in British life. They also contributed to a temporary set-back in form of the loss of his seat in the 1868 British general election. In this contest, Watkin's constituents had been influenced by John Bright, who had condemned Watkin for supporting the "Intercolonial guarantee, Confederation, etc." C.J. Brydges of the Grand Trunk observed that to some extent Watkin's "defeat at Stockport is due to his loyalty in the furtherance of Canadian interests."[21] In the decades after Confederation, Watkin was involved in a number of high-profile projects such as his abortive scheme for a tunnel under the English Channel and a plan to build a tower in London that would rival the Eiffel Tower, a structure he humbly styled the Watkin Tower.[22]

Watkin's vision of the Hudson's Bay Company never came to pass. Nevertheless, Confederation benefited the HBC by creating a willing buyer for Rupert's Land, namely, the Dominion government. Under the old constitutional framework, French-Canadian fears that the acquisition of the territories would dilute their voting strength would have complicated any sale to the Province of Canada.[23] By giving the French Canadians a homeland in which their language, religion, institutions, and laws were secure, federation opened the door to the western expansion so many in Upper Canada desired. Moreover, the Dominion had much deeper pockets than the old Province of Canada, for its Parliament was able to levy taxes over an area extending to the eastern tip of Cape Breton. In 1869–70, after years of complex three-way negotiations between the company, the Colonial Office, and the governments of the Province and then the Dominion of Canada, the HBC finally sold Rupert's Land to the Dominion government.

Was the Colonial Office an ally of the HBC in its bargaining with the Canadian authorities? The gentlemanly capitalist thesis of empire advanced by Cain and Hopkins might lead one to expect that the Colonial Office assisted the HBC at every possible turn. Moreover, there were many personal connections between the staff of the Colonial Office and the management of the HBC. For instance, Sir Edmund Head, governor of the HBC between 1862 and his death in 1868, was a retired colonial governor. Head's replacement at the helm of the HBC, Lord Kimberley, was a future Colonial Secretary. When the Liberals returned to power in 1868, Kimberley resigned from the company and joined Gladstone's cabinet.[24] His successor as governor was Sir Stafford Northcote, a Conservative MP who had helped redesign Britain's civil service and who had served in the British cabinet between 1866 and 1868.[25] The duke of Buckingham, who replaced Carnarvon as Colonial Secretary in March 1867, was the former chairman of the London and North Western Railway, an enterprise controlled by George Carr Glyn, a major investor in Canada. Several of Glyn's relatives had invested in the financial syndicate that acquired the HBC in 1862.

Given all of these connections, one would have expected the Colonial Office to have shown considerable bias towards the company in its struggle to obtain the highest possible price from the Canadian government. Today, such personal ties would be seized upon by muckraking journalists as proof of bias. In 1868 the Toronto *Globe* characterized Colonial Office officials as colluding with the HBC to drive the purchase price up to levels that would ensure that Canadian taxpayers were still paying for Rupert's Land for many years to come.[26] The reality, however, was far more complex than the *Globe* admitted, for the Colonial Office was seeking to balance the interests of both parties. The Colonial Office affirmed that the company was entitled to some compensation for its property rights and rejected the argument that its 1670 charter was a legal nullity, but it also undermined the HBC's bargaining position at key points in the process. As a result, the HBC got less for Rupert's Land that it had expected.

British politicians of both parties had long expressed dislike for the HBC. Sir Edward Bulwer-Lytton, the Conservative Colonial Secretary in 1858–59, regarded the company's title as illegitimate and had encouraged the government of Canada to launch a legal challenge.[27] Bulwer-Lytton's decision to create the colony of British Columbia was widely regarded as a move hostile to the company.[28] His successor, the duke of Newcastle, was no friend of the HBC. In fact, the draft bill he prepared in 1860 indicates that he considered the charter-based claim to Rupert's Land to be worthless and that the company was entitled to compensation only for the capital improvements it had made to the territory.[29] Newcastle's perspective was altered by the International Financial Society's purchase of the HBC, for at this point he ceased regarding the company as an impediment to European settlement.[30]

However, the distinction between the old and the new company seems to have been lost on the Colonial Secretaries who came after Newcastle. His successors included Lord Carnarvon, who was characterized as an "enemy" of the HBC by Governor Henry Hulse Berens in 1858. The takeover by Watkin's syndicate did nothing to change Carnarvon's view of the HBC.[31] Moreover, the duke of Buckingham's connection to the Glyns does not seem to have prevented him from taking a tough stand during the negotiations with Canada. Buckingham considered Kimberley's demands for a permanent tax exemption extravagant.[32] The HBC's deputy governor, Sir Curtis Lampson, even denounced Buckingham for neglecting to protect a British firm.[33] Lord Granville, Buckingham's Liberal replacement as Colonial Secretary, was the target of similar criticism.[34]

By 1867 public opinion in Britain was increasingly hostile to the HBC, with middle-of-the-road voices joining the chorus of condemnation led by the *Westminster Review* and the Liverpool Financial Reform Association.[35] The *Times*, the great barometer of English opinion, denounced the HBC as "the last great monopoly which the improvidence and reckless favouritism of Charles II inflicted upon the commercial world." Arguing that the HBC had been holding back settlement by the "landless poor" for too long, the paper advocated the immediate surrender to the Dominion of all of Rupert's Land save the soil underneath the trading posts.[36] Although London's *Money Market Review* supported the company's claims on the grounds that property rights were sacrosanct,[37] such expressions of support were rare. Few Britons appear to have bought the argument that the Upper Canadian assault on the HBC's rights threatened the security of property in general.

At the time of the takeover of the HBC, the leaders of the IFS did not envision a radical change in the constitutional status of Rupert's Land. Under their plan, the company would have moved from trading fur to dealing in land while continuing to govern the territory.[38] But as doubts grew about the company's ability to exercise control, the investors' strategy shifted to quicker ways of earning a return. The long-term approach implied in the original plans for a proprietary colony was abandoned.

In the discussions of the future of Rupert's Land that took place during Newcastle's tenure at the Colonial Office, various proposals for a Crown colony were made. Newcastle envisioned a scenario in which the company would have retained ownership of land and minerals while selling its right to govern the territory to a newly minted Crown colony. Upon coming into existence, the first act of this Crown colony would have been to issue bonds in London and use the proceeds to compensate the HBC for the loss of its right to govern. The cost of servicing this debt would have been born by the future inhabitants of the territory, not by taxpayers in Britain or Canada. Both Cartier and Macdonald endorsed Newcastle's Crown colony plan on the grounds that it was better to leave Rupert's Land as a separate colony for the time being. George Brown said he would support the Crown colony option provided the territory was tied to Canada by a *zollverein*.[39] However, the failure of the HBC and the Colonial Office to come to an agreement regarding a purchase price prevented the Crown colony option from being pursued.

Shortly before leaving office, Newcastle expressed great frustration at the intransigence of the HBC on the issue of the price.[40] The attitude of the HBC also frustrated the Toronto *Globe*, which denounced Sir Edmund Head, the "very unfit person" at its helm.[41]

Newcastle's successor, Edward Cardwell, believed that outright annexation to Canada was the only way to keep Rupert's Land out of grasping Yankee hands.[42] He put an end to planning for a Crown colony.[43] Although an offer to buy Rupert's Land was made by a London financial syndicate led by an obscure stock-jobber named Alexander McEwen, Cardwell killed the proposal by declaring that Canada had the right of first refusal to the territory.[44]

Some Canadians clung to the old belief that the HBC charter was legally void. These people hated the idea of paying a penny in compensation to the HBC.[45] During a December 1864 visit to London, George Brown flatly declared that the charter was worthless. He also argued that the company's estimate of the so-called "Fertile Belt" as being worth over a million pounds was vastly inflated.[46] In April 1865 Brown returned to London with Macdonald, Cartier, and Galt.[47] By this point, Brown had softened his opposition to any payment to HBC. The agreement that emerged from a meeting between Cardwell and the Canadians stipulated that "the indemnity, if any, should be paid by a loan to be raised by Canada under the Imperial guarantee."[48]

In the period immediately after Confederation, it was unclear what stance the new Dominion government would assume regarding the HBC's charter rights. In July 1867 Head and the directors found it necessary to assure shareholders that they would vigorously defend the interests of the company no matter what attitude Canada presented.[49] Given that the Canadian government now included William McDougall, whose newspaper had commenced the Upper Canadian assault on the chartered rights of the company in the 1850s, they had ample reason to be concerned.[50]

Head was even worried about the attitude of Sir John A. Macdonald,[51] who had made the Delphic suggestion that the company's property rights might be determined by a Canadian court. In its correspondence with the Colonial Office, the HBC reiterated that its title had been confirmed by the Law Officers of the Crown in 1857 and stated that the persistence of any doubts to the contrary "in the minds of the Canadian Ministers, or the Canadian people" threatened the general rights of property in the Dominion.[52] The Canadian government eventually announced its willingness to pay at least some compensation. Macdonald entrusted the bargaining to Cartier and McDougall, who thus embarked on a long and complex bargaining process.[53]

There was little discussion in 1868 when the British Parliament passed legislation authorizing the sale of Rupert's Land to the Dominion.[54] The Rupert Land Act stipulated that the transfer should be done in such a way that no expenditure was incurred by the British government.[55] This clause helps to explain why the legislation was ignored by Bright and the other self-appointed champions of the British taxpayer. The passage of the enabling legislation[56] does not seem to have accelerated the negotiations and after a period of fruitless bargaining, Granville imposed a settlement. He did so by declaring that if his terms were not accepted by both parties, he would have the courts determine the validity of the company's title.[57] Because they could either have upheld the full claims of the company or found them entirely worthless, going to law was a high-stakes gamble desired neither by Canada nor the HBC.

Preferring the certainty of a half-loaf, the management of the HBC accepted Granville's terms in March 1869. William McDougall also swallowed his pride and accepted the proposal, although as Granville recognized, doing so was far more difficult for him than for Cartier: "Although they are colleagues, they represent different parties in the State – the French and the English Canadians."[58] Under Granville's terms, Canada was to pay £300,000 for Rupert's Land. In return for surrendering jurisdiction and fee simple title, the company would receive blocks of land amounting to one-twentieth of the Fertile Belt. However, its demand for an exemption from Canadian taxation was not granted.[59]

The directors of the company had agreed to present the offer to the shareholders for ratification. This was destined to be more than a formality, however, for when the firm's general court assembled on 24 March 1869, many of the shareholders were disgusted that the directors had accepted a price that was a fraction of earlier estimates of the value of Rupert's Land.[60] The revelation of the terms of the offer pushed the long-festering shareholder revolt to feverish levels.[61] Although some shareholders, such as William Newmarch, defended the offer as the best that could be hoped for under the circumstances, many other investors were enraged and denounced Northcote for proposing it for approval.[62] Due to the unrest, the final decision was adjourned to 9 April. At this meeting, cooler heads prevailed and a large majority accepted the offer, albeit grudgingly.[63]

The accusations that Northcote had yielded too much were unwarranted, for his bargaining position had been weak to start with. Outside observers thought the level of compensation was adequate and the *Economist* felt little sympathy for the "grumbling" shareholders. It argued that they had obtained a "good bargain" and that Granville had been right to back the Canadian position.[64] The *Times* regarded the terms as fair because the company was merely giving up rights to land and jurisdiction that it could no longer effectively exercise. It also stressed the importance of Canadian recognition of the company's title to ten million acres in the Fertile Belt, suggesting that secure title to a smaller property was worth more than a large but disputed claim.[65]

In the long run, the *Economist*'s prediction that the HBC would benefit from the new arrangements proved correct. Deprived of its responsibility to govern, the HBC was able to devote itself to the pursuit of profit.[66] Its leading figures in the decades after Confederation included Donald Alexander Smith, a future participant in the CPR syndicate,[67] and C.J. Brydges, the former general manager of the Grand Trunk.[68]

In the interests of bringing Canada and the HBC to an agreement, the Colonial Office had promised the Dominion that the imperial government would help it to raise the compensation money by guaranteeing a loan. This offer was to prove very controversial in Britain because there were already concerns over the management of the money that had been raised under the terms of the 1867 Canada Railway Loan Act.

Borrowing the money to build the Intercolonial had begun soon after Confederation, but the delays in starting construction had left the proceeds languishing in accounts bearing low interest. John Rose, the Canadian minister of Finance, decided to apply part of the railway money to discharging some of the Dominion government's unrelated obligations. This commonsensical manoeuvre disturbed the staff of Britain's Treasury, some of whom wished to censure Rose in public.[69]

In the British Parliament, Rose's actions were seized upon by those who had formerly opposed the railway loan guarantee. In 1869 the Radical MP Roger Sinclair Aytoun introduced a resolution condemning the Canadian government and proscribing all future colonial loan guarantees.[70] In response, Thomas Baring defended Rose's conduct, praising his wise handling of the loan fund and affirming that Rose's abilities and great "personal worth" had impressed everyone he had met.[71]

It is not surprising that when the Rupert's Land loan guarantee was brought before Parliament in August 1869, Aytoun was savage in his attacks, condemning the loan on grounds that included the territory's manifest unsuitability for agriculture.[72] Aytoun's attack was supported by Sir Charles Dilke, a radical Liberal who was a noted admirer of the United States and who privately believed that Britain should scrap both its empire and the monarchy.[73] In *Greater Britain* (1868), a book on the expansion of the Anglo-Saxon races, Dilke had praised the Union Pacific and disparaged Canadian dreams of building a rival railway. In his eyes, the best thing for Canada would be to join the Republic.[74]

Gladstone's reply to the critics of the guarantee was convoluted and somewhat self-contradictory, as befitted someone who had formerly opposed the Intercolonial loan guarantee. He stated that while he disliked colonial loan guarantees in the abstract, this particular loan would assist Canada in becoming more self-sufficient in financial matters.[75] The loan guarantee was ultimately passed and the money was raised to pay the owners of the HBC for Rupert's Land. Although the investors did not receive quite as much as they had hoped, the level of compensation was generous given the political circumstances.

The details of the sale of Rupert's Land were not the only occasion for a divergence of opinion between British investors and the British government. In 1871 most of the British garrisons in Canada were closed on the orders of Gladstone's Liberal cabinet.[76] This decision was bitterly denounced by Watkin, who was never reconciled to it. In 1886 Watkin advocated the redeployment of British regulars to Canada on the grounds that the United States was becoming increasingly "socialist" and thus more of a threat to the Dominion.[77] Watkin argued that the removal of the troops would not have occurred had Newcastle lived longer: "If the Duke of Newcastle had been a member of that Cabinet such a miserable policy never could have been put in force; but he was *dead*."[78] After Disraeli's Conservatives returned to power in 1874, Carnarvon, the Colonial Secretary, discussed re-establishing major garrisons in Canada, but it proved impossible to turn the clock back on

Edward Cardwell's military reforms. The result was that Canada was left with only two small forces of British regulars at Esquimalt and Halifax.[79]

The decision to close the Canadian garrisons was connected to the thaw in Anglo-American relations that began in the early 1870s and that, in a roundabout way, made it possible to build the railway to the Pacific. The 1871 Treaty of Washington between Britain and the United States was a turning point in Canadian-American relations that marked the end of war as a serious possibility and the beginning of the era of the "undefended border."[80] This treaty altered Canada's security situation quite quickly. Just a year before its conclusion, the British Parliament had passed the Canada Defence Loan Act[81] to assist Canada in borrowing £1.5 million for the construction of the defensive works that had been proposed in 1864.[82] The treaty suddenly made these fortresses seem rather pointless. Reasoning that fortifications were now unnecessary, the Canadians argued that the aid previously committed to them should be converted into a loan guarantee to support the construction the Pacific railway.[83]

Canada was in a position to demand such a favour from the British government because sections of the treaty with the United States required the assent of the Canadian Parliament: the treaty's British negotiators had granted the United States some fishery privileges in Canadian waters. In June 1873 Gladstone's government introduced legislation to provide for an imperial guarantee on a Canadian railway loan of £3.6 million.[84] This legislation was denounced by the government's own supporters as a violation of Liberal principles. Sir Charles Dilke was particularly robust in his criticisms, declaring that each colony should borrow on its own credit and that imperial guarantees eliminated the incentive for a colony to improve its reputation in the money market. He added that the Canadians had misappropriated the money Parliament had intended for the railway between Halifax and Quebec. In any event, he concluded, the contemplated project was foolish, since much of the projected line ran through desolate territory unsuited for agriculture.[85]

It was left to Gladstone to respond to these criticisms because the Chancellor of the Exchequer, Robert Lowe, was opposed to colonial loan guarantees and conspicuously absented himself from the Commons while they were under discussion.[86] Gladstone explained that the railway was required by the terms of union between Canada and British Columbia. He declared that whether or not the northerly route selected for the Canadian Pacific was ideal was a decision for the Canadians to make. He also alluded to the complex diplomatic situation that had induced the British government to guarantee the loan.[87]

The imperial Parliament's approval of the 1873 loan guarantee marked the beginnings of London's active encouragement of a great imperial project that promised to connect Liverpool with Britain's Asian dominions. While the Canadian taxpayer provided the lion's share of the subsidies needed to build the Canadian Pacific, the imperial government also assisted the company, albeit in a more minor way.[88] In 1887 the Conservative government of Lord Salisbury granted the Canadian Pacific a contract to transport mail between Liverpool and Hong Kong via Montreal and Vancouver. Along with the railway's offices in Trafalgar Square, the Canadian Pacific's integrated land-sea transport system symbolized, in the eyes of many Canadians, the fundamentally imperial nature of the enterprise.[89]

One group in British society that definitely did not benefit from Canadian Confederation was the exporters of manufactured goods. Exports to British North America remained near their pre-Confederation levels: the North American colonies took only 3.05 percent of Britain's exports in the period 1867–79.[90] Over the course of the 1870s, the proportion of Canada's imports coming from the United States grew at the expense of British producers.[91] In other words, the taxes paid by British manufacturers helped to build up a transportation infrastructure in Canada that was increasingly used to ship the products of their American competitors.

Judging from Benjamin Forster's research on the origins of the National Policy, the Colonial Office does not appear to have been a significant factor constraining the making of tariff policy by the Dominion.[92] The failure of Britain to limit Canadian protectionism after Confederation[93] suggests that under the counterfactual scenario of Canadian political independence in the 1860s, British manufacturers would have faced similar if not identical tariffs. After all, the British had conceded the right of colonies to be protectionist as early as 1859. The 1879 tariff treated British and American goods identically and it was only during the Laurier era that there were modest steps towards imperial preference.[94] Andrew Carnegie sardonically observed in 1898 that Canada bought its Union Jacks in New York.[95] His point was that the British identity of the Dominion had little impact on its actual pattern of trade in visible goods.

Confederation did little to help Manchester mill owners, but the same cannot be said for London bankers and bond traders. Baring and Glyn both died in 1873 but Barings' continued to represent the Canadian government in the decades after Confederation. This period saw the public debt of Canada soar to new heights. In 1871 the national debt stood at just over twenty-six percent of Canada's gross national product, but by 1879 the figure had hit thirty-two percent, reaching thirty-seven at the time the last spike was driven in 1885.[96] Almost all of this debt was issued in London. The financial historian Ranald Michie notes that while Canadians held 9.3 percent of the Dominion's debt in 1870, "this proportion fell to 0.4 percent by 1914" because it became increasingly easy for Canada to issue bonds in Britain.[97] Although the commissions earned by marketing government bonds were typically low, Canada's borrowing requirements were massive in volume.

Until 1892 the Canadian government's lucrative London financial agency remained in the hands of Barings'. The transfer of the agency to the London branch of the Bank of Montreal in 1892 came about only because Barings' had precipitated a major financial crisis through its unwise investments in Argentina. Canada did not want its affairs in the hands of a bank that been saved from bankruptcy only by the kindness of the Bank of England.[98]

Canada's financial ties with Britain between 1867 and 1914 need to be understood with reference to both the underdevelopment of Canadian stock exchanges and the long-standing rivalry between the London and New York exchanges.[99] Ranald Michie has shown that in the years before 1914, London and New York competed for the business of trading in Canadian securities and that while New York enjoyed a geographical advantage, "Canada's position as an integral part of the British Empire"[100] served to direct Canadian business towards London. In other words, because Canada continued to be a British possession after 1867, commission income was gained by Londoners at the expense of the denizens of Wall Street. Trade in visible goods may not have followed the flag, but at least some brokerage fees did.[101]

Irving Stone estimates that between 1865 and 1914, British investment in Canada totalled £412 million. His figure for the much more populous United States in the same period is £836 million.[102] Discussing the fifty years before 1914, D.C.M. Platt writes that in Canada, New Zealand, and Australia, capital imports were generally about half of domestic savings, while in the United States, they amounted to less than five percent of all the capital used.[103] While American capital became increasingly important with the advent of the post-1879 branch-plant economy, more capital came to Canada from Britain than from the United States in every year before 1915. In fact, it was only in 1922 that the value of American assets in Canada outstripped those of the British.[104]

Of course, many variables influenced the allocation of British capital, and we must be careful about using the experiences of Canada and the United States as a sort of "natural experiment" for testing whether the empire's boundaries influenced capital flows. But whether we look at the slow-growth 1870s or the Laurier boom years, an interesting pattern emerges: in per capita terms, Canada received much more British capital than the United States (see Table 1). This pattern suggests that empire membership helped to incentivize British investment in Canada.

Historians disagree about whether the inflow of British investment into Canada was an entirely good thing. Donald Creighton's highly positive view of British investment was informed by a perspective that was both anglophile and anti-American. R.T. Naylor, a leftist nationalist sceptical of the benefits of foreign investment in general, argues that British investment was an instrument of economic imperialism that entrenched Canada's subordinate position in the international economic system: in the twentieth century, British masters were simply exchanged for American ones.[105] Niall Ferguson regards British investment in the white dominions as positive because he shares the neoliberal belief that capital mobility is inherently good.[106] A fourth perspective is provided by Rosemary Langhout, who argues that colonial government borrowing in London represented an attempt to establish the "autonomy" of the public sector from the local suppliers of capital. She suggests that it is better for the state to have a choice of money lenders than to be dependent on just a few local millionaires.[107]

Harold Innis praised Confederation as a measure that increased the creditworthiness of the colonies in the London bond market.[108] Although most economic historians believe that good public credit and low government borrowing costs create a virtuous circle leading

Table 1
British investment in Canada and the United States, selected periods.
£ Per Head of Population*

	1870–74	1890–94	1910–14
Canada	4.88	5.47	26.58
United States	2.17	1.23	2.29

* Refers to called up capital. Investment data from Irving Stone,
Table 45, "Major Recipients of British Overseas Investment."
Population data from United States Census, 1870, 1890, 1910;
Canadian Census, 1871, 1891, 1911.

to economic growth,[109] there may also have been a downside to the new Dominion's creditworthiness. After all, state borrowers compete with entrepreneurs for scarce capital and there is no guarantee that the social rate of return on money invested by governments will be higher than those that would come from the alternative uses of capital. Canadian historians should pay attention to the scholarly debate on whether the British state's improved creditworthiness after the Glorious Revolution actually helped to increase the productive resources of that country. There is a consensus that improved government creditworthiness after 1688 was important in financing British military and naval expenditure. But while crucial to realizing the ambitions of statesmen and admirals, government borrowing may have made life more difficult for private borrowers seeking to expand productive enterprises.[110]

Whether post-Confederation Canadian governments spent the money they borrowed in London wisely is an important and complex question. There can be no doubt that much of the borrowed money was directed into works that consolidated Canada as a political unit and allowed the central state to exert power over the heterogeneous population of a large landmass. However, whether the social rate of return on this massive expenditure was positive is a very different question.[111] Some individuals and firms clearly benefited from the construction of post-1867 engineering projects such as the Intercolonial and Pacific railways, but compiling a list of winners does not address the question whether overall economic growth would have been maximized by investing the money on other public goods or simply by leaving it in the pockets of taxpayers.[112]

In 1874 the London financial journalist Charles Fenn distinguished between borrowing by Britain's settlement colonies from the debt-fuelled militarism of the Americans and the continental Europeans. British subjects, he said, borrowed to invest in "reproductive" works such as railways and canals, while the silly foreigners squandered their borrowed money on warfare and the territorial ambitions of rulers.[113] The reality was that the Dominion's borrowing spree, focused as it was on constructing the nervous system of the Canadian Leviathan, may have been less different from foreign government borrowing than Fenn supposed. Projects like the Intercolonial did bring some commercial benefits, but the major motives for their construction centred on what H.G.J. Aitken called "defensive expansionism," namely, a desire to keep all of British North America out of the hands of the Americans. Estimating the social rate of return on the post-Confederation engineering projects is an important question, albeit one that lies outside the remit of this work.[114]

Confederation changed the scale on which economic policy in British North America was made. Political economists have advanced various theories for understanding the connection between the size of a nation and the incentives that influence the making of public policy.[115] Some scholars work on the premise that while benefits concentrated locally are easy to appreciate, costs dispersed nationally are harder to detect. They conclude that, *ceteris paribus*, increasing the size of the polity intensifies the incentives to support economically inefficient policies.[116] In other words, corporate welfare payments, protectionism, and other examples of rent-seeking behaviour are more likely to take place in a large polity than if the same territory is divided into several small polities.

This theory provides one possible lens for viewing Confederation and its legacies. It helps to explain Canada's drift to protectionism after 1867, for while the costs of the post-Confederation National Policy were externalized over a larger territory, the benefits were concentrated in particular firms and federal ridings. Patronage spending in the era of Macdonald and Laurier exhibited a pattern that can be summed up in an adage popular with political economists: "dispersed costs, concentrated benefits."[117] It is likely that British North America *sans* Confederation would have been less prone to protective tariffs and patronage spending. Economic theory suggests that protectionism and patronage spending tend to reduce the overall welfare of a society.

Whether or not the creation of a Dominion extending from Cape Breton to Vancouver Island was ultimately a good thing is perhaps more of a philosophical question than a strictly historical one. A follower of Jane Jacobs who thinks small is beautiful will doubtless have a different opinion than someone who believes that large polities deliver substantial economies of scale.[118] Quebec nationalists have a particular view of Confederation. First Nations people will also have their own perspectives, since Confederation paved the way for the dispossession of the native inhabitants of the Canadian West.

For people interested in the ways in which Canadian history intersects with the history of globalization, several features of Confederation stand out. The fact that the constitutional bond between Britain and Canada managed to survive the turbulent 1860s was important for the gentlemanly capitalists of the City of London. The colonies had been integrated into the gentlemanly capitalist order well before 1867, but Confederation was essential to the preservation of this important relationship. Had the British North American colonies become independent republics in the 1860s or part of the United States, New York rather than London would probably have become their financial capital at a comparatively early date. For better or worse, Canada would look to London to meet most of its capital requirements until 1914. Thereafter, Canada drifted away from Britain and into the American Empire.

Whether or not the Dominion's reliance on external sources of capital was a boon for Canada is a question outside the scope of this book. What is clear, however, is that a small group of investors influenced the British policies that resulted in the existence of the Dominion of Canada in the first place. Although it would be going too far to describe the investors as the unknown Fathers of Confederation, the role these capitalists played ought to be remembered by Canadians. In fact, Canadians would do well to reflect deeply on the importance of foreign capital in their history. Doing so will inform our understanding of many contemporary issues.

Note on Sources

The secondary literature on Confederation is extensive. The classic works on the topic include: W.L. Morton, *The Critical Years: The Union of British North America, 1857–1873* (Toronto: McClelland and Stewart, 1964); Donald Creighton, *The Road to Confederation: The Emergence of Canada, 1863–1867* (Toronto: Macmillan, 1964); and P.B. Waite, *The Life and Times of Confederation* (Toronto: University of Toronto Press, 1962). These works remain essential reading, although not all twenty-first-century readers will share their underlying premise that Confederation was a positive development and something to be celebrated. The assumption that the formation of larger political units is somehow progressive is ably challenged in Jane Jacobs, *Canadian Cities and Sovereignty Association* (Toronto: Canadian Broadcasting Corporation, 1980).

Much of the recent scholarship on Confederation has focused on what might be broadly defined as intellectual history. Among such works are Peter J. Smith, "The Ideological Origins of Canadian Confederation," *Canadian Journal of Political Science* 20 (1987): 3–29; and Janet Ajzenstat, Paul Romney, Ian Gentles, and William D. Gairdner, eds., *Canada's Founding Debates* (Toronto: University of Toronto Press, 2003). In sharp contrast, I focus on the role of economic factors in Confederation. The working assumption of this book is that the Fathers of Confederation and their friends in the British investment community were self-interested and rational economic actors. I do not dispute that the study of political ideas and culture has tremendous value and that intellectual shifts can sometimes be important drivers of political and constitutional change. I submit, however, that materialist approaches to history provide a far better paradigm for understanding why Canadian Confederation occurred and why it happened when it did.

One particularly important work on the political economy of Confederation is P.J. Cain and A.G. Hopkins, *British Imperialism, 1688–2000*, 2d ed. (New York: Longman, 2002). The first edition of this work (1993) spawned a whole series of scholarly debates. See *Gentlemanly Capitalism and British Imperialism: The New Debate on Empire*, edited by Raymond E. Dumett (London: Longman, 1999). Other important works on the economics of British imperialism include Niall Ferguson, *Empire: The Rise and Demise of the British World Order and the Lessons for Global Power* (New York: Basic Books, 2002); Lance E. Davis and Robert A. Huttenback, *Mammon and the Pursuit of Empire: The Economics of British Imperialism* (New York: Cambridge University Press, 1988); Paul Kennedy, "Debate; the Costs and Benefits of British Imperialism, 1846–1914," *Past and Present* (1989): 186–99; and Avner Offner, "The British Empire, 1870–1914: A Waste of Money?" *Economic History Review*, New Series 46 (1993): 215–38. Two particularly important works for understanding why the Fathers of Confederation supported continued membership in the British Empire are: Stéphane Kelly, *La petite loterie: comment la Couronne a obtenu la collaboration du Canada français après 1837* (Montreal: Boréal, 1997); and Peter Baskerville, "Imperial Agendas and 'Disloyal' Collaborators: Decolonization and the John Sandfield Macdonald Ministries, 1862–64," in *Old Ontario: Essays in Honour of J.M.S. Careless*, edited by David Keane and Colin Read, 234–56. (Toronto: Dundurn Press, 1990).

Excellent biographies have been written about many of the key players in Confederation. Among the most useful in the writing of this work were: Donald Creighton, *John A. Macdonald: The Young Politician* (Toronto: Macmillan, 1952); Brian Young, *George-Étienne Cartier: Montreal Bourgeois* (Montreal: McGill-Queen's University Press, 1981); J.M.S. Careless, *Brown of the Globe* (Toronto: Macmillan, 1963); F. Darrell Munsell, *The Unfortunate Duke: Henry Pelham, Fifth Duke of Newcastle, 1811–1864* (Columbia: University of Missouri Press, 1985); David Hodgkins, *The Second Railway King : The Life and Times of Sir Edward Watkin, 1819–1901* (Cardiff: Merton Priory Press, 2002); and J. Murray Beck, *Joseph Howe*, vol. 2, *The Briton Becomes Canadian* (Kingston: McGill-Queen's University Press, 1982).

I consulted a number of excellent unpublished dissertations in preparing this manuscript. They include: Donald Roman, "The

Contribution of Imperial Guarantees for Colonial Loans to the Consolidation of British North America, 1847–1865" (D.Phil. dissertation, University of Oxford, 1978); Gene Lawrence Allen, "The Origins of the Intercolonial Railway, 1835–1869" (PhD dissertation, University of Toronto, 1991); James M. Colthart, "Edward Ellice and North America" (PhD dissertation, Princeton University, Princeton, 1971); Colin C. Eldridge, "The Colonial Policy of the 5th Duke of Newcastle, 1859–1964" (PhD dissertation, University of Nottingham, 1966); and Rosemary Langhout, "Public Enterprise: An Analysis of Public Finance in the Maritime Colonies during the Period of Responsible Government" (PhD dissertation, University of New Brunswick, 1989).

Ged Martin has recently reminded Canadian historians of the important role played by Britain in Confederation in his *Britain and the Origins of Canadian Confederation, 1837–67* (Houndmills, Basingstoke, Hampshire: Macmillan, 1995). I certainly do not dispute Martin's thesis that British government policies were crucial to the achievement of Confederation: my aim is to provide a better explanation for why British government acted the way it did. The thesis of this book, namely, that the pressure from British investors influenced the course of the British government with regard to Confederation is not new. Anti-Confederates in the 1860s alleged that investors were behind the scheme for a colonial union and this idea has subsequently been repeated by various historians, such as Reginald G. Trotter, *Canadian Federation: Its Origins and Achievement, a Study in Nation Building* (Toronto: Dent, 1924); and R.T. Naylor, *The History of Canadian Business 1867–1914* (Toronto: Lorimer, 1975). Unfortunately, the proponents of the investor-influence thesis did not back up their claim with sufficient evidence. One of the aims of my work was to place this thesis on a more solid evidentiary foundation. R.T. Naylor dramatically overstated the bankers' power over British policy and made bold declarations on the basis of slender evidence. My research suggests that the bankers had real but limited influence over the British and Canadian governments.

This manuscript is based on printed and archival material found in libraries and archives in Canada and the United Kingdom. The most important source for my research was the Library and Archives of Canada (LAC) in Ottawa (formerly the National Archives). I consulted Colonial Office (CO) papers, including Colonial Office

217 (Nova Scotia) Colonial Office 42 (Province of Canada), Colonial
Office 188 (New Brunswick). Canadian government fonds that I ex-
amined included the Governor General's Correspondence, RG7 G17
A, the Minister of Finance Fonds, and the Canadian National Rail-
ways Fonds (Grand Trunk Series), RG 30-A. I also used many pri-
vate papers housed in LAC, particularly the A.T. Galt Fonds, MG 27,
I, D8; Baring Brothers and Company Fonds, MG24-D21; Charles
Stanley Monck, 4th Viscount Monck Fonds, MG27-IB1; Edward
Cardwell Fonds, MG27-IA1; George Brown Fonds, MG24-B40; Glyn
Mills and Company Fonds, MG24-D36; Joseph Howe Fonds, MG24-
B29; Samuel Leonard Tilley Fonds, MG27-ID15; Sir John A. Macdon-
ald Fonds, MG26-A; and the William McDougall Fonds, MG27-IC6.
Within the Hudson's Bay Company Records group, I examined the
International Financial Society Papers, MG20-F27. I also used the
Canada Company Fonds at the Archives of Ontario in Toronto.

In Britain, I used the Public Record Office (PRO) in Kew, now
called the National Archives (NA). There I examined PRO 30/6/
154, Henry Herbert, Fourth Earl of Carnarvon Papers; PRO BT 31,
Board of Trade, Companies Registration Office, Files of Dissolved
Companies; and RAIL 1007/348 Papers on Sir Edward Watkin.
The Manuscripts Room of the British Library in London contains
the John Bright Papers, Richard Cobden Papers, and the W.E.
Gladstone Papers. At London's Guildhall Library, I consulted the
papers of the Lloyd's Insurance syndicate and the records of the
Association of British Chambers of Commerce. The Guildhall
Library also houses copies of *The Course of the Exchange* (London:
Effingham Wilson, 1742–1889), the official register of prices on the
London Stock Exchange that was printed under the authority of
the Stock Exchange's committee. Several British banks kindly
granted access to their collections: ING Baring Archives in London
allowed me to use the House Correspondence within the Baring
Bros. Papers. The Royal Bank of Scotland Archives, also in Lon-
don, granted access to a variety of files, the most important being
the Glyn Mills and Co. Papers, GB 1502 RBS/GM. At the Borthwick
Institute at the University of York, I consulted the Hickleton
Papers, which can be found within the Wood Family Papers. The
University of Nottingham Library houses the papers of the fifth
duke of Newcastle. The Local Studies section of the Manchester
Library and Archives provided access to the Sir Edward Watkin
Papers M219/3/1–8.

Various published sources were essential to this study. The British parliamentary debates and the *Debates of the Legislative Assembly of United Canada*, General Editor, Elizabeth Nish (Montreal: Presses de l'École des hautes études commerciales, 1970–) were frequently consulted, as were various British Parliametary Papers and the *Parliamentary Debates on the Subject of the Confederation of the British North American Provinces, 3d session, 5th Provincial Parliament of Canada* (Quebec: Hunter, Rose, 1865). Unless otherwise noted, all references to *Hansard* are to be the British *Hansard*.

The British Newspaper Library at Colindale was essential to this work, as were the diffusion copies of Canadian newspapers on microfilm. Among the newspapers and serials that I consulted were the *Canadian News and British American Intelligencer* (London); *Daily News* (London); *Fenn's Compendium of the Funds* (London); *Globe* (Toronto); *Herapath's Railway and Commercial Journal* (London); *Illustrated London News*; *Le Pays* (Montreal); *Liverpool Journal of Commerce*; *Manchester Guardian*; *Mitchell's Steam Shipping Journal* (London); *Montreal Witness Protestant Review and Commercial Newspaper*; *Newsletter* (Belfast); *Northern Whig* (Belfast); *Sheffield and Rotherham Independent*; *Sheffield Daily Telegraph*; *Star and Dial* (London); *Bankers' Magazine* (London); *Bullionist* (London); *Course of the Exchange* (London); *Economist* (London); *Money Market Review* (London); and *The Times* (London).

I used several important reference works in the course of preparing this manuscript. I consulted the databases of the *Oxford Dictionary of National Biography* (Oxford: Oxford University Press, 2004) and the *Dictionary of Canadian Biography* (Toronto: University of Toronto Press, 1966–) between October 2004 and March 2005. I also made extensive use of John Orbell and Alison Burton, *British Banking: A Guide to the Historical Records* (London: Business Archives Council, 2001). Two contemporary sources were particularly important in researching the prosopography of the British North American Association (BNAA): *Bradshaw's Railway Manual, Shareholder's Guide, and Official Directory* (Manchester: Bradshaw and Blacklock, 1863); and *Dod's Parliamentary Companion* (London: Hurst Green, 1847–).

Notes

1 The phrase is taken from Jack M. Sosin, *Whitehall and the Wilderness: The Middle West in British Colonial Policy, 1760–1775* (Lincoln: University of Nebraska Press, 1961).

2 The focus of this book is on the political economy of British investments in this core region. Important works touching on the economic aspects of Confederation outside the core include J.K. Hiller, "Confederation Defeated: the Newfoundland Election of 1869," in *Newfoundland in the Nineteenth and Twentieth Centuries: Essays in Interpretation,* edited by J.K. Hiller and Peter Neary (Toronto: University of Toronto Press, 1980); Frederick Jones, "'The Antis Gain the Day': Newfoundland and Confederation in 1869," in *The Causes of Canadian Confederation,* edited by Ged Martin (Fredericton: Acadiensis Press, 1990), 142–7, 143; Ian Ross Robertson, *The Tenant League of Prince Edward Island, 1864–1867: Leasehold Tenure in the New World* (Toronto: University of Toronto Press, 1996), 27.

3 Donald Read, *Cobden and Bright: A Victorian Political Partnership* (London: Edward Arnold, 1967), 231.

4 The term "Centennial synthesis" refers to the standard or received account of Confederation as it appeared in such works as W.L. Morton, *The Critical Years: The Union of British North America, 1857–1873* (Toronto: McClelland and Stewart, 1964); Donald Creighton, *The Road to Confederation: The Emergence of Canada, 1863–1867* (Toronto: Macmillan, 1964); P.B. Waite, *The Life and Times of Confederation* (Toronto: University of Toronto Press, 1962). Like most English-language histories of Confederation, the works written around the time of the centennial displayed a strong pro-Confederation bias.

5 Ged Martin, *Britain and the Origins of Canadian Confederation, 1837–67* (Houndmills, Basingstoke, Hampshire: Macmillan, 1995). Martin advances similar arguments in "The Case against Canadian Confederation," in *The Causes of Canadian Confederation*, edited by Ged Martin, 19–50. It should be noted that Martin has also written on the formation of the Australian federation; see Ged Martin, *Australia, New Zealand and Federation, 1883–1901* (London: Menzies Centre for Australian Studies, 2001).

6 Martin, *Britain and the Origins of Canadian Confederation*, 34–5.

7 Ibid., 47.

8 For Martin's analysis of the economic arguments for and against Confederation, see ibid., 58–60.

9 Martin bases his analysis of the use of loan guarantees on Don Roman, "The Contribution of Imperial Guarantees for Colonial Loans to the Consolidation of British North America, 1847–1865" (D. Phil. dissertation, University of Oxford, 1978).

10 Martin, *Britain and the Origins of Canadian Confederation*, 238. In particular, Martin was referring to Arthur Lower, *Colony to Nation: A History of Canada* (Toronto: Longmans, Green, 1946), 316.

11 In addition to Ged Martin, see P.B. Waite, "Edward Cardwell and Confederation," *Canadian Historical Review* 43 (1962): 17–41.

12 Marcel Bellavance, *Le Québec et la confédération: un choix libre? Le clergé et la constitution de 1867* (Sillery: Septentrion, 1992).

13 Anthony Trollope, *The Prime Minister* (Toronto: Hunter Rose, 1876), 80.

14 Important works that interpret empire in cultural terms include Catherine Hall, Keith McClelland, and Jane Rendall, *Defining the Victorian Nation: Class, Race, Gender and the British Reform Act of 1867* (Cambridge: Cambridge University Press, 2000); Catherine Hall, *Civilising Subjects: Metropole and Colony in the English Imagination, 1830–1867* (Cambridge: Polity Press, 2002); Bill Ashcraft, Gareth Griffiths, and Helen Tiffin, *Post-Colonial Studies: The Key Concepts* (London: Routledge, 2000).

15 John Gallagher and Ronald Robinson, "The Imperialism of Free Trade," *Economic History Review* 6 (1953):1–15; cf. Oliver MacDonagh, "The Anti-Imperialism of Free Trade," *Economic History Review* 14 (1962):489–501.

16 Niall Ferguson, "Globalisation in Interdisciplinary Perspective," in *Globalization in Historical Perspective*, edited by Michael Bordo, Jeffrey G. Williamson, and Alan Taylor (London: University of Chicago Press, 2003), 549–70.

17 C.D.W. Goodwin, *Canadian Economic Thought: The Political Economy of a Developing Nation, 1814–1914* (Durham: Duke University Press, 1961), 55–8, 64, 111, 126.

18 Oliver MacDonagh, "The Anti-Imperialism of Free Trade", 489–501.
19 See Peter Cain, "Jeremy Bentham and the Radical Critique of 'Colonialism,'" paper delivered to the Department of Economic History, London School of Economics, 23 November 2006.
20 Ellen Meiksins Wood, The Empire of Capital (London: Verso, 2003); Norman Etherington, Theories of Imperialism: War, Conquest, and Capital (London: Croom Helm, 1984), 40–61, 165–74.
21 Gallagher and Robinson, "The Imperialism of Free Trade," 1–15; Peter Harnetty, "Imperialism of Free Trade: Lancashire and the Indian Cotton Duties, 1859–1862," Economic History Review 18 (1965):333–49.
22 Authors who believe that the empire harmed Britain's overall economy include Lance E. Davis and Robert A. Huttenback, Mammon and the Pursuit of Empire: The Economics of British Imperialism (New York: Cambridge University Press, 1988); P.K. O'Brien, "The Costs and Benefits of British Imperialism, 1846–1914," Past and Present (1988): 163–200, and Andrew Porter, "The Balance Sheet of Empire, 1850–1914," Historical Journal 31 (1988):685–99. This viewpoint was challenged by Paul Kennedy, "Debate; The Costs and Benefits of British Imperialism, 1846–1914," Past and Present (1989): 186–99; Avner Offner, "The British Empire, 1870–1914: A Waste of Money?" Economic History Review, New Series 46 (1993): 215–38.
23 The relationship of different social classes in Britain to the empire is discussed by Bernard Porter in The Absent-Minded Imperialists: Empire, Society, and Culture in Britain (Oxford: Oxford University Press, 2004). Porter convincingly argues that it was the landed aristocracy that was most involved in empire and that middle and lower classes were largely indifferent to the project of empire. Acknowledging his debts to the anti-imperialist economist J.A. Hobson, Porter takes issue with postcolonial theorists who see imperialism as an essentially cultural phenomenon, maintaining that the empire was mainly about perceived economic advantages.
24 P.J. Cain and A.G. Hopkins, British Imperialism, 1688–2000, 2d ed. (New York: Longman, 2002). The first edition of this work in 1993 spawned a whole series of scholarly debates. See Raymond E. Dumett, ed., Gentlemanly Capitalism and British Imperialism: The New Debate on Empire (London: Longman, 1999).
25 Geoffrey Ingham, Capitalism Divided?: The City and Industry in British Social Development (London: Macmillan, 1984).
26 Anthony Sampson, Anatomy of Britain (London: Hodder and Stoughton, 1962).

27 Cain and Hopkins, *British Imperialism*, 235–6. They base their view that British acquiescence in higher tariffs was dictated by a preference for the interests of finance over manufacturing on Glen Williams, "The National Policy Tariffs: Industrial Underdevelopment through Import Substitution," *Canadian Journal of Politics* 12 (1979): 333–8.

28 Cain and Hopkins, *British Imperialism*, 231–5.

29 Ibid., 138, 143, 206–8.

30 The limitations on City power are discussed by David Kynaston, *The City of London: A World of Its Own, 1815–90* (London: Pimlico, 1995), vol. 1, 125; A.C. Howe, "Free Trade and the City of London, c.1820–1870," *History* 77 (1992):391–410.

31 The hatred some people in the City felt for Gladstone was palpable. One financial publication referred to Gladstone's "hallucinations" in an article congratulating the "banking interest" for its successful campaign against some changes to the banking law that Gladstone has proposed. See "Withdrawal of Mr Gladstone's Bank of Issue Bill," in *Bankers' Magazine*, June 1865, 801–4.

32 David Kynaston, "The Bank of England and the Government" in *The Bank of England: Money, Power, and Influence 1694–1994*, edited by Richard Roberts and David Kynaston (Oxford: Oxford University Press, 1995), 22–3.

33 R.T. Naylor, *The History of Canadian Business 1867–1914* (Toronto: Lorimer, 1975), 27–35. This work's harshest critic is Michael Bliss, who writes: "It is an eclectically Marxist work, factually unreliable, and it was of no use in the preparation of this history." Michael Bliss, *Northern Enterprise: Five Centuries of Canadian Business* (Toronto: McClelland and Stewart, 1987), 585.

34 E.g., Baring Brothers to Colonial Secretary, 6 August 1859 in National Archives (NA), Kew, Colonial Office (CO) 42/621. An exception to this generalization is the BNAA's November 1862 memorial stressing the importance of preserving reciprocity with the United States. The Colonial Office forwarded this memorial to both houses of Parliament and to the Foreign Office. J.C.D. Hay, Chairman of the BNAA to Newcastle, 6 November 1862, NA CO 42/636.

35 For example, one individual wrote under a pseudonym to tell the Colonial Office that "a monarchy or Empire à la Mexico would be the thing for Canada." See "The Hermit of London" to Cardwell, 3 August 1864, NA CO 42/646.

36 The role of New Brunswick's mercurial lieutenant-governor is described in J.K. Chapman, "Arthur Gordon and Confederation,"

Canadian Historical Review 37 (1956): 141–57. The distribution of knighthoods and other honours to Canadians at the time of Confederation was another delicate question that confronted the Colonial Office. In 1867 Cartier was incensed when he was offered a lesser honour than Macdonald and was only satisfied when he was granted a baronetcy in 1868. See Cartier to Watkin, 22 September 1867, in Edward Watkin, *Canada and the States: Recollections, 1851 to 1886* (London: Ward, Lock, 1887), 458, and Tupper to Macdonald, 25 April 1868, in Macdonald Fonds, LAC 282: 129095.

37 It is tempting to relate Cardwell's support for Confederation to the policies he later pursued as secretary of state for war after 1868. Cardwell's biographer, however, believes that he was largely indifferent to military matters until he was given this cabinet portfolio in 1868. Arvel B. Erickson, "Edward Cardwell: Peelite," *American Philosophical Society Transactions* (Philadelphia: American Philosophical Society, 1959).

38 E.J. Feuchtwanger, "Grenville, Richard Plantagenet Campbell Temple-Nugent-Brydges-Chandos-, third duke of Buckingham and Chandos (1823–1889)," in *Oxford Dictionary of National Biography*, edited by H.C.G. Matthew and Brian Harrison (Oxford: Oxford University Press, 2004).

39 Speech at Niagara, 18 September 1862, in Joseph Howe, *The Speeches and Public Letters of Joseph Howe*, edited by Joseph Andrew Chisholm, vol. 2, 372–83, 375 (Halifax: Chronicle Publishing, 1909). To make his point, Howe cited George Hudson, MP, the scandalous railway promoter at the centre of the railway bubble of the 1840s.

40 Colin C. Eldridge, "The Colonial Policy of the 5th Duke of Newcastle, 1859–1964" (PhD dissertation, University of Nottingham, 1966), 61.

41 Fortescue was a meticulous diarist and his journal is a useful source for exploring the private world of British politics. Unfortunately, Fortescue later destroyed the passages of his diary relating to early 1862. The destruction of the diaries was likely related to Fortescue's pursuit of Lady Waldegrave, but it eliminated a valuable resource that could have illuminated informal and verbal communication between investors and policy makers. For the defaced Lord Carlingford diaries, see British Library Manuscripts Room, Add. Mss 63676.

42 Patrick Jackson, *Education Act Forster: A political Biography of W.E. Forster* (Cranbury, NJ: Associated University Presses, 1997), 100.

43 Joseph Howe, *A Letter to the Right Honourable C.B. Adderley M.P. on the Relations of England with Her Colonies* (London; Edward Stanford, 1863).

44 C.B. Adderley, *Letter to the Right Hon. Benjamin Disraeli, M.P. on the Present Relations of England with the Colonies* (London: Stanford, 1861).

45 Of the three most senior civil servants in the Colonial Office, Under-Secretary Frederic Rogers and Assistant Under-Secretary Henry Taylor were separatists. Henry Taylor, *Autobiography of Henry Taylor, 1800–1875*, vol. 2 (London: Longmans Green, 1885); Lord Blachford, *Letters of Frederic Lord Blachford: Under Secretary of State for the Colonies: 1860–1871* (London: J. Murray, 1896). However, the assistant under-secretary with responsibility for the British North American file, T.F. Elliot, shared Newcastle's strong commitment to preserving the empire. Employees below the rank of assistant under-secretary exercised essentially clerical functions.

46 Newcastle to Palmerston, 11 November 1861, in the University of Nottingham Library, 5th Duke of Newcastle Papers (hereafter Newcastle Papers), NEC 10890. In reality, Palmerston's suspicions were largely correct. The inclinations of the senior civil servants at the Colonial Office are discussed in Colin C. Eldridge, "The Colonial Policy of the 5th Duke of Newcastle, 1859–1964" (PhD dissertation, University of Nottingham, 1966), 64; D.M.L Farr, *The Colonial Office and Canada, 1867–1887* (Toronto University of Toronto Press, 1955). It is significant that Newcastle was in the dark as to the private opinions of his subordinates.

47 Newcastle to Monck, 29 May 1863, in University of Nottingham Library, Newcastle Papers, NEC 11223. Discussing default on payments to British bondholders by the City of Hamilton, an annoyed Newcastle remarked that the municipality's action had depreciated the value of other Canadian securities, including some that Newcastle had put up for sale at that very moment. For Newcastle's political career, see F. Darrell Munsell, *The Unfortunate Duke: Henry Pelham, Fifth Duke of Newcastle, 1811–1864* (Columbia: University of Missouri Press, 1985).

48 J.M.S. Careless, *The Union of the Canadas; The Growth of Canadian Institutions* (Toronto: McClelland and Stewart, 1867), 193.

49 Joseph Howe to Leonard Tilley, 19 January 1862, Library and Archives Canada (LAC), Joseph Howe Fonds, 7:182.

50 Elaine A. Mitchell, "Edward Watkin and the Buying-Out of the Hudson's Bay Company," *Canadian Historical Review* 34 (1953): 219–44, 219. Two biographies of Watkin have appeared recently: David Hodgkins, *The Second Railway King: The Life and Times of Sir Edward Watkin, 1819–1901* (Cardiff: Merton Priory Press, 2002); John Neville Greaves, *Sir Edward Watkin, 1819–1901: The Last of the Railway Kings* (Lewes: Book Guild, 2005).

51 Edward Ellice; Sr, to Charles Wood 11 November 1862, 30 August
    1863, Hickleton Papers, Borthwick Institute of Historical Research,
    A4/D3A. In 1861 Ellice wrote a lengthy memorandum advising
    Newcastle to federate the North American colonies. Historian James
    Colthart points out that Ellice's proposed constitution was similar to
    the eventual British North America Act in that it gave the residuary
    power to the federal government rather than to the states. However,
    the difference in intent between Ellice's proposal and the Quebec
    scheme is even more striking than this similarity; for while the Fa-
    thers of Confederation explicitly stated that their goal in drafting a
    new constitution was to preserve the British connection, Ellice be-
    lieved that Britain should sever its ties with Canada. It is unclear
    whether this unsolicited memorial was even read by Newcastle, a
    man with scant time for the Little England ideas espoused by Ellice.
    James M. Colthart, "Edward Ellice and North America" (PhD disser-
    tation, Princeton University, Princeton, NJ 1971), 204, 287, 296, 312.
    The 1861 memorandum is preserved in the Edward Ellice Papers at
    the National Library of Scotland in Edinburgh.
52 Newcastle to Gladstone, 2 February 1863, University of Nottingham
    Library, Newcastle Papers, NEC 10,891.
53 Michael P. Costeloe, *Bonds and Bondholders: British Investors and Mexico's
    Foreign Debt, 1824–1888* (Westport: Praeger, 2003).
54 Frank Griffith Dawson, *The First Latin American Debt Crisis: The City of
    London and the 1822–25 Loan Bubble* (New Haven: Yale University
    Press, 1990).
55 Paolo Mauro and Yishay Yafeh1, "The Corporation of Foreign Bond-
    holders," IMF Working Paper, Washington, DC, 2004; Albert Fishlow
    "Lessons from the Past: Capital Markets during the 19th Century and
    the Interwar Period," *International Organization* 39 (1985):383–439.
56 H.S. Ferns, *Britain and Argentina in the Nineteenth Century* (Oxford:
    Clarendon Press, 1960), 301.
57 Ibid., 306.
58 BNAA members who later sat on the council of the Corporation of
    Foreign Bondholders included T.M. Weguelin, A.F. Kinnaird, Philip
    Rose, and the transplanted Canadian, Sir John Rose. *First Report of the
    Council of the Corporation of Foreign Bondholders* (London: Corporation
    of Foreign Bondholders, 1874).
59 Ibid. The Corporation of Foreign Bondholders may even have been
    conceived by Thomas Baring, judging from comments made at the
    organization's meeting immediately after his death in 1873. Baring's

relationship with the Mexican bondholders is discussed in *Money Market Review*, "Acceptance of the Agency of the Mexican Bondholders," 18 January 1862, 45. On the political consequence of Mexico's repudiation of its sovereign debt in July 1861, see Steven C. Topik, "When Mexico Had the Blues: A Transatlantic Tale of Bonds, Bankers, and Nationalists, 1862–1910," *American Historical Review* 105 (2000): 714–38.

60 Donald Creighton, "Economic Nationalism and Confederation," *Canadian Historical Association Report* (1942): 44–51; Harold A. Innis, *Essays in Canadian Economic History*, edited by Mary Q. Innis (Toronto: University of Toronto Press, 1956). D.A. Muise, *Elections and Constituencies: Federal Politics in Nova Scotia, 1867–1878* (PhD dissertation, University of Western Ontario, 1971), is a study of the economic determinants of attitudes to Confederation in Nova Scotia.

61 Stéphane Kelly emphasizes the role of self-interest in *La petite loterie: comment la Couronne a obtenu la collaboration du Canada français après 1837* (Montreal: Boréal, 1997).

62 Barbara J. Messamore, *Canada's Governors General, 1847–1878: Biography and Constitutional Evolution* (Toronto: University of Toronto Press, 2006), 5.

63 Robert A. McGuire, *To Form a More Perfect Union: A New Economic Interpretation of the United States Constitution* (New York: Oxford University Press, 2002).

64 "Quebec Resolutions," in Sir Joseph Pope, ed., *Confederation: Being a Series of Hitherto Unpublished Documents Bearing on the British North America Act* (Toronto: Carswell, 1895), 38–52.

65 Peter J. Smith, "The Ideological Origins of Canadian Confederation," *Canadian Journal of Political Science* 20 (1987): 3–29.

66 Colonial reactions to the visit of the Prince of Wales in 1860 are discussed in Ian Radforth, *Royal Spectacle: The 1860 Visit of the Prince of Wales to Canada and the United States* (Toronto: University of Toronto Press, 2004).

67 Janet Ajzenstat, Paul Romney, Ian Gentles, and William D. Gairdner, eds., *Canada's Founding Debates* (Toronto: University of Toronto Press, 2003); Janet Ajzenstat and Peter J. Smith, "Liberal-Republicanism: The Revisionist Picture of Canada's Founding," in *Canada's Origins: Liberal, Tory, or Republican?*, edited by Janet Ajzenstat and Peter J. Smith (Ottawa: Carleton University Press 1995), 367–8.

68 Simon J. Potter, *News and the British World: The Emergence of an Imperial Press System, 1876–1922* (Oxford: Clarendon Press, 2003). Philip Buckner demonstrates the strength of the British identities in the colonies,

suggesting that the colonists' sense of being British intensified rather than decreased in the period 1815 to 1860. See his "Making British North America British, 1815–1860," in Colin Eldridge, ed., *Kith and Kin: Canada, Britain and the United States from the Revolution to the Cold War* (Cardiff: University of Wales Press, 1997), 11–44.

69 Brian Young, *George-Etienne Cartier: Montreal Bourgeois* (Kingston: McGill-Queen's, 1981), 114–15.

70 J.K. Johnson, "John A. Macdonald, the Young Non-Politician," *Canadian Historical Association Historical Papers* (1971): 138–53.

71 Tupper's investment in the Springhill colliery is mentioned in *Dictionary of Canadian Biography*, s.v. "Sir Charles Tupper."

72 Peter Baskerville, "Imperial Agendas and 'Disloyal' Collaborators: Decolonization and the John Sandfield Macdonald Ministries, 1862–64," in *Old Ontario: Essays in Honour of J.M.S. Careless*, edited by David Keane and Colin Read (Toronto: Dundurn Press, 1990), 234–56, 234. For Robinson's theory, see Ronald Robinson, "Non-European Foundations of European Imperialism: Sketch for a Theory of Imperialism," in *Studies in the Theory of Imperialism*, edited by Roger Owen and Bob Sutcliffe (London: Longman, 1972), 117–42.

73 "British North American Association," *Globe* (Toronto), 29 September, 1863, 2.

74 J.M.S. Careless, *Brown of the Globe* (Toronto: Macmillan, 1963), vol. 2, 206–7.

75 Alexander Mackenzie, ed., *The Life and Speeches of Hon. George Brown* (Toronto: Globe Publishing, 1882), 152–3.

76 Elisabeth Wallace, "The Origin of the Social Welfare State in Canada, 1867–1900," *Canadian Journal of Economics and Political Science* 16 (1950): 383–93.

77 Lowe to Monck, 11 November, 1863, LAC Lord Monck Fonds.

78 Contemporary references to the role of British investors in Confederation that are not mentioned elsewhere in this book include: Montreal's *Le Pays*, "Aux Electeurs de Comté d'Hochelaga," 8 November 1864, 2; Benjamin Seymour, *Confederation Debates*, 15 February 1865, 199. The secondary literature dealing with the role of British business in Confederation includes: Reginald G. Trotter, *Canadian Federation: Its Origins and Achievement, a Study in Nation Building* (Toronto: Dent, 1924), and Tom Naylor, *History of Canadian Business*.

79 *Montreal Witness*, 19 January 1867, "Confederation," 44.

80 *Le Pays* (Montreal), "La confédération et le Grand Tronc," 29 May 1866, 2. Writing in the 1850s, the Canadian historian F.X. Garneau

had blamed the 1841 union on the influence of "la maison Baring" and this accusation was pointedly repeated in the summer of 1864 in"Une conclusion d'histoire: Revue, Corrigée et Augmentée," *La Revue Canadienne*, 1 (1864), 424; *Montreal Witness, Commercial Review and Family Newspaper*, article on "La Revue Canadienne," 10 September 1864, 2.

81 *Parliamentary Debates on the Subject of the Confederation of the British North American Provinces* (Quebec: Hunter, Rose, 1865), 15 February 1865, 199.

82 John Stuart Mill, *Principles of Political Economy with Some of Their Applications to Social Philosophy*, 7th edition (London: Longmans Green, 1870), Book 4, chapter 4.

CHAPTER TWO

1 The impact of the end of mercantilism on Canada is discussed in Gilbert Norman Tucker, *The Canadian Commercial Revolution, 1845–1851* (New Haven: Yale University Press, 1936).

2 Goldwin Smith, *The Empire: A Series of Letters Published in "The Daily News,"* 1862, 1863 (Oxford: J.H. and J. Parker, 1863).

3 Harnetty, "Imperialism of Free Trade."

4 United Kingdom, House of Commons, "Annual Statement of the Trade and Navigation of the United Kingdom with Foreign Countries and British Possessions in the Year 1860" (hereafter UK, "ASTNUK 1860"), *Parliamentary Papers* (1861) 60, Tables 4 and 5.

5 This pattern endured for a long time. See Davis and Huttenback, *Mammon*, 159.

6 I derived the numbers from UK, "ASTNUK 1860," Table 6.

7 Peter Marsh suggests that British manufacturers and traders in the Victorian era were less interested in empire and other non-European trade than either previous or subsequent generations of businessmen had been or would be. See Peter Marsh, *Bargaining on Europe: Britain and the First Common Market, 1860–92* (New Haven: Yale University Press, 1999).

8 See UK, "ASTNUK 1860." Exports are defined as products of Great Britain and Ireland and do not include foreign goods transhipped through the United Kingdom.

9 Harold A. Innis, *The Cod Fisheries: The History of an International Economy* (New Haven: Yale University Press, 1940). Also see table detailing British imports from Newfoundland in "Annual Statements of

Trade and Navigation for 1858," *Parliamentary Papers* (1859, session 2) 28: 49–238.

10 A.R.M. Lower, *Great Britain's Woodyard: British America and the Timber Trade, 1763–1867* (Montreal: McGill-Queen's University Press, 1973); Graeme Wynn, *Timber Colony: A Historical Geography of Early Nineteenth Century New Brunswick* (Toronto: University of Toronto Press, 1981).

11 John McCallum, *Unequal Beginnings: Agricultural and Economic Development in Quebec and Ontario until 1870* (Toronto: University of Toronto Press, 1980).

12 However, the tendency to focus on a few staples has been criticized on the grounds that it provides an oversimplified view of Canadian economic history. Douglas McCalla, *Planting the Province: The Economic History of Upper Canada, 1784–1870* (Toronto: University of Toronto Press, 1993).

13 See also the table "Computed Real Value of Corn and Grain Wheat Imported to the United Kingdom in 1858," in UK, "ASTNUK 1860."

14 After 1851 token colonial preference continued but likely had a negligible effect because the degree of preference was so small. The last remaining protection for colonial timber was eliminated in 1860. Lower, *Great Britain's Woodyard*, 91.

15 Gary M. Anderson and Robert D. Tollison, "Ideology, Interest Groups, and the Repeal of the Corn

16 Laws," *Journal of Institutional and Theoretical Economics* 141 (1985): 197–212; A.C. Howe, "Free Trade and the City of London, c. 1820–1870," *History* 77 (1992):391–410.

17 *Canadian News* (London), "The British North American Association," 30 January 1862, 73. For the names of these companies, see Lower, *Great Britain's Woodyard*, 141.

18 For the use of this argument, see Archibald Hamilton, "On the Economic Progress of New Zealand," *Journal of the Royal Statistical Society* 32 (1871): 293f, and "On the Colonies," ibid. 35 (1874): 107f; J. Beaufort Hurlbert, *Britain and her Colonies* (London: Edward Stanford, 1865), 117.

19 John Plummer, Factory Operative, *Our Colonies: Being an Essay on the Advantages Accruing to the British Nation from Its Possession of the Colonies* (London: W. Tweedie; Kettering, Thomas Waddington; 1864). Plummer was a stay maker in the Midlands town of Kettering.

20 My calculation is based on UK, "ASTNUK 1860" and population data from the 1860 United Status census and "Report on the State of the Colonies" in *Parliamentary Papers*, various years.

21 D.F. Barnett, "The Galt Tariff: Incidental or Effective Protection?," *Canadian Journal of Economics* 9 (1976): 389–407.

22 *Economist,* "Canada and England: The Connection and the Value,"
    22 April 1865, 463–5.
23 My calculation based on UK, "ASTNUK 1860."
24 See "Report of the Committee on the Expenses of Military Defence in the
    Colonies," *Parliamentary Papers* (1861), vol. 13, 69–466, especially 411–18.
    See also the anonymous article by Sir George C. Lewis, "Military De-
    fence of the Colonies," *Edinburgh Review* 115 (January 1862) 104–26.
25 "Report of the Committee on the Military Expenses of the Colonies,"
    Parliamentary Papers (1860), vol. 41, 572–9.
26 Martin Daunton, *Trusting Leviathan: The Politics of Taxation in Britain,
    1799–1914* (Cambridge: Cambridge University Press, 2001), 102;
    Barry Baysinger and Robert Tollison, "Chaining Leviathan: The case
    of Gladstonian Finance," *History of Political Economy* 12 (1980): 206–
    13; H.C.G. Matthew, "Disraeli, Gladstone, and the Politics of Mid-
    Victorian Budgets," *Historical Journal* 22 (1979): 615–44.
27 G.R. Searle's *Entrepreneurial Politics in Mid-Victorian Britain* (Oxford:
    Oxford University Press, 1993) is useful in understanding their over-
    all world view. See also, William D. Grampp, *The Manchester School
    of Economics* (Stanford: Stanford University Press, 1960); Nicholas C.
    Edsall, *Richard Cobden, Independent Radical* (Cambridge: Harvard
    University Press, 1986); Donald Reed, *Cobden and Bright: A Victorian
    Political Partnership* (London: Arnold, 1967).
28 For the details of this meeting, see *Speech of the Hon. A.T. Galt, at the
    Chamber of Commerce, Manchester, September 25, 1862* (London: British
    North American Association, 1862), as well as the *Money Market
    Review,* "Mr Galt, Late Finance Minister of Canada," 11 October 1862,
    314. The members of the Manchester Chamber of Commerce
    complained about the high Canadian duties, suggesting that they had
    set a precedent that India had then followed.
29 G.M. Trevelyan, *The Life of John Bright* (London: Constable, 1913), 274.
30 Daniel Drezner, *All Politics Is Global: Explaining, International Regula-
    tory Regimes* (Princeton: Princeton University Press, 2007), 119–48.
31 UK, "ASTNUK 1860."
32 Much of the timber exported to Britain was in the form of
    wooden ships. See Cecil J. Houston and William J. Smyth, "New
    Brunswick Shipbuilding and Irish Shipping: The Commissioning of
    the Londonderry, 1838," *Acadiensis* 16 (1987): 95–106; Eric W. Sager
    and Gerald E. Panting, *Maritime Capital: The Shipbuilding Industry in
    Atlantic Canada, 1820–1914* (Montreal: McGill-Queen's University
    Press, 1990), 35.

33 See the "Report from the Select Committee Appointed to Inquire into the State of Merchant Shipping," *Parliamentary Papers* (1860), vol. 13, 1–789, 418.

34 The company had offices throughout British North America and the West Indies but not in the US. The capital of the Colonial was one million pounds sterling in 1854. In that year, the main Canadian board, which met in Montreal, was chaired by Peter McGill. The local boards also included important figures in Canadian business and politics, such as William Proudfoot of the Bank of Upper Canada, Jason F. Smith of the Bank of Montreal, Sir Allan MacNab, and J.A. Macdonald. See the prospectus of *The Colonial Life Assurance Company* (Edinburgh, 1846).

35 Michael Moss, *Standard Life: 1825–2000, the Building of Europe's Largest Mutual Life Company* (Edinburgh: Mainstream, 2000), 80.

36 Most of the historians who have looked at this topic agree that the status of the British North American colonies qua colonies influenced the decisions of private investors. Trotter, *Canadian Federation*, passim; H.C. Pentland, "The Role of Capital in Canadian Economic Development before 1875," *Canadian Journal of Economics and Political Science* 16 (1950): 457–74. Cf. Roderick Norman Beattie, "Some Aspects of British Investment in British North America 1850–1864" (MA thesis, University of Toronto, 1949), 16.

37 Samuel Orchart Beeton, *Guide to Investing Money with Safety and Profit* (London: Ward Lock, 1870), 27.

38 Leading article, *Daily News*, 8 November 1866, 4. The London paper was responding to the Toronto *Globe's* accusation that it had besmirched the honour of the colonists by alleging that Canada might repudiate its financial obligations just as Mexico and Pennsylvania had done. The *Daily News* clarified its position, stating that while a British colony would never default on its sterling bonds, it might try to shift the burden of part of its public debt onto the back of the British taxpayer.

39 L.E. Davis and R.J. Cull, *International Capital Markets and American Economic Growth, 1820–1914* (Cambridge University Press, 1994), 1, argue that most capital used in the United States in this period was domestic rather than imported. See also Irving Stone, *The Global Export of Capital from Great Britain, 1865–1914: A Statistical Survey* (New York: St Martin's Press, 1999), Tables 1 and 2. D.C.M. Platt argues that the experiences of the Dominions (Canada, Australia, and New Zealand) were essentially different from those of the United States; see Platt's *Foreign Finance in Continental Europe and the United*

States, 1815–1870 Quantities, Origins, Functions, and Distributions (London: George Allen, 1984), 141.

40 Mira Wilkins, *The History of Foreign Investment in the United States to 1914* (Cambridge, MA: Harvard University Press, 1989); John J. Madden, *British Investment in the United States, 1860–1880* (New York: Garland Publishing, 1985; originally completed in Cambridge, 1957), 2. John Madden argues that save for a brief period between 1870 and 1875, British capital played a minor role in American economic growth.

41 Madden, *British Investment*, 78.

42 Charles Fenn, *Fenn's Compendium of the Funds*, 12th ed. (London: Effingham Wilson, 1874), 148.

43 In 1848, on the eve of the Guarantee Act, Canada's sovereign debt had been about £3.93 million sterling. Of this, £3.06 million was in the form of sterling debentures payable in London while the rest was payable to Canadians. Platt and Adelman, "London Merchant Bankers," 212. The massive borrowing of the 1850s probably increased Canada's demand for capital much faster than the rate at which domestic savings grew. In the early 1860s, A.T. Galt referred to the growing market for provincial bonds in Canada (see A.T. Galt to George Glyn, 19 May 1862, Royal Bank of Scotland Archives, GB 1502 RBS/GM/108) but it is clear from his comments that this was a new and somewhat feeble development. In 1874 it was estimated that £17.7 million of the Dominion's public debt of £26.6 million was domiciled in London. Fenn, *Fenn's Compendium* (1874), 148. A few of the registers of the sterling bonds indicate that the interest payments were made to people in the colonies, but the overwhelming majority do not give any hint of the interest payments occurring anywhere but London. Registers for bonds domiciled in the colonies are in Sterling Debentures, LAC, D-4, vol. 2, 375, Ministry of Finance Record Group, RG19.

44 The statement is based on the prices of Canadian bonds recorded in *The Course of the Exchange*. Prices of the leading British North American securities between 1853 and 1869 were sampled at monthly intervals.

45 H.C. Pentland, "The Role of Capital in Canadian Economic Development before 1875," *Canadian Journal of Economics and Political Science* 16 (1950): 457–74, 464.

46 Platt and Adelman, "London Merchant Bankers," 211. Of course, these estimates are tentative, but even if it turned out that the United States took the majority of British investment in North American in the period 1860–1912, it would still be hard to accept A.A. Den Otter's statement that "the United States was the favoured destination" for British

capital in this period. A.A. Den Otter, *The Philosophy of Railways: the Transcontinental Railway Idea in British North America* (Toronto: University of Toronto Press, 1997), 254, note 7.

47 Perhaps because of the Grand Trunk debacle of the 1850s, Herman Merivale worried about artificially high British investment in the colonies; see his *Lectures on Colonization and Colonies*, 2d ed. (London: Longman, Green, 1861), 673–7. Merivale served as the permanent undersecretary for the colonies from 1848 to 1860.

48 On the relationship between constitutions, commitments, and borrowing, see Douglass North and Barry Weingast, "Constitutions and Commitment: The Evolution of Institutions Governing Public Choice in Seventeenth-Century England," *Journal of Economic History* 49 (1989): 803–32; John Wells and Douglas Wills, "Revolution, Restoration, and Debt Repudiation: The Jacobite Threat to England's Institutions and Economic Growth," *Journal of Economic History* 60 (2000): 418–41.

49 Madden, *British Investment*, 231. Wilkins, *Foreign Investment*, 71. On the problems faced by British holders of American bonds, see Reginald McGrane, *Foreign Bondholders and American State Debts* (New York: Macmillan, 1935).

50 Levi, *International Commercial Law*, 32. The complications for British investors created by American federalism is relevant when looking at British business reactions to the Quebec Resolutions.

51 Madden, *British Investment*, 231. The author of one 1860 investors' manual recommended investing in firms that had British participation in management. "Anglo-American," *American Securities: Practical Hints on the Test of Stability and Profit* (London: Mann Nephews, 1860).

52 Peter Baskerville, "Americans in Britain's Backyard: The Railway Era in Upper Canada," *Business History Review* 55 (1981): 314–36.

53 *Bradshaw's Railway Manual, Shareholder's Guide, and Official Directory for 1863 Containing the History and Financial Position of Every Company, British, Foreign and Colonial* (Manchester: Bradshaw and Blacklock, 1863). Hereafter *Bradshaw's*.

54 NA BT 31 Box 1166 co.2496c, Edward Miall and Co. Limited. By 1866 just under two hundred pounds in capital had been called up on Bright's shares.

55 For the rights conferred by this charter, see *An Alphabetical List of the Proprietors of the Bank of British North America on the 1st January, 1867* (London: Waterlow, 1867).

56 E.E. Rich, *The Hudson's Bay Company, 1670–1870* (London: Hudson's Bay Record Society, 1958–1959), vol. 2, 817, discusses the profitability

of the HBC. Watkin's role is discussed by Elaine Allan Mitchell, "
Edward Watkin and the Buying-out of the Hudson's Bay Company,"
Canadian Historical Review 34 (1953): 219–44.

57 Edward Ermatinger, *The Hudson's Bay Territories: A Series of Letters on this Important Question* (Toronto: Maclear, Thomas, 1858).

58 Liverpool Financial Reform Association, *The Hudson's Bay Company versus Magna Charta, and the British People* (Liverpool: N.p., 1857).

59 The criticisms of the company in the 1830s are discussed in Roger D. Hall, "The Canada Company: 1826–1843" (PhD dissertation, Cambridge, 1974), 302–16. The basic idea was that the Anglican church in Upper Canada would sell the reserves to British investors. The clergy would get ready cash, while the investors would gain an asset that would pay dividends in the longer term.

60 Hall, ibid., 422 attributes the company's "solid prosperity" in the 1850s to Frederick Widder's efforts.

61 "Historical Note" by R.W. Heneker, the company's commissioner in Canada, 1855–1902, in British American Land Company Fonds, LAC, pp. 149–62.

62 See Canada, Vict. 22 (1858), cap. 85.

63 Peter Baskerville, "John A. Macdonald: the Young Non-Politician," *Canadian Historical Association Historical Papers* (1971): 138–53, 143.

64 *Prospectus of the Canada Landed Credit Company* (Toronto: Thompson, 1859); *Money Market Review,* "The Proposed Issue of Land Debentures in This Country: The Plan of the Canada Landed Credit Company," 12 April 1862, 327; *The Canada Landed Credit Company Almanack* (Toronto: Globe, 1869); D.C. Masters, "Canadian Bankers of the Last Century, vol. 1: William McMaster," *Canadian Banker* 49 (1942): 389–96; Peter Baskerville, in *Dictionary of Canadian Biography,* vol. 11, s.v. "Robert Cassels."

65 Anglo-Canadian, *The Landed Credit System of Canada: Explained and Recommended as the Surest and Most Profitable Medium for the Investment of British Capital* (London: Effingham Wilson, Royal Exchange, 1860), 4.

66 *The Trust and Loan Company of Upper Canada: Statement of the Objects of the Company* (London: Trust and Loan Company of Upper Canada, 1851), 1.

67 *Money Market Review,* "The Trust and Loan Company of Upper Canada and the Other Companies Founded on the Same Principle," 27 June 1863, 607. The paper reported that £666,267 in debentures had been sold to the public.

68 The Upper Canada Consolidated Municipal Fund is discussed in Albert Faucher, "Le fonds d'emprunt municipal dans le Haut-Canada,

1852–1867," *Recherches Sociographiques* 1 (1960): 7–32. To see how bonds were issued under this legislation, see Thomas Ridout to Glyn, 16 June 1856, Royal Bank of Scotland Group Archives, GB1502 /GM/68. It is important to point out that the City of Hamilton's bonds fell outside the terms of the 1852 provincial legislation and did not enjoy a provincial guarantee.

69 Huttenback and Davis, *Mammon*, 138.

70 *Money Market Review*, "A Defaulting Canadian Municipality," 11 January 1862, 26–7.

71 The incident with the "lost" assessment roll is discussed in the *Money Market Review*, "The Hamilton Bondholders- Canada West," 31 January 1863, 105–7. The paper also mentioned that many of the British investors had purchased their bonds from the late Sir Allan MacNab. See ibid., "What Will the Government of Canada Do With the Bondholders of Hamilton, CW," 11 April 1863, 337.

72 *Money Market Review*, "The Hamilton Bondholders, Canada West" 28 February 1862, 202.

73 *Money Market Review*, "Privileges and Duties of Our Colonies: The Recent Case of Attempted Repudiation," 22 February 1862, 158–9.

74 Because this was a matter of public interest, much of the relevant Colonial Office correspondence was printed. See United Kingdom, House of Commons, "Correspondence between the Colonial Secretary and the Governor-General on Hamilton Municipal Bonds," *Parliamentary Papers* (1863), vol. 38, 301–58, especially T.F. Elliot to Messrs Dawes and Sons, 21 February 1863; Albert Faucher, "Le problème financier de la Province du Canada (1841–1867)," *Recherches sociographiques* 1 (1960): 343–62.

75 *Money Market Review*, "A Proposition for a Settlement With the Bondholders of Hamilton, Canada West," 12 April 1862, 328; ibid., "The Hamilton Bondholders (Canada West)," 1 October 1864, 396.

76 The bonds of Galt, Upper Canada, continued to sell during this period. Thomas Sparrow, Treasurer of Galt, to Glyn Mills and Co., 11 July 1860, Royal Bank of Scotland Group Archives, GB1502 /GM/33; Thomas Sparrow to Glyn Mills and Co., 5 January 1862, ibid.; Thomas Sparrow, Treasurer of Galt, to Glyn Mills and Co., 4 July 1863, ibid. It is uncertain whether sharing a name with the provincial minister of Finance made the municipality's bonds easier to sell.

77 Michael J. Piva, *The Borrowing Process: Public Finance in the Province of Canada, 1840–1867* (Ottawa: University of Ottawa Press, 1992), xiii; Rosemary Langhout, "Public Enterprise: An Analysis of Public

Finance in the Maritime Colonies during the Period of Responsible
Government" (PHD dissertation, University of New Brunswick, 1989).

78 Phillip Ziegler, *The Sixth Great Power, Barings, 1762–1829* (London:
Collins, 1988), 10. Niall Ferguson emphasizes that the combined re-
sources of the various branches of the Rothschild families were always greater than those of Barings'. Niall Ferguson, *The House of
Rothschild: The World's Banker 1849–1998* (London: Penguin Books,
2000), xxv. Richard Roberts, "What's in a Name? Merchants,
Merchant Bankers, Accepting Houses, Issuing Houses, Industrial
Bankers, and Investment Bankers," *Business History* 35 (1993): 22–38.
The world of Baring and Glyn is described by Walter Bagehot, *Lombard Street: A Description of the Money Market* (London: Henry S. King,
1873), 268–9. As a private banker who wrote books on the English
constitution and edited *The Economist*, Bagehot was a well-informed
commentator. Alistair Buchan, *The Spare Chancellor: The Life of Walter
Bagehot* (London: Chatto and Windus, 1959).

79 Ziegler, *Sixth Great Power*, 161.

80 Ralph W. Hidy, *The House of Baring in American Trade and Finance: English Merchant Bankers at Work, 1763–1861* (Cambridge, MA: Harvard
University Press, 1949), 52.

81 *Times*, letter to the editor, 18 January 1843, 5; ibid., "House of Commons," 22 March 1843, 2.

82 Ziegler, *Sixth Great Power*, 151–2, 156–7.

83 The Pennsylvania debacle and its role in reorienting the firms towards British North America is discussed in Hidy, *House of Baring*,
310–30.

84 See article on "Repudiation" in John Lalor, *Cyclopaedia of Political Science* (New York: Maynard, Merrill, 1899). For the relationship with
the Bank of the United States, see Ziegler, *Sixth Great Power*, 75–6.

85 Michael Reed, "Glyn, George Carr, First Baron Wolverton (1797–
1873)," in *Oxford Dictionary of National Biography*, Reed, like most historians, considers both men to have been the province's official
agents.

86 Michael J. Piva, "Financing the Union: The Upper Canadian Debt and
Financial Administration in the Canadas, 1837–45." *Journal of Cana-
dian Studies* 25 (1990): 82–98; M.L. Magill, "John H. Dunn and the
Bankers," *Ontario History* 62 (1970): 83–100.

87 Roger Fulford, *Glyn's 1753–1953: Six Generations in Lombard Street* (London: Macmillan, 1953), 121; Anonymous, "Glyns and the Grand Trunk
Railway," *Three Banks Review* 52 (1961): 28–40; Clement E. Stretton, *The*

History of the Amalgamation and the Formation of the London and North-Western Railway Company (Leeds: Goodall and Suddick, 1901), R.A. Ashbee, "George Carr Glyn and the Railways," *Three Banks Review* 46 (1960): 34–47; Thomas Wrigley, *London and North-Western Railway* (Manchester: s.n., 1862); Sir Francis Bond Head, *Stokers and Pokers: or the London and North-Western Railway, the Electric Telegraph and the Railway Clearing House* (London: John Murray, 1849).

88 Ronald Stewart Longley, *Sir Francis Hincks: a Study of Canadian Politics, Railways, and Finance in the Nineteenth Century* (Toronto: University of Toronto Press, 1943). See also Peter Baskerville, "Americans in Britain's Backyard: The Railway Era in Upper Canada," *Business History Review* 55 (1981): 314–36; Peter Baskerville, "Transportation, Social Change, and State Formation, Upper Canada, 1841–1864," in *Colonial Leviathan: State Formation in Mid-Nineteenth-Century Canada,* edited by Allan Greer and Ian Radforth (Toronto: University of Toronto Press, 1992), 230–56; Douglas McCalla, "Railways and the Development of Canada West, 1850–1870" in ibid., 190–229.

89 Joseph Nelson, *On the Political and Commercial Importance of Completing the Line of Railway from Halifax to Quebec* (London: W. Penny, 1860); Grey to Elgin, 17 November 1848; Elgin to Grey 30 April 1849, in *The Elgin-Grey Papers, 1846–1852,* edited by Sir Arthur Doughty (Ottawa: The King's Printer, 1937), 1,379–81, 1458–63. For an account of the Intercolonial discussions during Grey's term at the Colonial Office, see Den Otter, *Philosophy,* 51–61.

90 The promoters only managed to raise £2.78 million of the £3.6 million originally expected and within a few weeks the securities were selling at a steep discount.

91 Under the provincial Guarantee Act of 1849 the Canadian government guaranteed interest payments of six percent on railways over seventy-five miles in length. The Guarantee Act was supported by all parties in the legislature. It was inspired by American precedents: many American states had provided public underwriting for private railway bonds. For more detailed information regarding this crucial legislation see George Parkin de Twenebroker Glazebrook, *History of Transportation in Canada* (Toronto: McClelland and Stewart, 1964), 163–4.

92 David Kynaston, *Cazenove and Co., a History* (London: Batsford, 1991), 44.

93 D.C.M. Platt and Jeremy Adelman, "London Merchant Bankers," 208–27; Currie, *Grand Trunk,* 33–52.

94 Probate records indicate that Baring was worth less than £1,500,000 upon his death in 1873. John Orbell, "Baring, Thomas (1799–1873),"

in *Oxford Dictionary of National Biography*. Orbell takes this figure
from the records of the Principal Civil Registry. However, it reflects
the nominal value of many of the securities Baring owned. For Peto's
bankruptcy, see M.H. Port, "Peto, Sir (Samuel) Morton, First Baronet
(1809–1889)," in *Oxford Dictionary of National Biography*.

95 Cain and Hopkins, *British Imperialism*, 263.

96 Ann M. Carlos and Frank Lewis, "The Profitability of Early Canadian
Railroads: Evidence from the Grand Trunk and Great Western Rail-
way Companies," in *Strategic Factors in Nineteenth Century American
Economic History*, edited by Claudia Goldin and Hugh Rockoff
(Chicago: University of Chicago Press, 1992), 401–26.

97 The Toronto *Globe* reported that there were "seven or eight hundred"
gentlemen at a meeting of the Grand Trunk's share and bondholders.
Globe, "Mails by the Europa," 23 August 1862, 1.

98 Davis and Huttenback, *Mammon*, 164–70, 273–6.

99 *Economist*, "The Influence of Increased Education upon the Stock
Market," 7 May 1864, 575–6.

100 Walter Arnstein, "The Myth of the Triumphant Victorian Middle
Class," *The Historian* 37 (1975): 205–21.

101 One Grand Trunk investor, James Newall of the British Linen Co.
Bank, was reduced to outright pleading. See Newall to Thomas
Baring, 9 March 1859, in ING Baring Archives, HC5.15.34.

102 A.J. Johnson to Thomas Baring, 9 March 1859, in ibid.

103 J.C. Conybeare, *Mr Baring and the Grand Trunk* (London, s.n., 1863), 20–1.

104 *Money Market Review*, 16 August 1862. See also letter from Henry
Chapman and Co., Montreal 13 October 1860, "Letters from Henry
Cleaver Chapman" ING Baring Archive, HC5.15.39; *Gore's Liverpool
Directory* (Liverpool: Henry Young and Sons, 1857).

105 Chapman's investigations are discussed in "Grand Trunk Railway,"
Herapath's Railway and Commercial Journal, 15 September 1860, 936
(hereafter *Herapath's*). Chapman's brother Henry was a wine merchant in Montreal. *Mackay's Montreal Directory* (Montreal: Owler
and Stevenson, 1861), 76.

106 Henry C. Chapman to Thomas Baring, 13 October 1860, ING Baring
Archive, HC5.15.39. The two brothers had been confirmed in this
opinion after having seen Blackwell in action at the Pointe St Charles
locomotive works.

107 T.E. Blackwell to Baring, 22 September 1858, ING Baring Archive,
HC5.15.26.

108 "Plan for the relief of the Grand Trunk: Mr Newmarch's Scheme."
February-March 1861, ING Baring Archive, HC5.15.64. The Ontario,

Simcoe and Huron, a railway between Toronto and Collingwood that had been rescued by the province in 1858–59, was the probable model for this plan. Its affairs are discussed in "Papers Concerning the Formation of the Northern Railway of Canada," Royal Bank of Scotland Archives, GB 1502 RBS/GM/75; Currie, *Grand Trunk*, 255–65.

109 Joseph Schumpeter, *Imperialism and Social Classes; Two Essays*, introduction by Bert Hoselitz; translated by Heinz Norden (New York: Meridian Books, 1951).

110 Anne O. Krueger, "Why Crony Capitalism Is Bad for Economic Growth," in *Crony Capitalism and Economic Growth in Latin America: Theory and Evidence*, edited by Stephen Haber (Stanford: Hoover Institution Press, 2002), 1–25.

111 For a general description of firms of this type, see Robert B. Ekelund and Robert D. Tollison, *Mercantilism as a Rent-Seeking Society: Economic Regulation in Historical Perspective* (College Station: Texas A&M University Press, 1981), and James M. Buchanan, *Constitutional Economics* (Oxford: Blackwell, 1991).

112 Earl Grey, *Parliamentary Government Considered with Reference to Reform*, 2d ed. (London: John Murray, 1864), 94-7; Peter Burroughs, "Liberal, Paternalist or Cassandra? Earl Grey as Critic of Self-Government," *Journal of Imperial and Commonwealth History* 18 (1990): 33-60.

113 F.X. Garneau, *Histoire du Canada depuis sa découverte jusqu'à nos jours* (Montreal: Editions de l'Arbre, 1944–46, vol. 9, 138); D.G.G. Kerr, *A Scholarly Governor: Sir Edmund Head* (Toronto: University of Toronto Press, 1954), 192.

114 For these allegations, see *Globe*, "Sir E. Head's Closet Councillors", 7 August 1858, 2. The short-lived government led by Brown collapsed because Sir Edmund refused to grant a dissolution of Parliament: when Brown and his allies had taken cabinet positions in the course of forming a ministry, they had automatically vacated their seats, thereby eliminating their majority in the legislature. This had allowed the old Conservative-Bleu alliance to win a no-confidence vote, bring down the government, and then return to power, albeit with a shuffled cabinet.

115 Head to Thomas Baring and George Carr Glyn, 19 July 1856 in RG7 G17 A, 3:243–9, LAC.

116 In 1861 Frederic Algar, the paper's publisher, implausibly claimed that the *Canadian News* was a strictly apolitical publication. Frederic Algar to Leonard Tilley, 17 September 1861, LAC, Leonard Tilley Fonds, vol. 10. Given the importance of the *Canadian News*, it is unfortunate that more information on Algar's background is not available.

CHAPTER THREE

1 The visit of the prince is discussed in Ian Radforth, *Royal Spectacle: The 1860 Visit of the Prince of Wales to Canada and the United States* (Toronto: University of Toronto Press, 2004).

2 Thomas Galt to A.T. Galt, Quebec, 25 September 1860, in "Letters from Thomas Galt, QC," ING Baring Archive, HC5.15.41. Other correspondence about the court cases can be found in HC5.15.40 and HC5.15.45. See also Thomas Galt to George Carr Glyn, 5 January 1861, in Royal Bank of Scotland Group Archives, GB1502 /GM/99; Thomas Galt to Glyn, 30 November 1861, ibid., and "Report of the Arguments and Judgement in Herrick v the Grand Trunk Railway of Canada." heard 17 June 1861, before the Court of Chancery in Upper Canada (Toronto: Rowsell and Ellis, 1861), in ibid.

3 John Ross to Thomas Baring, 28 September 1860 and 4 October 1860, ING Baring Archive, HC5.15.27.

4 For the attempt by bondholders to seize the railway, see *Herapath's*, "Grand Trunk," 30 November 1861, 1,222–4; letter to editor from bondholder, "Grand Trunk and Buffalo and Lake Huron Railways," in ibid., 11 June 1864, 678. *Herapath's* advised the holders of GTR bonds to be patient: interest payments would soon be restored, and the railway would become profitable in the longer term: "There is a great future for the Grand Trunk, to be realised when Canada is a little more populated and the line extended to Halifax."

5 Thomas Galt to Thomas Baring, 20 July 1861, in ING Baring Archive, HC5.15.41.

6 Ziegler, *Sixth Great Power*, 179–80.

7 "A Barrister," *Overend, Gurney, and Co., Limited. A Plain Statement of the Case* (London: James Gilbert, 1867).

8 Watkin, *Canada and the States*, 5. Watkin's Canadian activities are described in David Hodgkins, *The Second Railway King: The Life and Times of Sir Edward Watkin, 1819–1901* (London: Merton, 2002), 177–241. See also NA RAIL 1007/348 "Papers on Sir Edward Watkin."

9 Sir E. Watkin. *Absalom Watkin: Fragment No. 1* (Manchester: Alex Ireland, 1874).

10 Cobden to E. Watkin, 6 March 1857, in Manchester Library and Archives, Local Studies, Sir Edward Watkin Papers M219/3/1–8 .

11 *Hansard*, 3d ser., 186 (1867): 1,054–5. Watkin's ideas on state ownership are explored more fully in the conclusion.

12 Edward Watkin, *Canada and the States: Recollections, 1851 to 1886* (London: Ward, Lock, 1887), 5.

13 Watkin, *Canada and the States*, 3.

14 In this context, constitutional political economy denotes theories that link comparative economic performance with structural differences in political systems.

15 Morton H. Halperin, Joseph Stiegle, and Michael M. Weinstein, *The Democracy Advantage: How Democracies Promote Prosperity and Peace* (London: Routledge, 2004).

16 The Glorious Revolution of 1688 established the principle of parliamentary supremacy in England and was a stepping stone to liberal democracy. Thomas Babbington Macaulay, *The History of England from the Accession of James the Second* [1848, 1855, 1861] (New York: Twentieth Century Editions, 1900), vol. 1, 322–3.

17 On the continued aristocratic dominance of British society and politics, see Walter Arnstein, "The Myth of the Triumphant Victorian Middle Class," *The Historian* 37 (1975): 205–21

18 *Herapath's,* leading article on the "Grand Trunk" 4 October 1862, 1,046–7. "We can assert that there would have been little or no difference in the actual value of the Indian or Canadian railways under the same treatment ... what renders the Indian railways good investments and the Canadian bad? Nothing but the conduct of the two governments." The paper had a point: because the Grand Trunk was operating in a democratic environment, it had incurred all sorts of political expenses in defending its privileges (campaign donations, free passes for MLAS and ministers of religion, etc.) that a railway in India would not have faced. For a similar argument about democracy's impact on railway finances, see *Money Market Review,* "Grand Trunk Railway of Canada," 14 February 1863, 152–3.

19 Letter to the editor from Thomas Adams, *Herapath's,* 14 April 1860, 387.

20 Christopher Moore, *1867: How the Fathers Made a Deal* (Toronto: McClelland and Stewart, 1997), 170–6.

21 *Canadian News,* "Hamilton Municipal Indebtedness," 3 April 1862, 215. The *Canadian News* followed the *Montreal Gazette* in arguing that the Canadian legislature's decision to establish a "low franchise" was the ultimate cause of the default. See also "City of Hamilton Bonds," in *Canadian News,* 23 January 1862, 73–4, letter to the editor from Veritas dated 24 January 1862.

22 *Bankers' Magazine,* May 1861, "Grand Trunk Railway of Canada", 345–8. The subsidized immigration from the British Isles to Canada

discussed by the *Bankers' Magazine* would have killed two birds with one stone, helping to put emigrant bums into Grand Trunk seats while addressing domestic social concerns. The *Bankers' Magazine* conceded that the the Grand Trunk bondholders did not have a "strictly legal" claim on the Canadian provincial treasury, the people of Canada were refusing to discharge a "debt of honour" to the investors because "things have turned out differently from what the Canadian people and Canadian government said they would do."

23 There have been no studies of the role of class ideas in British perceptions of the colonies of settlement, but considering that the colonists were economic migrants or their descendents, it is reasonable to suppose that class ideology coloured elitist contempt for the people of the colonies.

24 See the *Minutes of the Political Economy Club* (London, s.n., 1921). On 3 March 1859, the club discussed "What would be the probable Economical consequences in this Country of a Government based on Universal Suffrage?"

25 Daunton, *Trusting Leviathan*, 69.

26 John Stuart Mill, *Considerations on Representative Government* (London: Longmans, Green, 1861), chapter 6, sec. 2. Because it assumes that states are Leviathans intent on expanding as much as possible, this viewpoint is similar to that articulated by the modern Public Choice constitutional theorists who search for constitutional ways of chaining Leviathans; see for example James M. Buchanan, *The Limits of Liberty: Between Anarchy and Leviathan* (Chicago: University of Chicago Press, 1975).

27 *Financial Reformer*, Letter from Lawrence Heyworth, "The Real Interest of the Working Classes in Parliamentary Reform," June 1861, 507.

28 Herbert Spencer, "Parliamentary Reform: The Dangers and the Safeguards," *Westminster Review* (April 1860): 486–507. later reprinted in *Man Versus the State* (London: Williams and Norgate, 1892, reprinting articles that appeared in the *Contemporary Review*, 1884).

29 John Austin, *A Plea for the Constitution*, 2d ed. (London: John Murray, 1859). A former Benthamite, Austin had re-examined his commitment to democracy. Looking at the United States for evidence of democracy's dangers, Austin remarked on the impolite behaviour of guests from the "humbler classes" at presidential functions.

30 Henry Fawcett, *Free Trade and Protection: An Inquiry into the Causes Which Have Retarded the General Adoption of Free Trade Since Its Introduction into England* (London: Macmillan, 1878). Fawcett's argument

appeared in an earlier form in "The Riddle of Australian Politics," *The Exchange: A Home and Colonial Monthly Review of Commerce, Manufactures and General Literature* (April 1862).

31 Earl Grey, *Parliamentary Government Considered with Reference to Reform*, 2d ed. (London: John Murray, 1864), 94–7, 160, 175, 352. For the increasingly conservative drift of Grey's thinking on colonial and other matters, see Peter Burroughs, "Liberal, Paternalist or Cassandra? Earl Grey as Critic of Self-Government," *Journal of Imperial and Commonwealth History* 18 (1990): 33–60.

32 Income tax would have been anathema to most Canadians, a political attitude disapprovingly noted by Gladstone and by other British observers convinced that income tax was both socially just and a necessary corollary of free trade. Gladstone to Newcastle, 14 December 1861, "Memorandum on Intercolonial Railway," Newcastle Papers NEC 11252/1. The great organ of British free trade opinion noted that the Canadians had "a dread of direct taxation, which seems to Englishmen morbid." *Economist*, "The Canadian Proposal to Purchase the Hudson's Bay Company," 14 October 1865, 1,236.

33 John Ross to Thomas Baring, undated but probably 1860, "John Ross Correspondence," ING Baring Archive, HC15.25.

34 *Globe*, "Grand Trunk Railway of Canada: A Special General Meeting in London," 23 August 1862, 2–3.

35 Similarly incendiary accusations had been made by investor J.C. Conybeare in *Herapath's*, "Grand Trunk Railway of Canada," 20 July 1861, 729.

36 *Money Market Review*, "Grand Trunk Railway of Canada," 25 October 1862, 356; *Canadian News*, "Grand Trunk of Canada," 14 August 1862, 102–3. The *Times*, "Railway and Other Companies" 9 August 1862, 14, attributed the fact that the act had been passed at all to the efforts of Watkin.

37 Watkin made this comment at a special meeting of bond and shareholders held 9 June 1864 and reported in *Herapath's*, "Grand Trunk of Canada," 11 June 1864, 675–6 . The meeting had been held to ratify an agreement with the Buffalo and Lake Huron Railway for "conjoint working." *Herapath's* argued that while Confederation would benefit the provinces, the construction of the Intercolonial would be equally profitable for the Grand Trunk.

38 Watkin also thought that the amalgamation of the Grand Trunk with its competitors, the Great Western, and the Buffalo and Lake Huron railways, was essential. Opposition in the Canadian legislature to

such a "monopoly" frustrated his 1862 plan for amalgamation. See
Currie, *Grand Trunk*, 105.

39 "A British Railway from Atlantic to Pacific," in the *Illustrated London
News*, 16 February 1861, 135–6, mentioned in Watkin, *Canada and the
States*, 57.

40 John Ross to Eliza Ross, 8 October 1858, LAC, Baldwin Family Fonds, 9.

41 13 November 1860. The addressee of this letter is unknown and the
original is no longer extant. It was probably part of the collection of
Watkin correspondence destroyed in the 1940s. However, it was reprinted in Watkin, *Canada and the States*, 12.

42 John Murray Gibbon, *Steel of Empire: The Romantic History of the Canadian Pacific, the Northwest Passage of Today* (New York: Bobbs-Merrill,
1935), 335.

43 Edward Watkin to Newcastle, 30 September 1861, University of
Nottingham Library, Newcastle Papers, NEC 11270. This letter was
written in the Executive Council Office, Quebec.

44 Sandford Fleming, *The Intercolonial: A History, 1832 to 1876* (Montreal:
Dawson Bros, 1876), 56–7.

45 Watkin to T. Baring, undated but 1862, LAC, Baring Brothers and Co.
Fonds, 3:1,474–7, 3:1,609–11; William Chapman to Macdonald,
24 January 1862, LAC, Sir John A. Macdonald Fonds, 337:153705.

46 Harold Pollins, "Aspect of Railway Accounting before 1868," in *Railways in the Victorian Economy: Studies in Finance and Economic Growth*,
edited by M.C. Reed (Newton Abbot: David and Charles, 1969), 138–
61. Watkin was an early example of a salaried, non-shareholding Canadian business executive. The rise of the "visible hand" in a British
context is discussed by T.R. Gourvish, *Mark Huish and the London and
North Western Railway: A Study of Management* (Leicester: Leicester
University Press, 1972). The American story is discussed in Alfred
Chandler, "Railroads: Pioneers in Modern Management," *Business
History Review* 39 (1965): 16–40.

47 Although the amount of traffic generated by the Intercolonial in the
1870s proved to be quite modest, Watkin lacked the benefit of hind-
sight. In retrospect, it would have been much better if Watkin had adopted the policy eventually pursued by President Richard Potter after
1872. Currie, *Grand Trunk*, 119.

48 Palmerston felt that if a penny-pinching policy had not been pursued
in the past, the railway would already exist. Palmerston to Sir George
C. Lewis, 26 August 1861, Papers of Henry John Temple, Third Viscount Palmerston, Broadlands Archive, University of Southampton.

I am grateful to the trustees of the papers for permission to quote this letter.

49 Newcastle to Gladstone, n.d. but 1861, University of Nottingham Library, Newcastle Papers, NEC 11756/1–2.

50 Cobden to John Bright, dated Midhurst, 7 December 1861, British Library Manuscripts Room, Cobden Papers, Add MSS 43651, f.304

51 Cobden to John Bright, dated Midhurst, 11 December 1861, British Library Manuscripts Room, Cobden Papers, Add MSS 43651, f.308.

52 Edward Watkin to Newcastle, 26 December 1861, LAC, Joseph Howe Fonds, 3:279. Howe was writing from Rose Hill near Manchester.

53 Morton, *Critical Years*, 120–4; Roman, "Imperial Guarantees," 256–9; Gene Lawrence Allen, "The Origins of the Intercolonial Railway, 1835–1869," (PHD dissertation, University of Toronto, 1991), 285–96.

54 It does not appear that the existing personality disputes within the cabinet were relevant to the making of North American colonial policy. According to Colin C. Eldridge, "The Colonial Policy of the Fifth Duke of Newcastle, 1859–1964" (PHD dissertation, University of Nottingham, 1966), 72, relations between the Colonial Office and the Treasury were bad, despite Newcastle's personal friendship with Gladstone. Treasury relations with the Foreign Office were good, even though Lord John Russell disliked Gladstone.

55 Newcastle to Gladstone, 23 February 1863, University of Nottingham Library, Newcastle Papers, NEC 10891.

56 Howe to Gladstone, 10 January 1862, British Library Manuscripts Room, Gladstone Papers, 44398, f. 24. This appeal did not change Gladstone's mind, although he does appear to have enjoyed the interview with Howe that resulted from this letter. See Sir Morton Peto to Howe, 13 January 1862, LAC, Howe Fonds, 3:322. See also Gladstone's "Memorandum on Intercolonial Railway, British North America," 14 December 1861, Private and Confidential, in Newcastle Papers, University of Nottingham Library, NEC 11252/2/1–4.

57 On the cleavages within the Liberal party and the tendency of the more moderate Liberals to think like the Conservatives on colonial matters, see C.J. Brydges to Tilley dated Boston, 14 December 1863, LAC, Samuel Leonard Tilley Fonds, LAC 15.

58 This phrase was used by Samuel Laing, a Liberal, in the April 1867 debate on government aid for the most heavily indebted British railways. United Kingdom, *Hansard*, 3d series, 186 (1867): 1,051–4.

59 Newcastle to Palmerston, 11 November 1861, Newcastle Papers, University of Nottingham Library, NEC 10890/1.

60 For Gladstone's testimony, see "Report of the Committee on the Military Expenses of the Colonies," *Parliamentary Papers* (1861), vol. 13, 255–70. The generally imperialist character of Gladstone's public and private statements is clear. In 1904 Goldwin Smith claimed that Gladstone had proposed ending the Civil War by giving Canada to the United States as a gift. If true, this anecdote would suggest that Gladstone was a covert anti-colonialist. However, Paul Knaplund is very sceptical of this claim. Paul Knaplund, *Gladstone and Britain's Imperial Policy* (London: George Allen and Unwin, 1927), 91.

61 John Strachan to Gladstone, 5 January 1864, British Library Manuscripts Room, W.E. Gladstone Papers, Add MSS 44402, f.22. On Gladstone's opposition to state aid to the colonies and the evolution of his colonial principles, see Alan Shaw, *Gladstone at the Colonial Office, 1846* (London: Australian Studies Centre, Institute of Commonwealth Studies, University of London, 1986), 9, 13, 18.

62 Adderley made this argument in his *Review of "The Colonial Policy of Lord J. Russell's Administration"* (London: E. Stanford, 1869), 49. Adderley's other works on colonial relations include *Letter to the Right Hon. Benjamin Disraeli, M.P. on the Present Relations of England with the Colonies* (London: E. Stanford, 1861); *Europe Incapable of American Democracy* (London: E. Stanford, 1867); *Imperial Fellowship of Self-Governed British Colonies* (London: Rivington, 1903). His belief in colonial military self-sufficiency was challenged by Joseph Howe, *A Letter to the Right Honourable C.B. Adderley M.P. on the Relations of England with Her Colonies* (London: Edward Stanford, 1863, published for the British North American Association).

63 Morton, *Critical Years*, 123.

64 David Bebbington goes so far as to describe Gladstone's economic ideas as communitarian and anti-individualist; D.W. Bebbington, *The Mind of Gladstone: Religion, Homer, and Politics* (Oxford: Oxford University Press, 2004), 306–14. Other works dealing with his economic principles include Richard Shannon, *Gladstone* (London: Hamilton, 1982–1999); Roy Jenkins, *Gladstone: A Biography* (London: Macmillan, 1995), 215–29; H.C.G. Matthew, *Gladstone, 1809–1874* (Oxford: Oxford University Press, 1986), 119–20.

65 See 2 April 1862, *The Gladstone Diaries*, edited by H.C.D. Matthew (Oxford: Clarendon Press, 1968), vol. 6, 112; David Kynaston, *The Chancellor of the Exchequer*, (Lavenham: T. Dalton, 1980), 51.

66 Richard Cobden, *How Wars Are Got Up in India* (London: F. and W.G. Cash, 1853); *Three Panics: An Historical Episode* (London: Ward, 1862).

In 1864 Cobden retired from politics for health reasons, but upon learning in 1865 that there was going to be a debate in the Commons on imperial aid to build fortifications in Canada, he was roused to travel to London against medical advice. For the details of his last days, see Wendy Hinde, *Richard Cobden: A Victorian Outsider* (New Haven: Yale University Press, 1987), 325.

67 G.R. Searle, *Entrepreneurial Politics in Mid-Victorian Britain* (New York: Oxford University Press, 1993).

68 Cobden to Bright, 21 November 1861, British Library Manuscripts Room, Cobden Papers, Add MSS 43651, f.295; Cobden to Bright, 11 December 1861, ibid, f.308; Cobden to Gladstone, 11 December 1861, ibid., Gladstone Papers, Add MSS 44136, f.146; Gladstone to Cobden, 13 December 1861, ibid., f.155.

69 11 June 1859, *The American Diaries of Richard Cobden*, edited by Elizabeth Hoon Cawley (Princeton: Princeton University Press, 1952, based on Cobden Papers, British Library Manuscripts Room, Add MSS 43808), 211.

70 Bright to Cobden, 9 December 1861, British Library Manuscripts Room, John Bright Papers, Add MSS 43384, f. 280.

71 Robertson Gladstone had pursued a career in business in Liverpool. His relationship with his brother remained close but was strained by Robertson's conversion to Unitarianism. S.G. Checkland, *The Gladstones: A Family Biography, 1764–1851* (Cambridge: Cambridge University Press, 1971), 376–8. In the 1870s Gladstone, dispirited about the prevailing political climate, became a recluse.

72 *Financial Reformer*, "The Financial Reform Association," June 1861, 508; ibid., "The Colonial Incubi," 1 September 1864, 494.

73 The committee was divided on this issue, but its final report was a triumph for the duke of Newcastle's position that primary responsibility for the defence of Canada and other self-governing colonies still rested with the imperial government. Eldridge, "Colonial Policy," 260.

74 *Financial Reformer*, "Our Paradoxical Chancellor," June 1862, 607–8; ibid., "What Mr Gladstone has Done for England?" November 1866, 433: "Mr Gladstone will dwarf all that he has hitherto done, and become excepting ONE only, the greatest benefactor of mankind the world has ever saw, if he live to crown his work with the abolition of Customs and Excise and the establishment of perfect freedom of trade."

75 *Financial Reformer*, July 1861, "British Invasion of America," 509.

76 Quotation from *Financial Reformer*, "Our Colonial Wars," May 1862, 591–2. For the expression of similar anti-colonial sentiments, see

Tracts of the Liverpool Financial Reform Association, tracts no. 11
and 12, "Speech of Sir William Molesworth Bart MP delivered in the
House of Commons, 25 July 1846." Another anti-colonial tract distributed by the LFRA was the paper on colonies delivered by Henry Ashworth, president of the Manchester Chamber of Commerce, at a
meeting of the Society of Arts, on 26 March 1861. *Financial Reformer,*
"Our Colonial Wars," May 1862, 591–2.

77 Cobden to E. Watkin, 9 July 1840, Manchester Library and Archives,
Local Studies, Sir Edward Watkin Papers M219/3/1–8.

78 See F.M.L. Thompson, *Gentrification and the Enterprise Culture: Britain,
1780–1980* (Oxford: Oxford University Press, 2001).

79 Howe to Tilley, 19 January 1862, LAC, Howe Fonds 7:182.

80 Colthart, "Edward Ellice and North America," 99–101, 204, 266, 285,
296–301, 326.

81 Edward Ellice, Sr, to Charles Wood, 23 November 1861, Hickleton
Papers, Borthwick Institute of Historical Research, A4/D3A. The activities of the Canada Club in the 1860s remain a mystery due to the
loss or destruction of the papers dealing with this period.

82 *Gladstone Diaries*, edited by H.C.D. Matthew, 14 December 1861,
vol. 6, 6:82. The Canada Club's Minute Books for the 1860s have not
survived, although papers from preceding and subsequent decades
have. J.G. Colmer, *The Canada Club, London: Some Notes on Its Origins,
Constitution, and Activities* (London: Canada Club, 1934).

83 Ellice to Wood, 11 November 1862, Hickleton Papers, Borthwick Institute of Historical Research, A4/D3A.

84 Ellice to Wood, 30 August 1863, ibid.

85 Joseph Nelson reported that while some members of the Canada
Club did join the association, they were averse to its political
agenda; in 1864 Joseph Nelson blamed the Canada Club for the
British North American Association's problems. J. Nelson to Howe,
23 January 1864, LAC, Howe Fonds 4:13; Watkin, *Canada and the
States,* 139.

86 *Canadian News* "The Intercolonial Railway," 23 January 1862, 57.

CHAPTER FOUR

1 W.L. Morton, *The Critical Years,* 120; A.A. Den Otter, *The Philosophy
of Railways: The Transcontinental Railway Idea in British North America*
(Toronto: University of Toronto Press, 1997), 115; Roman, "Imperial
Guarantees," 226–37.

2 John Gallagher and Ronald Robinson, "The Imperialism of Free Trade," *Economic History Review* 6 (1953): 1–15.
3 Edward Watkin to Howe, dated New York, 15 February 1862, LAC, Howe Fonds, 3:365. Upon landing at New York that morning Watkin telegraphed Howe to inform him of the association's excellent start.
4 "Despatch of the Duke of Newcastle to the Earl of Mulgrave, Lieutenant-Governor of Nova Scotia, dated 6th July 1862, on the subject of the Confederation of the B.N.A. Provinces," in *Confederation: Being a Series of Hitherto Unpublished Documents Bearing on the British North America Act,* edited by Joseph Pope (Toronto: Carswell, 1895), 303–4. Hereafter Pope, ed., *Confederation.*
5 Ged Martin, *Origins of Confederation,* 114, 232–3. Cf. Creighton, *Road to Confederation,* 187–219.
6 Newcastle to Mulgrave, 6 July 1862, LAC CO 217/230. The despatch was reprinted in Pope, ed., *Confederation,* 303–4.
7 See discussion on 11 October 1864 in "Discussions in Conference of the Delegates from the Provinces of British North America," in Pope, ed., *Confederation,* 59.
8 Howe to Thomas Baring, 31 December 1861, LAC, Joseph Howe Fonds, 8:166.
9 William Charles Wentworth, *Representation of the Australian Colonies in Parliament: Report of the Proceedings at a Meeting of the General Association for the Australian Colonies Held at the London Tavern, Bishopsgate Street, Wednesday July 15th 1857* (London: Edward Stanford, 1857).
10 Nelson sought the assistance of the colonial governments in assembling a library on British North America. In particular, he asked Howe for publications dealing with the Nova Scotia goldfields. J. Nelson to Howe, 26 July 1862, LAC, Howe Fonds, 3:471.
11 The membership list appears in *Rules of the British North American Association* (London: s.n., 1862).
12 Edward Watkin to Howe, dated New York, 15 February 1862, LAC, Howe Fonds, 3:365.
13 *Dictionary of Canadian Biography,* vol. 9:348–57, S.V. "Thomas Chandler Haliburton."
14 For the backgrounds of the three Canadian commissioners, Chamberlin, Gillespie, and Wier, see Elspeth Heaman, *The Inglorious Arts of Peace: Exhibitions in Canadian Society during the Nineteenth Century* (Toronto: University of Toronto Press, 1999), 167, 170–5.
15 Freda Harcourt, "British Oceanic Mail Contracts in the Age of Steam, 1838–1914," *Journal of Transport History* 9 (1988): 1–18; *Conveyance of*

Mails (North America): Return to an Address of the Honourable the House of Commons, dated 7 July 1859, for, Copies of all Correspondence between Her Majesty's Government and the Provincial Government of Canada, in Reference to the Conveyance of Mails between this Country and British North America (London: HMSO, 1859); Francis E. Hyde, *Cunard and the North Atlantic, 1840–1973: A History of Shipping and Financial Management* (London: Macmillan, 1975), 36.

16 Hyde, *Cunard*, 36. See "Canada and the Cunard Contract" in *Mitchell's Steam Shipping Journal*, 14 October 1859, 145, and "The Late Government and the Subsidizing System," in ibid., 2 September 1859, 48–9; "Memorandum in Reference to the Cunard Contract for American Mails," 7 November 1866, in NA PRO 30/6/162; Edmund Head to Henry Labouchere, 3 September 1856, LAC, CO 42/605.

17 T.E. Appleton, *Ravenscrag: The Allan Royal Mail Line* (Toronto: McClelland and Stewart, 1974); see also *Dictionary of Canadian Biography*, vol. 11, s.v. "Sir Hugh Allan."

18 Grand Trunk figures who joined the BNAA included Kirkman Daniel Hodgson, MP, and Thomas Matthias Wegeulin, MP, John M. Grant, H. Wollaston Blake, William Chapman, and James Hodges.

19 Information about the members of the BNAA derives from a number of sources. The biographical details of members of Parliament comes from Michael Stenton, ed., *Who's Who of British Members of Parliament: A Biographical Dictionary of the House of Commons Based on Annual Volumes of Dod's Parliamentary Companion and Other Sources* (Atlantic Highlands, NJ: Humanities Press, 1976), vol. 1, 1832–1885; *Kelly's Post-Office Directory* (London: s.n., 1860); *Oxford Dictionary of National Biography*; George Bradshaw, *Bradshaw's Monthly General Railway and Steam Navigation Guide, for Great Britain and Ireland* (London: W.J. Adams, 1861); *Grand Trunk Railway of Canada Prospectus*, 1853, LAC; Canadian National Railway Fonds, LAC; and other sources where noted.

20 Kynaston, *The City of London*, 1:250.

21 For Franks' background, see G.L. Lee, *The Story of the Bosanquets* (Canterbury: Phillimore, 1966). For a discussion of the City as a community, see R.C. Michie, "The Social Web of Investment in the Nineteenth Century," *Revue Internationale d'Histoire de la Banque* 18 (1979): 158–75. See the entry for Herries, Farquhar and Co. in John Orbell and Alison Burton, *British Banking: A Guide to the Historical Records* (London: Business Archives Council, 2001). For the financial ties between the Canada Company and the Grand Trunk, see 11 July 1861,

"Court of Directors Records (Minutes), Canada Company Papers,
Archives of Ontario, Ms564 r.9,10, vol. 9.

22 Stanley Chapman, *The Rise of Merchant Banking* (London: Allen and
Unwin, 1988), 129. Kynaston, *The City of London*, 1:223.

23 Gladstone was willing to tolerate imperial subsidies for telegraph
lines under the sea (e.g., the transatlantic telegraphs) but not for ones
on land. For this distinction, see Gladstone to Newcastle, 16 February
1863, British Library Manuscripts Room, Gladstone Papers, Add MSS
44263, f.176; Newcastle to Gladstone, 23 February 1863, University of
Nottingham Library, Newcastle Papers, NEC 10891.

24 For this overview of the IFS, I am indebted to P.J. Cottrell, *Investment
Banking in England: 1856–1881. A Case Study of the International
Financial Society* (London: Garland, 1985). However, I have
supplemented it with IFS papers held in Canada to which Cottrell did
not have access: International Financial Society Papers, in Hudson's
Bay Company Papers LAC microform reel HBC 5M43. Other investors
in the IFS included J.S. Morgan and the banking house of Frühling
and Göschen that was the home of a future Chancellor of the
Exchequer. E.E. Rich, *The Hudson's Bay Company, 1670–1870* (London:
Hudson's Bay Record Society, 1958–1959), vol. 2, 833. For the rapid
turnover of shares, see "Register of Transfers," in International
Financial Society Papers, LAC reel 5M43 F/28. The details of Watkin
and Potter's negotiations with the HBC are given in W.B. Drake to
Maynard, 13 June 1863, International Financial Society Papers, in
ibid., F/27.

25 The role of lawyers in the incorporation process is discussed in Kostal, *Law and English Railway Capitalism*, 14–15, 23–5, 110–27.

26 On 11 November 1858, Charles Bischoff attended a banquet given by
Lord Bury and the Canada Club for visiting colonial delegates. This
banquet was connected with Bury's Intercolonial scheme. *Canadian
News*, 24 November 1858. Bischoff was also involved in the British
legal aspects of the attempted 1862 merger of the Grand Trunk and
the other two Canadian lines.

27 *Oxford Dictionary of National Biography*, s.v. "Rose, Sir Philip, First
Baronet (1816–1883)."

28 Kostal, *Law and English Railway*, 323–33. Robert Baxter was called to
describe his lobbying activities to the parliamentary committee set up
in the aftermath of the collapse of the bubble. "Minutes of Evidence
Taken Before the Select Committee on Private Bills," *Parliamentary
Papers* (1847), vol. 12, 155–38.

29 See a privately printed work by his widow, "In Memoriam R. Dudley Baxter, M.A." (London: n.p., 1878).

30 Phillip Cazenove and William Chapman are discussed in chapter 1.

31 For the involvement of the firm of James Capel, Norburry, Trotter in the sale, see ING Baring Archive, HC5.15.8.

32 M.C. Reed, *A History of James Capel and Co.* (London: Printed by James Capel and Co., 1975).

33 *Canadian News*, "The British North American Association," 6 March 1862, 152. The controversy over Cunard's mail contract is discussed comprehensively in "Canada and the Cunard Contract," *Mitchell's Steam Shipping Journal*, 14 October 1859. Francis E. Hyde, *Cunard and the North Atlantic, 1840–1973: A History of Shipping and Financial Management* (London: Macmillan, 1975); Samuel Cunard to Watkin, 5 June 1858, LAC, Sir Edward Watkin Fonds.

34 Charles Edward Mangles and George F. Young.

35 Macdonald thought that the Canadian Post Office could count on the "whole influence of the Grand Trunk Shareholders" being "brought to bear on the British Government" in favour of the amalgamation of the shipping lines. Head also appears to have thought this policy would have been of electoral assistance to Palmerston. Macdonald to Sidney Smith, Postmaster General of Canada, 21 August 1861, in *The Letters of Sir John A. Macdonald*, edited by J.K. Johnson and Carol B. Stelmack (Ottawa: Public Archives of Canada, 1969), vol. 2, 390.

36 See *Canadian News*, "British North American Association," 6 February 1862, 90. Thomas Baring expressed his appreciation for Crawford's efforts on behalf of the BNAA in Baring to Watkin, 27 February 1862, LAC, Baring Brothers and Co. Fonds.

37 Hugh Culling Eardley Childers was MP for Pontefract. Childers would have known Sir Cusack Roney of the Grand Trunk because they both sat on the board of the ill-fated London, Chatham and Dover railway, which went bankrupt in 1866. Childers' Australian mission on behalf of the Baring railway loan is discussed in *The Life and Correspondence of Hugh C.E. Childers, 1827–1896*, edited by Edmund Spencer Childers (London: John Murray, 1901), 82–8.

38 J.A. Roebuck, *The Colonies of England: A Plan for the Government of Some Portion of Our Colonial Possessions* (London: J.W. Parker, 1849); *Oxford Dictionary of National Biography*, s.v. "Roebuck, John Arthur (1802–1879)."

39 Head to Thomas Baring, MP, and George Carr Glyn, 19 July 1856, LAC, Governor General's Correspondence, A 3:243–9.

40 While the failed confederation initiative of 1858 was mainly the work of A.T. Galt, Head privately approved of it. On the 1858 federation initiative and the controversy it created in the Colonial Office, see the hostile minute by Herman Merivale dated 30 August on a letter by Head to Lytton, 16 August 1858, LAC, CO 42/614; Bruce A. Knox, "Conservative Imperialism: Bulwer-Lytton, Lord Carnarvon, and Canadian Confederation," *International History Review* 6 (1984) 333–57; Bruce A. Knox, "The Rise of Colonial Federation as an Object of British Policy, 1850–1870," *Journal of British Studies* 11 (1971): 92–112.

41 Sir Francis Bond Head, 1816–1875, no relation of Sir Edmund and lieutenant-governor of Upper Canada at the time of the 1837 rebellion, attended several BNAA meetings, *Canadian News*, 6 February 1862, 90, and 10 January 1867, 24, but does not seem to have taken an active role in organization.

42 While there was some debate over whether the Grand Trunk should own or merely manage the line between Rivière-du-Loup and Truro, the promoters of the Intercolonial at this time clearly believed that the railway would be part of an integrated Grand Trunk system running from Windsor to Halifax. See Watkin to Newcastle, 2 February 1862, University of Nottingham Library, Newcastle Papers, NEC 11262.

43 *Herapath's*, "British North America" 8 February 1862, 141. The paper described the membership of the BNAA as "ranking A1 in the City". Two years later E.J. Herapath, the paper's editor, remarked that completing the Intercolonial would make the Grand Trunk a "great property" by serving as a traffic "feeder." *Herapath's*, "Grand Trunk of Canada," 4 June 1864, 658–9.

44 *Canadian News*, "The Intercolonial Railway," 9 January 1862, 124, untitled leading article, 20 March 1862, 184.

45 *Canadian News*, "The British American Federation," 3 July 1862, 7.

46 Howe to Tilley, 19 January 1862, LAC, Howe Fonds, 7:182.

47 Nelson to Howe, 22 March 1862, LAC, Howe Fonds, 3:384. *Canadian News* declared: "We are glad to learn that the Governments of the several provinces have promised the Association substantial support, by way of subsidy, and every other assistance in their power to promote its objects" (30 January 1862, "The British North American Association," 73).

48 This campaign has been mentioned by a number of historians but never discussed in depth. See Den Otter, *Philosophy*, 115; Allen, *Origins*, 291–3; Roman, *Imperial Guarantees*, 215–19.

49 Gladstone to Newcastle, 14 December 1861, "Memorandum on Intercolonial Railway," University of Nottingham Library, Newcastle

Papers, NEC 11252/1. Gladstone also referred to the "plundered creditors of the City of Hamilton."

50 Joseph Nelson to Macdonald, dated Ottawa 19 December 1867, LAC, Macdonald Fonds, 340:155721; Joseph Nelson to Macdonald, 12 December 1867, ibid., 340:155725. Unfortunately, Macdonald's reply, if any, has not survived. For Howe's description of the lobbying see Howe to T. Baring, 31 December 1861, LAC, Baring Brothers and Co. Fonds, 3:1458–1469; T. Baring to Watkin, 27 January 1862, ibid., 3:155411.

51 Joseph Nelson, *The Hudson's Bay Company and Sir Edward Watkin: A Statement in Support of An Application for the Appointment of a Select Committee of the House of Commons to Inquire into and Report upon all the Circumstances respecting the Reconstruction of the Hudson's Bay Company by Mr Edward Watkin in 1863, by which the Capital of the Company was Thereby Increased from £500,000 to £2,000,000 Without Adding in any Material Way to the Resources of the Company* (London: R.D. Madden, 1877). Joseph Nelson's publications on Grand Trunk matters included *The Present and Future Prospects of the Grand Trunk* (London: s.n., 1860); *Grand Trunk Railway of Canada: Address to the Bond and Stockholders* (London: Abbott and Barton, 1869).

52 Charles Bischoff to Macdonald, 3 July 1867, LAC, Macdonald Fonds, 340:155411.

53 Joseph Nelson to Tilley, 10 August 1865, LAC, Tilley Fonds 18. In the 1890s Nelson published a pamphlet proposing a transcontinental railway to compete with the Canadian Pacific Railway.

54 See shareholder register in NA BT 31 CO. 342C Canada Landed Credit Company Ltd.

55 NA BT 31 Box 342 co. 1238, "Halifax and Quebec Railway Company Ltd." The company was wound up after the failure of the Intercolonial negotiations of 1858. See also *Minutes of Proceedings of a Meeting Held at the Thatched House Tavern, St James's Street, on Saturday, the 5th June 1858 Relative to the Formation of the Halifax and Quebec Railway* (London: W. Penny, 1858); see also Allen, *Origins*, 270. Bury called for closer ties between metropolis and colony in "Notes on Canadian Matters," *Fraser's Magazine* 56 (1857): 90–105. In his *Exodus of the Western Nations* (London: R. Bentley, 1865), Bury invoked the old idea that the seat of civilization was constantly moving westward (e.g., from Athens to Rome).

56 Joseph Nelson, *A Letter Addressed to the Right Honourable the Earl of Donoughmore, President of the Board of Trade on the Trade of British North America* (London: William Penny, 1859), 6.

57 Joseph Nelson, *Grand Trunk Railway of Canada: An Address to the Bond and Stockholders* (London: Abbott, Barton, 1869).

58 Ibid., 5.

59 Thomas Evans of the Bristol Chamber of Commerce to Howe, 28 December 1861, LAC, Howe Fonds, 3:291; Tilley to Bristol Chamber of Commerce, 31 December 1861, LAC, Tilley Fonds, 8:162; Howe to Tilley, 19 January 1862, LAC, Howe Fonds 7:182. Edward Watkin sat on the Manchester city council, which passed a resolution in 1861 endorsing imperial government financial assistance to the line. Watkin to Newcastle, 19 November 1861, University of Nottingham Library, Newcastle Papers, NEC 11274/1–2.

60 "Halifax-Quebec Railway Memorials," *Parliamentary Papers* (1862), vol. 36, 619–29.

61 The line of business of the signatories has been determined by using the *Post-Office Annual Directory* (London: Kelly, 1861).

62 Gibbon, *Steel of Empire*, 118–20.

63 The two men had drifted apart ideologically over the years and John was now extremely conservative. "English and Canadian Mining Co.," NA BT 31 Box 350, co. 1268; and S.G. Checkland, *The Gladstones: A Family Biography, 1764–1851* (Cambridge: Cambridge University Press, 1971), 240–54.

64 Nelson to Howe, 22 March 1862, LAC, Howe Fonds, 3:384.

65 Clyde Binfield and David Hey, *Mesters to Masters: A History of the Company of Cutlers in Hallamshire* (Oxford: Oxford University Press, 1997).

66 The mayor of Sheffield, John Brown owned the Atlas Iron and Steel Works, a massive enterprise employing thousands. See Allan John Grant, *Steel and Ships: A History of John Brown's* (London: Michael Joseph, 1950). For the history of Sheffield steel in this period, see J.D. Scott, *Vickers: A History* (London: Weidenfeld and Nicolson, 1963); Geoffrey Tweedale, *Steel City: Entrepreneurship, Strategy, and Technology in Sheffield, 1743–1993* (New York: Oxford University Press, 1995), 65; Clive Trebilcock, *The Vickers Brothers: Armaments and Enterprise, 1854–1914* (London: Europa, 1977).

67 Adolphus M. Hart, *Practical Suggestions on Mining Rights and Privileges in Canada* (Montreal: n.p., 1867); Jacob Houghton, *The Mineral Region of Lake Superior: Comprising its Early History* (Buffalo: O.G. Steele, 1846).

68 Tweedale, *Steel City*, 36.

69 J. Shortridge to Watkin, dated 7 February 1862, Hartford Steel Works and Rolling Mills, Sheffield, LAC, Howe Fonds 3:355.

70 *Sheffield Daily Telegraph*, "British North American Association," 31 January 1862, 2.

71 Ibid., 13 February 1862.

72 This account of the council meeting is based on *Sheffield Daily Telegraph*, "Sheffield Town Council," 13 March 1862, 3; *Sheffield and Rotherham Independent*, 13 March 1862.

73 The flurry of articles in the *Sheffield Daily Telegraph* on British North America and the benefits to Britian of possessing it include: "Troops for Canada," 22 January, 1862, 4; "What Captain Wilkes Has Done," 23 January 1862, 4; "Gold Fields in British Columbia," 6 February, 3; "The Despatch of Troops and Stores to Canada," 11 February, 6; "The Canadian Expedition," 25 January 1862, 8. "British North American Association," 2; ibid., "Mr Seward on the Destiny of Canada," 31 January 1862, 4; ibid., "Railway Communication with Canada," 19 February 1862, 2, under "Local and General." The leading article on 21 February 1862 (p. 2) was a robust refutal of Goldwin Smith's separatist argument. It praised the "entente cordiale" with the colonies (Australia and Canada) and expressed hope for a permanent union between "the Australians and Canadians and ourselves." The intellectual roots of liberal imperialism are explored by Jennifer Pitts in *A Turn to Empire: The Rise of Liberal Imperialism in Britain and France* (Princeton: Princeton University Press, 2004). While Pitts focuses on the liberal imperialism of leisure-class intellectuals rather than businessmen, her work is a corrective to Bernard Porter's view that empire had few attractions for the liberal middle classes.

74 "Goldwin Smith and His Colonies," *Sheffield and Rotherham Independent*, 10 February 1862.

75 Henry Ashworth to Cobden, 27 January 1862, British Library Manuscripts Room, Cobden Papers, Add MSS 43654, f.142. Quotation from f. 146.

76 While port-level data regarding the value of the cargoes sent and received from British North America is not available, the records of the total tonnage sent and received can be used as a rough proxy, keeping in mind that some ships returned with ballast, or low-value bulky goods. The figures given here have been derived from "Annual Statement of the Trade and Navigation of the United Kingdom with Foreign Countries and British Possessions in the Year 1860," Table 41, "Number and Tonnage of British and Foreign Vessels, Entered and Cleared, with Cargoes and Ballast, from and to various countries, at Each of the Principal Ports of the United Kingdom," *Parliamentary Papers* (1861), vol. 60, 401–32.

77 The "Annual Statement of the Trade and Navigation of the United Kingdom" shows that in Belfast and Cork an overwhelming majority of the wooden shipping had been built in British North America. In Glasgow, a majority of the wooden tonnage was BNA-built and in Liverpool about half the wood tonnage had been built in the North American colonies. For a description of Ireland's reliance on colonial-built ships, see Houston and Smith, *New Brunswick Shipbuilding*.

78 "The Gold Regions of British Columbia," *Belfast News-Letter*, 18 February 1862, 2; "British Columbia," ibid., 6 February 1862, 2.

79 *Northern Whig* (Belfast), "The Belfast Harbour Commissioners," 19 February 1862, 3.

80 *Belfast Newsletter*, editorial 19 February 1862, 2.

81 Minutes of the Standing Committee, 1861–67, in Association of British Chambers of Commerce Papers, Guildhall Library Manuscripts, MS 17594.

82 Several contemporaries regarded the *Times* as biased towards the Rothschilds and their Brazilian railways and against Barings and their Canadian ventures. See letter to the editor from Acadia dated 18 April 1860 in *Herapath's*, 21 April 1860, 401. The *Money Market Review*, " The Financial Department of the Times," 10 May, 412–13, also saw the Rothschild influence in the City columns of the *Times*. One correspondent to the latter journal alleged that the financial editor of the *Times* was himself a director of a Rothschild-controlled railway in Brazil. See letter to the editor from A. Fitzadam in *Money Market Review*, 17 May 1862, 437–8.

83 Ged Martin, "Our Advices from Canada are Unimportant: The *Times* and British North America, 1841–1861," in *Kith and Kin: Canada, Britain, and the United States from the Revolution to the Cold War*, edited by Colin Eldridge (Cardiff: University of Wales Press, 1997), 61–94.

84 Martin, *Britain and the Origins of Canadian Confederation*, 230.

85 Ibid., 56.

86 Philip Buckner, "The Maritimes and Confederation: A Reassessment," *Canadian Historical Review* 71 (1990): 1–30.

CHAPTER FIVE

1 One exception to this is J.M.S. Careless, "Mid-Victorian Liberalism in Central Canadian Newspapers, 1850–67," *Canadian Historical Review* 31 (1950): 221–36.

2 Glazebrook, *History of Transportation*, 184, argues that the Grand Trunk was initially open-minded about the new ministry, hoping that

a fresh set of faces would have better lucking passing the aid package. However, this attitude quickly turned to hostility.

3 For Monck's account of the defeat of the bill, see Monck to Newcastle, 30 May 1862, LAC, CO 42/634. For a general overview of the factors leading to the fall of the Cartier-Macdonald ministry, see W.L. Morton, *The Critical Years*, 105–14.

4 *Globe*, "Defeat of the Ministry: Ministerial Crisis," 21 May 1862, 3, "Mr Galt's Budget," 2, "J. Sandfield Macdonald Sent For," 22 May 1862, 3; *Perth Courier*, "The Provincial Finances," 6 June 1862, 2.

5 Baskerville, "Imperial Agendas," 247.

6 The ministry's efforts to curtail government expenditure were praised by the *Globe*, "Another Good Deed," 7 October 1863, 2.

7 Henry C. Klassen, "Luther Hamilton Holton Montreal Businessman and Politician, 1817–1867" (PhD dissertation, University of Toronto, 1970), 159. Holton's free trade ideas are discussed by Ben Forster, *A Conjunction of Interests: Business, Politics, and Tariffs, 1825–1879* (Toronto: University of Toronto Press, 1986), 66, 80, 128, 142.

8 Lowe to Monck, 11 November 1863, LAC, Lord Monck Fonds.

9 See *Globe*, "Independence of the Press," 16 September 1863, 3.

10 Watkin to a Mr Wright, n.d., University of Nottingham Library, Newcastle Papers, NEC 13840/1.

11 George Brown to Gordon Brown, 11 May 1863, LAC, George Brown Fonds, 4:751–6.

12 *Globe*, "Sir E. Head's Closet Councillors," 7 August 1858, 2.

13 Lowe to Monck, 11 November 1863, LAC, Monck Fonds. For the 1863 election, see J.M.S. Careless, *Brown of the Globe* (Toronto: Macmillan, 1959–63), vol. 2, 96–7.

14 A.W. Currie, *Grand Trunk*, 86.

15 *Globe*, "The Idea of Galt," 23 September 1863, 2.

16 Morton, *Critical Years*, 125; Careless, *Brown of the Globe*, vol. 2, 87–95.

17 Bruce W. Hodgins, *John Sandfield Macdonald, 1812–1872* (Toronto: University of Toronto Press, 1971), 55–74.

18 Holton's steps towards retrenchment, balanced budgets, and free trade were praised in the *Economist*, "The Progress of Sound Financial Views in Canada," 10 October 1863, 1,124–5. The *Economist* had earlier condemned the fiscal policy of the Cartier-Macdonald regime and had advocated a shift from reliance on customs duties to direct taxation as a way of building up the commerce of the St Lawrence; See "The New Channels of Trade with the Western and Central States of North America," 6 September 1862, 983–5, "The New

Channels of Trade with the Western and Central States of North America," 13 September 1862, 1,013–14.

19 *Globe*, "The Budget," 16 September 1862, 2.

20 Holton's budget speech and subsequent debate, 15 September 1863, in *Globe*, "Parliament Last Night," 16 September 1863, 3. Holton's comment regarding the regeneration of England drew forth an exclamation from Isaac Buchanan. *Globe*, "Provincial Parliament," 19 September 1863, 1. Buchanan was a strong protectionist who had opposed the end of the Old Colonial System and detested the memory of Peel. For Buchanan's view, see Isaac Buchanan, *The Moral Consequences of Sir R. Peel's Unprincipled and Fatal Course: Disquiet, Overturn and Revolution* (Greenock [Scotland]: Advertiser, 1850) *The British American Federation a Necessity: Its Industrial Policy Also a Necessity* (Hamilton: Spectator Steam Press, 1865), and *The Relations of the Industry of Canada with the Mother Country and the United States* (Montreal: J. Lovell, 1864).

21 *Globe*, "The Budget," 16 September 1863, 2, and "The Spirit of Faction," 18 September 1863, 2.

22 Ibid., "The Idea of Galt," 23 September 1863, 2.

23 Klaussen, *Holton*, 230. The Bank of Upper Canada closed its door in 1866. *The Bank of Upper Canada: A Collection of Documents*, edited by Peter Baskerville (Toronto: Champlain Society, 1987). George Brown agreed with the principle of borrowing internally but disliked the fact that Holton was favouring Montreal at the expense of Toronto institutions. Brown to Holton, 23 October 1863, in *The Life and Speeches of Hon. George Brown*, edited by Alexander Mackenzie, 207–8.

24 According to Piva, *Borrowing Process*, 3, Upper Canada had done most of its borrowing internally before the late 1830s.

25 *Globe*, "British North American Association," 29 September 1863, 2.

26 *Globe*, "The Ideas of Galt," 23 September 1863, 2.

27 The *Globe* also appears to have connected the BNAA to a proposal for imperial federation. For the genesis of this concept, see Ged Martin, "The Idea of 'Imperial Federation'," in Ronald Hyam and Ged Martin, *Reappraisals in British Imperial History* (London: Macmillan, 1975), 121–38

28 *Globe*, "Mails by the Europa," 23 August, 1, "The Grand Trunk Meeting," 2 October 1862, 4. The paper's complaint that the BNAA was unauthorized and unrepresentative parallels the criticisms later made of the Colonial Society established in London in 1869; see J.E. Tyler, *The Struggle for Imperial Unity, 1868–1896* (London: Longmans, 1938), 2.

29 *Globe*, "The Idea of Galt," 23 September 1863, 2.

30 George Carr Glyn to Thomas Galt, 4 June 1862, LAC, Glyn Mills and
Co. Fonds, Letter book 6, p. 19–20; A.T. Galt to Glyn, Mills, and Co.,
12 November 1862, Royal Bank of Scotland Group Archives GB1502 /
GM/37.

31 John Ross to Thomas Baring, 18 May 1863, "John Ross Correspondence," ING Baring Archive, HC15.25.

32 Rose to Thomas Baring, 25 October 1862, LAC, Baring Brothers and
Company Fonds. Whether or not they were utopian, the end of large-
scale Canadian borrowing in London would have thwarted Rose's
future business career; for in the late 1860s, Rose moved to London
and began peddling Canadian securities. M.H. Long, "Sir John Rose
and the Informal Beginnings of the Canadian High Commissioner-
ship," *Canadian Historical Review* 12 (1931): 23–43; *Dictionary of Canadian Biography,* vol. 11, s.v. "Sir John Rose, 1820–1888."

33 Brydges to Macdonald, 16 January 1864, LAC, Macdonald Fonds 191:
79423–6.

34 *Globe,* "Parliament Last Night," 7 October 1863, 2.

35 Ibid., "Provincial Parliament," 10 October 1863, 1. George Brown repeated the accusation that the Grand Trunk investors were attempt-
ing to depreciate the price of provincial government bonds. See *Globe,*
"Parliament Last Night," 16 September 1863, 2.

36 *Globe,* "The Grand Trunk Conspiracy," 8 September 1863, 2.

37 Edward Manning Saunders, *Three Premiers of Nova Scotia: The Hon.
J.W. Johnstone, the Hon. Joseph Howe, The Hon. Charles Tupper, M.D.,
C.B.* (Toronto: W. Briggs, 1909), 228–42; J. Murray Beck, *Joseph Howe*
(Kingston: McGill-Queen's University Press, 1982) 2: 67–75.

38 It is noteworthy that Howe justified public ownership as a way of
keeping the railway from falling into the hands of "American capitalists." Glazebrook, *History of Transportation,* 158. British capitalists were
fine in his books. Discussing the relations of the North American colonies with British financiers, Rosemarie Patricia Langhout, "Public Enterprise: An Analysis of Public Finance in the Maritime Colonies
during the Period of Responsible Government" (PhD dissertation, University of New Brunswick, 1989), 30, regards the differences between
government and private ownership of railways as immaterial.

39 Killam's career is described in *Dictionary of Canadian Biography,* vol. 9,
s.v. "Thomas Killam."

40 Saunders, *Three Premiers,* 224–41, 287.

41 Langhout, *Public Enterprise,* 169. Langhout, who sees government
borrowing in London as an attempt by the provincial governments

to establish their "autonomy" from local suppliers of capital, argues
that Tupper advanced this autonomy-seeking agenda.

42 C.M. Wallace, "Albert Smith, Confederation, and Reaction in New
Brunswick, 1852–1882," *Canadian Historical Review* 44 (1963): 285–312;
Oxford Dictionary of National Biography, s.v. "Smith, Sir Albert James
(1822–1883)."

43 A different form of economic decolonization was underway on
Prince Edward Island, where a radical movement of tenants was intent on reshaping property rights. However, in the 1860s island issues
remained distinct from the politico-economic questions confronting
the mainland. Moreover, the British economic interest involved, a
group of absentee landlords, was separate from the investors connected with the Province of Canada. For the landlord-tenant issue,
see Robertson, *Tenant League.*

44 10 April 1862, *Gladstone Diaries*, edited by H.C.G. Matthew, vol. 6, 114.
For G.C. Lewis's view on the issue, see Lewis to Newcastle, 25 Sep-
tember 1861, University of Nottingham Library, Newcastle Papers,
NeC 12655.

45 10 April 1862, *Gladstone Diaries*, edited by H.C.G. Matthew, vol. 6.

46 The terms of the offer are given in Sandford Fleming, *The Intercolonial:
A Historical Sketch of the Inception, Location, Construction and Comple-
tion of the Line of Railway Uniting the Inland and Atlantic Provinces of the
Dominion* (Montreal: Dawson, 1876), 60–1.

47 Waite, *The Life and Times of Confederation*, 50.

48 The rules regarding the sinking fund that would likely accompany
the Intercolonial loan guarantee had been a source of controversy
since the negotiations of 1861; Newcastle to Gladstone [n.d. but
December 1861], University of Nottingham Library, Newcastle
Papers, NeC 11756/1–2.

49 Howe described the meetings in Howe to Earl Mulgrave, Lt. Gov. of
Nova Scotia, dated Halifax, January 1863, LAC, Tilley Fonds, 13.

50 One of the Treasury officials involved in the negotiations, Assistant
Secretary George Alexander Hamilton, had advocated colonial self-
sufficiency at the time of the 1859–60 interdepartmental committee on
colonial defence. Eldridge, "Colonial Policy," 260, argues that its report
was a triumph for the advocates of the status quo and a blow to the advocates of colonial self-sufficiency. Hamilton and another treasury official, J.R. Godley, wrote an appendix to the report highly critical of the
Colonial Office's defence of the existing arrangements; see "Report of
the Committee on the Expenses of Military Defence in the Colonies,"

Parliamentary Papers (1861), vol. 13, 69–466, especially 411–18. See also the anonymous article by Sir George C. Lewis, "Military Defence of the Colonies," *Edinburgh Review* 115 (1862 January): 104–26.

51 Howe to Tilley, 10 January 1863, LAC, Tilley Fonds, 13; Watkin to Howe, 19 January 1862, LAC, Howe Fonds, 3:334. The offensive letter does not seem to have survived.

52 W.L. Morton, *Critical Years*, 124, argues that Howland and Sicotte were sincere supporters of the Intercolonial and were not using the issue of the Sinking Fund to derail the project. However, given their demeanour as recorded by the other colonists, their unwillingness to seize the opportunity of pressing their case informally at Clumber, and the opposition to the railway of many *rouge* and Grit politicians, this view is very hard to accept.

53 Tilley to Gordon, 2 February 1863 (copy), University of Nottingham Library, Newcastle Papers, NEC 11177/2/1–4.

54 Newcastle to Gladstone, n.d., ibid., NEC 11756/1–2. Newcastle was probably using the word Canadian in its older sense of a francophone.

55 Howe to Tilley, 10 January 1863, LAC, Tilley Fonds, 13.

56 *Canadian News*, 1 January 1863.

57 The speeches of Howe and Tilley were printed in the *Canadian News*, "The British North American Association," 15 January 1863, 40–1. The speeches had been transcribed by the editor of the *Montreal Gazette*, who had also attended this dinner.

58 Joseph Nelson, *The Very Latest Grand Trunk Scheme*, 17. The purchase of the HBC by the IFS is discussed in the *Economist*, "The Hudson's Bay Company," 5 July 1863, 729–30.

59 Alexander McEwen to Head, 18 January 1866, Thomas Fraser to McEwen, 24 January; W.E. Forster to Head, 20 February; Head to Forster, 1 March 1866, in Canada, *Sessional Papers*, 1867–68, no. 19, 3–13.

60 Nelson to Howe, 23 January 1864, LAC, Howe Fonds, 4: 13. For earlier complaints about the failure of the Canadian government to contribute, see J. Nelson to Howe, 13 July 1862, ibid., 3: 466.

61 Nelson to Howe, 6 February 1864, ibid., 4: 18. While Howe's reply is no longer extant, he appears to have agreed to this request, because Nelson sent him the articles of association for inclusion in the legislature's act of incorporation. Nelson to Howe, 20 February 1864, ibid., 4:20.

62 *Canadian News*, "British American Association," 27 February 1862, 137.

63 Nelson to Howe, 23 January 1864, LAC, Howe Fonds, 4:13.

64 Nelson to Howe, 6 February 1864, ibid., 4:18.
65 *Canadian News*, "The Intercolonial Railway," 13 August 1863, 104. The *Canadian News* also endorsed Maritime union, seeing no contradiction in these two positions. Another article sympathetic to Maritime union appeared in the *Canadian News*, 17 March 1864.
66 Ibid., 20 August 1863, 115.
67 Ibid., "British North America," 3 September 1863, 151, 153–4. McGee was conflating Smith's advocacy of colonial independence with Adderley's belief in colonial self-sufficiency. The *Canadian News* did not identify its source for McGee's speech, aside from noting it was delivered in New Brunswick.
68 Ibid., "Alleged Treason in Canada," 17 September 1863, 184.
69 Ibid., "The Colonial Connection," 20 August 1863, 121.
70 Ibid., "Annual dinner of the Loyal Canadian Society," 5 November 1863, 293.
71 Ibid., 17 December 1863, "Hamilton City Debt," 393. It should be pointed out that this rate was to be levied on the assessed values of properties and not their real values.
72 Ibid., "The Hudson's Bay Company and its Future," 10 March 1864, 153–4, excerpt of story in *Money Market Review*. The article suggested that the railway should be built even if state guarantees were not forthcoming, using "Anglo-Saxon self-help."
73 Figures present at the meeting included Arthur Kinnaird, MP, as well as Sir J. Synge, Bart., E.W. Watkin, Arthur Mills, MP, William Newmarsh, and Joseph Nelson's replacement as secretary of the association, Irving Hare. In 1863 Watkin had intended to visit Red River with Synge in connection with his abortive transcontinental telegraphy scheme. See Rich, *Hudson's Bay Company*, vol. 2, 844.
74 Newcastle to Monck, 29 May 1863, University of Nottingham Library, Newcastle Papers, NEC 11223.
75 Brydges to Tilley, 20 June 1864, LAC, Tilley Fonds, 17.
76 Careless, *Brown of the Globe*, vol. 2, 116–17. Brydges had formally been employed by the Great Western, a company supported by the *Globe*. This may have been a factor in his ability to open a dialogue with Brown.
77 *Herapath's*, "Grand Trunk of Canada," 11 June 1864, 675–6; *Canadian News*, "Grand Trunk of Canada," 16 June 1864, 373–4.
78 Brydges to Tilley, 20 June 1864, LAC, Tilley Fonds, 17.
79 Brydges to Macdonald, 24 February 1864, LAC, Macdonald Fonds, 191: 79437–43.

CHAPTER SIX

1 On 12 October 1864, the correspondent of the *Times* and several Canadian newspapers asked for permission to publish a daily abstract of the proceedings in which comments would not be attributed to particular speakers. However, the request was denied. See the printed proceedings of the Quebec Conference in Sir Charles Tupper Papers, LAC.

2 See *Montréal Gazette*, 26 September 1864.

3 Donald Creighton, *The Road to Confederation: The Emergence of Canada* (Toronto: Macmillan, 1964), 99. *Montreal Gazette*, "Confederation," 10 December 1864, 2. Given that the United Kingdom was able to accommodate Scots law, bijuralism was not inherently incompatible with a legislative union.

4 Charles Bischoff of the British American Land Company complained of this. Bischoff to Galt, 24 November 1864, LAC, Galt Fonds, 2:901.

5 Paul Romney has convincingly argued that many of the Upper Canadian Reformers who supported Confederation envisioned a genuine federation in which the autonomy of the provincial governments would be respected. See Paul Romney, Getting It Wrong: How Canadians Forgot Their Past and Imperilled Confederation (Toronto: University of Toronto Press, 1999). As the head of such a movement, it was natural for Brown to arouse the suspicions of people in Britain sympathetic to centralization.

6 The Quebec Resolutions appeared in the *London Standard*, "The New Canadian Constitution," on 24 November 1864, 2–3. See Bischoff to Galt, 24 November 1864, LAC, Galt Fonds, 2:901. Bischoff said that it was the first regular and complete description of the proposed constitution he had read.

7 Bischoff to Galt, 24 November 1864, Galt Fonds, 2:901.

8 See Chapter 2.

9 "Quebec Resolutions," in *Confederation: Being a Series of Hitherto Unpublished Documents Bearing on the British North America Act,* edited by Sir Joseph Pope (Toronto: Carswell, 1895), 38–52.

10 McCully's speech at Halifax, see *Canadian News*, "Confederation of the British North American Provinces," 12 January 1865, 26–9, 28.

11 R.T. Naylor, "The Rise and Fall of the Third Commercial Empire of the St Lawrence," in *Capitalism and the National Question in Canada*, edited by Gary Teeple (Toronto: University of Toronto Pres, 1972), 15.

12 Macpherson had stated that news of the Quebec agreement had raised the price of Canadian securities "15 or 17 percent" and had

connected this improvement with the urgent need of the province for public works. *Parliamentary Debates on the Subject of the Confederation of the British North American Provinces* (Quebec: Hunter, Rose, 1865), 10 February 1865, 150. Macpherson was a contractor who had been paid in Grand Trunk bonds and who attended the first meeting of the BNAA. In the parliamentary debates, he discussed the Intercolonial Railway and harbour construction on Lake Huron.

13 *Parliamentary Debates on the Subject of Confederation*, 15 February 1865, 203. Seymour showed that on 7 November, Canadian stock stood at eighty-six or ninety. On 25 November (the trading day after the resolutions were published in London), it was selling between eighty-eight to ninety-two. "And now, with a strong probability of the measure passing, what is the price? The last quotation is 81 to 83."

14 *Nova Scotia House of Assembly, Debates and Proceedings*, 12 April 1865 (Halifax, s.n., 1865), 234.

15 Calculations by author based on prices quoted in *The Course of the Exchange* (London: Effingham Wilson, 1860–1869). The full text of the Quebec Resolutions first appeared in the Quebec City papers on 8 November 1864 and were reported in the London *Standard*, 24 November 1864. The *Standard* cited the *Quebec Mercury* as its source. The spread in current yields between Canadian and Victorian bonds exhibited a similar pattern, narrowing in late November 1864 and then widening again in early 1865. These calculations have been based on prices quoted in *The Course of the Exchange*. The bond yields narrowed after 1867. The approach adopted here was inspired by Marc Weidenmier, "The Market for Confederate Bonds," *Explorations in Economic History* 37 (2000): 76–97, and Bruno S. Frey and Marcel Kucher, "Wars and Markets: How Bond Values Reflect the Second World War," *Economica* 68 (2001): 317–33.

16 *Economist*, "The New Programme of the Canadian Ministry," 16 July 1864, 892–3; "Difficulties in the Way of the New Federation of Canada," 27 August 1864, 1,080–1; "The Progress of the Scheme for the Federation of Canada," 15 October 1864, 1,279–80; "The Text of the Federal Constitution for the American Colonies," 26 November 1864, 1,455–6. The *Economist* was edited by Walter Bagehot, who also wrote extensively on constitutional and financial topics.

17 *Herapath's*, "The Canadian Confederation," 16 July 1864, 831. Herapath's "The Intercolonial Railway," 5 November 1864, 1,276; "Trust and Loan Company of Upper Canada," 3 December 1864, 1,363–4.

18 *Canadian News*, "The Proposed Confederation of the British North American Provinces," 4 August 1864, 72–4.

19 Ibid., "The Question of Canadian Confederation," 13 October 1864, 226.

20 *Canadian News,* "Confederation of the North American Provinces," 20 October 1864, 250

21 "A.A.B. of Warrington," "Why a Federation? Why Not a United Monarchy?" *Canadian News,* 15 September 1864, 168–70; "The Confederation of the British North American Provinces: A Federation Is a Republic," ibid., 13 October 1864, 233–4; Rev. A.A. Bridgeman, "The British North American Confederation," ibid.,16 February 1865, 108–9.

22 *Canadian News,* "Something More Wanted," 12 July 1866, 25–6. Bridgeman had lived in Australia and had developed pronounced views on the operation of responsible government in the colonies.

23 "A Backwoodsman" was Thomas D'Arcy McGee of Montreal, who used the same pseudonym in publishing *The Crown and the Confederation: Three Letters to the Hon. John Alexander McDonald, Attorney General for Upper Canada* (Montreal: J. Lovell, 1864).

24 Dunning's 1780 resolution had been made in the context of the American Revolution and the struggle of the Whigs with royal authority. It was discussed by Erskine May, *Constitutional History of England since the Accession of George the Third* (London: Longmans, Green, 1861), vol. 1, 51–61.

25 "Backwoodsman," "The Proposed Confederation – the Crown and the People," *Canadian News,* 27 October 1864, 259.

26 Mulgrave to Newcastle, 1 March 1860, LAC, CO 217/226, f.174.

27 Charles Bowyer Adderley, *The Colonial Policy of Lord John Russell's Administration* (London: R. Bentley, 1853), vol. 1, 34–5.

28 Algar did so in an article comparing the projected federation to the *Westminster Review*'s 1854 proposal for the conversion of the United Kingdom into a federal state. Under this plan, Britain would have been divided into units of roughly five counties, with each region having a local legislature. The existing Parliament in London would retain jurisdiction over national issues. Algar's comment suggests that he feared that the provincial governments would probably be dominated by the lower classes. *Canadian News,* 5 January 1865, "Confederation," 9–10.

29 Bischoff to Galt, 24 November 1864, LAC, Galt Fonds vol. 2: 901.

30 Bischoff to Galt, 3 November 1864, ibid. vol. 2: 890.

31 Bischoff to Galt, 15 December 1864, vol. 2, 913, 17 December 1864, vol. 2: 917, ibid. Bischoff suggested that George Carr Glyn would

want to borrow his copy of the Sherbrooke speech, suggesting that the banker was without a copy of his own.

32 In 1861 he chaired the parliamentary committee on colonial military expenditures. Mills was a moderate advocate of colonial military self-sufficiency. Mills attended a meeting of the BNAA dealing with colonial defence; *Canadian News*, "The Hudson's Bay Company and Its Future" 10 March 1864, 153–4.

33 Arthur Mills, "The British North American Federation," *Edinburgh Review* 121 (January 1865): 181–99. The tendency for horizontal integration of British firms detected by Mills is discussed in Alfred D. Chandler, Jr, *Scale and Scope: The Dynamics of Industrial Capitalism* (Cambridge: Belknap Press, 1990), 378–89.

34 Goldwin Smith, "The Proposed Constitution for British North America," *Macmillan's Magazine* 11 (March 1865): 407–12.

35 Arnold Haultain, *Goldwin Smith, His Life and Opinions* (London: T. Werner Laurie, 1913), 57–8.

36 *Canadian News*, "Confederation in New Brunswick," 23 March 1865, 186–7.

37 Ibid., "Confederation of the British North American Provinces," 27 April 1865, 264–5.

38 Ibid., "The Canadian Delegates," 15 June 1865, 264–5, and "The British American Confederation," 22 June 1865, 393.

39 For Gordon's view that the New Zealand provincial system should be the model for the new constitution, see Gordon to Cardwell, 5 December 1864, LAC, Cardwell Fonds, f.26. Gordon flushed out his reasons for disliking the Quebec scheme and preferring Maritime union in Gordon to Cardwell, n.d., December 1864, ibid., f. 21, and Gordon to Cardwell, 2 January 1865, ibid., f.34. In the undated letter, he complained that the proposed union was a federation "not only in name but in fact." See also P.B. Waite, "Edward Cardwell and Confederation," *Canadian Historical Review* 42 (1962): 17–41; James Keith Chapman, *The Career of Arthur Gordon, First Lord Stanmore* (Toronto: University of Toronto Press, 1964), 32–44.

40 Edward Watkin to Tilley, 30 March 1865, LAC, Tilley Fonds 17.

41 Nelson to Tilley, 4 August 1865, ibid.

42 Printed copy of Cardwell to Monck, 17 June 1866, LAC, Cardwell Fonds, f. 75. Cardwell point out that this correspondence had been published in Cardwell to Gordon, 24 June 1865, ibid., f. 1865.

43 Cardwell to Gordon, 24 June 1865, LAC, CO 189/21, f.110.

44 Cardwell to Gordon, 13 May 1865, ibid., f. 78. (similar in Cardwell to Gordon, 12 April 1865, Ibid., f. 95. Emphasis in the original. It should be noted that Cardwell thought that legislative union was clearly preferably to federation and interpreted the opposition of the New Brunswickers to the "complete fusion" desired by the Canadians as motivated by the fear of unemployment on the part of their salaried parliamentarians. Cardwell to Gordon, 14 October 1864, Cardwell Fonds, LAC f. 5.

45 G.E. Wilson, "New Brunswick's Entrance into Confederation," *Canadian Historical Review* 8 (1928): 4–24.

46 Currie, *Grand Trunk*, 96.

47 Tilley to Macdonald, 17 April 1866, LAC, Macdonald Fonds, 51: 20,164–9.

48 For Queen Victoria's alleged support for Tilley and the pro-confederates, see copy of a letter by David P. Kerr to the editor of the *Saint John Morning Telegraph*, 19 June 1866, LAC, Tilley Fonds 19.

49 *Bankers' Magazine* [London], "Bank of British North America," July 1865, 846–8.

50 *Canadian News*, "Commercial," 7 June 1866, 365. The issue of the usury laws of the colonies had also been raised by a shareholder at the 1865 annual general meeting of the Bank of British North America, a director replying that the management had taken advantage of the recent visit of the Canadian ministers to impress upon them the importance of abrogating the usury laws. In 1865–66, there had been an unsuccessful campaign to lower the legal maximum non-bank institutions could charge to six percent. See "An Act to Amend the Act Respecting Interest" (Ottawa: Hunter, Rose, 1865).

51 The usury laws of the Lower Provinces were considered even worse by some people in London. See C.D. Archibald to Tilley, London, 3 March 1864, LAC, Tilley Fonds, 17.

52 In early 1867 the *Montreal Trade Review* published an article attacking the "usury law advocates" and proposing that the Canadian Parliament leave "the rate of interest to be regulated by the law of supply and demand." Quoted in *Canadian News*, "Surplus Capital," 16 May 1867, 308

53 *Confederation Debates*, 7 March 1865, 738.

54 Ibid., 9 March 1865, 859.

55 The eventual BNA Act gave the federal government jurisdiction over "interest"; see s. 91(19) and s. 91(21).

56 20 December 1866, British Library Manuscripts Room, Carnarvon Diary, Carnavon Papers, Add MSS 60899.

57 Carnarvon to Cardwell, 20 July 1866, LAC, Cardwell Fonds, 43.

58 Ibid. This bill would have left the number of members of the federal House of Commons to the discretion of the Colonial Secretary. The general government would have had wide powers to make laws for the "peace, order, and good government of the United Provinces" Cardwell's draft bill can be found in ibid., Cardwell Fonds, f. 71.

59 See Carnarvon Diary, 22 January 1867; in British Library Manuscripts Room, Carnarvon Papers, Add MSS 60899; Monck to Carnarvon, undated but clearly written in January 1867, "Letters to and from Lord Monck, Captain-General and Governor of Canada," NA, Carnarvon Papers, 30/6/151, p. 180; Monck to Carnarvon, 3 January 1867, ibid. These efforts to increase the power of Canada's central legislature are mentioned in Rogers to Carnarvon, 18 January 1867, NA, Carnavon Papers. In the debates on the British North America bill, Cardwell praised Carnarvon's efforts to move the Canadian constitution in the direction of centralization, stating that while he would have preferred a Canadian central legislature with all the powers of the New Zealand legislature, he entirely understood why the Colonial Secretary, had not pressed "the question more at the present time." *Hansard Parliamentary Debates*, 3^d series, vol. 185 (1867), col. 1174.

60 Carnarvon appears to have toyed with the idea of having federal "Superintendents" in each province. Although the more grandiose office of lieutenant-governor was provided for in the final version of the bill, the tendency of Carnarvon's thinking was clear: the provinces were to be degraded into mere municipalities as far as possible. Compare "First Draft of Bill" in Pope, *Confederation*, 141–57, with "Third Draft of Bill" in *Documents on the Confederation of British North America*, edited by G.P. Browne (Toronto: McClelland and Stewart, 1969), 158–76. After 1867 the claim that the provincial legislatures were genuine parliaments deserving of respect had been buttressed with the idea that lieutenant-governors were direct representatives of the queen, not the federal government. In effect, it was an argument in favour of states' rights in a monarchist idiom. Christopher Armstrong, *The Politics of Federalism: Ontario's Relations with the Federal Government, 1867–1942* (Toronto: University of Toronto Press, 1981), 22–4.

61 Globe, "London Correspondence," 22 February 1867, 1; ibid., "Confederation Bill," 2. The negotiations that modified the Quebec scheme of union were recorded in "Minutes of the Proceedings in Conference of the Delegates from the Provinces of Canada, Nova Soctia, and New Brunswick, Held in London, December 1866," in Pope, *Confederation*, 94–7.

62 3 February 1867, British Library Manuscripts Room, Carnarvon
    Diary, Carnavon Papers.

CHAPTER SEVEN

1   Donald Creighton, *The Road to Confederation: The Emergence of Canada,*
    1863–1867 (Toronto: Macmillan, 1964), 429–30. Creighton's often-
    quoted reference to the "dog tax" appears in his *Dominion of the*
    North: A History of Canada, 2d ed. (London: Macmillan, 1958), 313.
2   There were, however, various minor criticisms and helpful amend-
    ments. These included E.W.T. Hamilton's suggestion that the adjec-
    tive "male" be inserted before the word "person" into the electoral
    qualifications established for the District of Algoma. UK, *Hansard*
    Parliamentary Debates, 3^d series, vol. 185 (1867), col. 1316.
3   For accounts of the passage of the Second Reform Bill, see Cowling,
    1867; F.B. Smith, *The Making of the Second Reform Bill* (Melbourne:
    Melbourne University Press, 1966); Catherine Hall et al., *Defining The*
    Victorian Nation; J.R. Vincent, *The Formation of the British Liberal Party:*
    1858–1867 (London: Constable, 1966).
4   Catherine Hall, "The Nation Within and Without," in *Defining the*
    Victorian Nation: Class, Race, Gender and the Reform Act of 1867, edited
    by Catherine Hall, Keith McClelland, and Jane Rendall (Cambridge:
    Cambridge University Press, 2000): 179–233, 231.
5   J.A. Froude, "The Canadian Confederacy," *Westminster Review* 83,
    Old Series and 27, New Series (1865): 533–60, 533.
6   As the marquess of Salisbury, he served as prime minister, 1885–86,
    1886–1892, and 1895–1902.
7   *Globe,* "London Correspondence," 22 February 1867, 1.
8   Cowling, *1867,* 143–4, 164–5.
9   20 December 1866, British Library Manuscripts Room, Carnarvon Diary,
    Carnavon Papers, Add MSS 60899.
10 28 December 1866, ibid.
11 For instance, when Danby Seymour voted in favour of imperial aid to
    the Intercolonial, he was joined by his brother, George H. Seymour.
12 Examples of this accusation being made are discussed in the intro-
    ductory chapter.
13 Charles Bischoff to Galt, 15 December 1864, LAC, Galt Fonds, 2: 913.
    Bishcoff's subsequent correspondence with Galt, however, does not
    reveal whether Baring or Glyn actually assisted with the costs of
    printing such a statement.

14 Joseph Howe, *Confederation Considered in Relation to the Interests of the Empire* (London: E. Stanford, 1866), 23–4. Howe's reasons for opposing Confederation in 1865–68 have been a matter of considerable historiographic controversy and will probably always be a matter for debate, given the lack of definitive evidence. Howe was probably motivated by a mixture of self-interest and high political principle. Contemporaries used Howe's earlier statements to charge him with being inconsistent, thereby suggesting that his opposition to Confederation was opportunistic and connected to his quest for salaried office. In the 1930s, this view of Howe was repeated in James A. Roy, *Joseph Howe: A Study in Achievement and Frustration* (Toronto: Macmillan, 1935). J. Murray Beck sought to rehabilitate Howe's reputation on this point, arguing that his opposition to the Quebec scheme had been principled. Beck, *Howe*, 244–50.

15 See leading article in *Morning Star and Dial*, 10 November 1866, 4. The paper's view that Howe was insincere in his opposition to Confederation was accurate: a few weeks later, Howe even offered to comment on the draft of the BNA Act. See Howe to Carnarvon, 21 December 1866, in NA, Carnavon Papers, PRO 30/6/146.

16 Garvie's Statement, 15 March 1867, in "Joseph Howe and the Anti-Confederation League," edited by Lawrence J. Burpee, *Transactions of the Royal Society of Canada*, 3rd series (March 1917), 461.

17 In 1862, *Dod's Parliamentary Companion* described Sir Minto Farquhar, MP, a BNAA member, as being in favour of a working-class franchise. Henry Paull, another BNAA member of the Commons, had voted in favour of Lord Derby's 1859 reform bill.

18 *Hansard*, 3d series, 186 (1867): 51–2. Baring's ultimate decision to support the bill is discussed by Maurice Cowling, *1867: Disraeli, Gladstone and Revolution – The Passing of the Second Reform Bill* (Cambridge: Cambridge University Press, 1967), 176.

19 Howe to Normanby, 22 November 1866, in Burpee, *Joseph Howe*, 440.

20 *Financial Reformer*, "A Fiscal Fallacy," July 1866, 334. Aside from this article, the *Financial Reformer* paid little attention to Confederation, perhaps because its liberal editors had become preoccupied by the Governor Eyre controversy.

21 *Daily News*, "What are we to think of this project of Confederation, which Canadian delegates are coming hither to advocate?" 9 November 1866, 4.

22 Howe to William J. Stairs, 30 August, 10 September, 28 September 1866, in Burpee, *Joseph Howe*, 431–5.

23 Howe to Stairs, 9 November 1866, in Burpee, *Joseph Howe*, 437. For the Nova Scotia electoral law, see John Garner, *The Franchise and Politics in*

British North America, 1755–1867 (Toronto: University of Toronto Press, 1969), 44–52.

24 William Frederick, Lord Stratheden and Campbell, 1824–1893, had sat in the Lords since 1860. He was the son of a famous Whig lord chancellor. The origins of his interest in Nova Scotia are hard to determine, for his other speeches in the Lords were unconnected to colonial policy. *Hansard*, 3d series, 181 (1866): 503. He was harshly dismissed as "Lord Campbell's brainless son" by the Toronto *Globe*, "London Correspondence," 14 March 1867, 2.

25 Although he expressed regret that the central government had not been made more powerful, Herbert had praised Confederation, predicting that it would lead to a form of imperial federation in which the new "England of the West" would send representatives to Westminster. Auberon Herbert, "The Canadian Confederation," *Fortnightly Review* 7, Old Series, and 1 New Series (1867): 480–90. *Canadian News*, "Canadian News," 21 February 1867, 120, described the Lords as being "somewhat full" during Carnarvon's speech, with fifty-two peers on hand.

26 It should be noted that property qualification for elected members of the legislative council of Canada had been set in 1856 at $8,000 (19 and 20 Vic. Canada c. 140), the $4,000 established in 1867 marking a reduction in the requirement.

27 *Hansard*, 3d series, 185 (1867): 557–76.

28 Shaftesbury's support for Confederation as a general concept was entirely consistent with his long-standing sympathies for centralization within Britain. See Robert M. Gutchen, "Local Government and Centralization in Nineteenth-Century England," *Historical Journal* 4 (1961): 85–96, 86; Joshua Toulmin Smith, *Local Self-Government Un-Mystified: A Response to the Manifesto of Centralization Delivered at the Social Science Association meeting in 1857* (London: N.p., 1857); John Wesley Bready, *Lord Shaftesbury and Social-Industrial Progress* (London: Allen and Unwin, 1926).

29 *Hansard*, 3d series, 185 (1867): 1,011–17.

30 Ibid., 579–81. Monck was a new member of the Lords, having recently been promoted from the Irish peerage to a British title. As an Anglo-Irish aristocrat, Monck had a particular reason to dislike the notion of popular sovereignty. Monck had earlier sent C.B. Adderley a lengthy memorandum using the Scottish and Irish unions as precedents for the current treatment of Nova Scotia. Adderley to Monck, 5 March 1867, LAC, Monck Fonds.

31 *Hansard*, 3d series, 185 (1867): 557–76.

32 In an effort to understand the socioeconomic roots of imperialism, Davis and Huttenback analyzed 125 divisions on colonial issues in the period 1860–1910, assigning each MP a social category related to the sources of his income. Of these divisions, forty-eight dealt with loan guarantees and non-military subsidies. Their research reveals that in this period, Liberal members who were lawyers or came from the landed aristocracy were more likely to support such imperialist measures as colonial loan guarantees than Liberals who came from manufacturing backgrounds. Davis and Huttenback, *Mammon*, 215–41, especially 235–6. Other works dealing with the relationship between middle-class liberalism and the political economy of imperialism are discussed in Bernard Porter, *Absent-Minded Imperialists*, and in Peter Marsh, *Bargaining on Europe: Britain and the First Common Market, 1860–92* (New Haven: Yale University Press, 1999).

33 See 23 December 1866 in British Library Manuscripts Room, 425 Carnarvon Diary, Carnarvon Papers, Add MSS 60898.

34 James E. Thorold Rogers, ed., *Speeches on Questions of Public Policy by the Rt Honourable John Bright, MP.* (London, Macmillan, 1869), viii.

35 Ibid., 1,164–81.

36 In March 1859, Bright had lectured the Commons on the benefits of political decentralization and had urged that the principle be introduced into the administration of India. *Hansard*, 3d series (152): 1,359–73.

37 *Times*, "Messrs. Bright And Scholefield At Birmingham," 19 January 1865, 9. "Proportional representation," Upper Canada's grievance, was an issue in Britain too: one vote, one value Proportional representation as determined by census was only achieved in Britain in 1885. Andrew Jones, *The Politics of Reform, 1884* (Cambridge: Cambridge University Press, 1972), 104, 108, 196–202.

38 *Hansard*, 3d series, 177 (1865): 1,613–33. The £43million figure had been supplied by Sir Minto Farquhar, a supporter of the expenditure and a member of the BNAA. Ibid., 1,662–5. Other BNAA members who spoke on this occasion included Sir James Ferguson (ibid., 1,585–7), Watkin (ibid., 1,598–1605), and Seymour Fitzgerald (ibid., 1,539–55). Spending on the fortifications was also endorsed in the *Economist*, "Mr Buxton on Canada," 9 September 1865, 1,086. Cobden, who was very ill, had wished to speak against this measure but had died before reaching London. Donald Read, *Cobden and Bright: A Victorian Political Partnership* (London: Edward Arnold, 1967), 231.

39 *Hansard*, 3d series, 185 (1867): 1,181–7.

40 The *Bullionist*, "The British American Confederation Act," 23 March 1867, 312–14, thought the bill was excellent, as the proposed constitution preserved the relationship between the mother country and the colonies while promising future increases in the power of the federal government. It also stated that federation would help protect the colonists from Yankee attacks: "Even while Mr Bright spoke, his Transatlantic friends were giving the lie to his pacific promises on their behalf, by insolently declaring in Congress itself that the union of the British provinces was an act unfriendly and menacing to the United States."

41 *Hansard*, 3d series, 185 (1867): 1,187–91. The Toronto *Globe*, 14 March 1867, reported the attendance of roughly 150 members.

42 *Morning Star and Dial*, leading article, 1 March 1867, 3.

43 *Hansard*, 3d series, 185 (1867): 1,192–3. M.G. Wiebe, *Oxford Dictionary of National Biography*, s.v. "Baillie, Alexander Dundas Ross Cochrane-Wishart-, First Baron Lamington (1816–1890)."

44 *Hansard*, 3d series, 185 (1867): 1,181–5. Chichester Samuel Fortescue (1823–1898) had served as under-secretary of state for the colonies in 1857–58 and from 1859 to 1865. H.C.G. Matthew, "Fortescue, Chichester Samuel Parkinson, Baron Carlingford and second Baron Clermont (1823–1898)," in *Oxford Dictionary of National Biography*.

45 *Hansard*, 3d series, 185 (1867): 1,185–7. Sir John Pakington had changed his last name from Russell to Pakington in 1831 for political reasons. *Oxford Dictionary of National Biography*, s.v. "Pakington, John Somerset, First Baron Hampton (1799–1880)."

46 Russell to Carnarvon, 25 July [n.y., but 1866], LAC, Cardwell Fonds. Russell's signature was illegible, but it is clear from the address that he was the author.

47 27 January 1867, Carnarvon Diary, Carnarvon Papers, Add MSS 60899, British Library Manuscripts Room.

48 *Hansard*, 3d series, 185 (1867): 1,320. Roger Sinclair Aytoun was MP for Kirkcaldy from 1862 to 1874. A Liberal, he supported the Disestablishment of the Irish church. In June 1868 he took up Nova Scotia's cause; *Hansard*, 3d series, 192 (1868): 1687–1688.

49 *Hansard*, 3d series, 185 (1867): 1,322. Jonathan Parry, "Lowe, Robert, Viscount Sherbrooke (1811–1892)," in *Oxford Dictionary of National Biography*,

50 25 December 1866, Carnarvon Diary, Carnarvon Papers, Add MSS 60898.

51 George Hadfield (1787–1879) was a Congregationalist, the son of a Sheffield manufacturer, and a leading advocate of Disestablishment.

Oxford Dictionary of National Biography, s.v. "Hadfield, George (1787–1879.)"

52 Howe to Bright, 8 March 1867, LAC, Howe Fonds, 10:180.

53 Martin, *Britain and the Origins,* 285.

54 See Garvie's 15 March 1867 report in Burpee, *Joseph Howe,* 409–73. In November 1864, Mill has expressed his approval of the "confederation plan for British America." See Mill to J.E. Cairnes, 8 November 1864, in *The Later Letters of John Stuart Mill* (Toronto: University of Toronto Press, 1972), 965.

55 House of Commons, *Divisions,* 1867 (London: HMSO, 1867), 41.

56 *Hansard,* 3d series, 186 (1867): 735–44.

57 Ibid., 744–7. In the mid-1860s, fears about the size of the national debt had been given added impetus by alarmist predictions that Britain's coal would soon be exhausted, a situation that seemed to require the accelerated repayment of the national debt. See M.J. Daunton, *Trusting Leviathan,* 120; W.S. Jevons, *The Coal Question: An Inquiry Concerning the Progress of the Nation, and the Probable Exhaustion of our Coal Mines* (London: Macmillan, 1865), chapter 17, "Of Taxes and the National Debt."

58 *Daily News,* leading article, 8 November, 1866, 4. The *Daily News* also endorsed the criticisms of Confederation offered by the *Montreal Herald* (a Presbyterian, laissez-faire oriented paper). See *Daily News,* "What are we to think of this project of Confederation, which Canadian delegates are coming hither to advocate?" 9 November 1866, 4.

59 Henry Parris, *Government and the Railways in Nineteenth Century Britain* (London: Routledge and Paul, 1965), 212, states that "1867 wasa turning point in relations between railways and the state," the threshold of an era of greater state involvement.

60 *Hansard,* 3d series, 185 (1867): 747–9.

61 Gladstone had favoured the colonial federation initiative of the Great Coalition from moment he had heard about it, believing that consolidating the British North American colonies would lead to their assuming the responsibility for their own defence, "the Alpha and almost the Omega" of colonial policy. Gladstone to Cardwell, 25 October 1864, quoted in Knaplund, *Gladstone,* 92. See also Gladstone's memorandum on the defences of Canada, 12 July 1864, reprinted in ibid., 228–42.

62 *Hansard,* 3d series, 186 (1867): 762–3.

63 Ibid., 757–62.

64 Adderley's request was doubtless superfluous and was probably mentioned simply to project the image of a disinterested individual.

It had been made through John A. Macdonald, see Adderley to
Macdonald, n.d., LAC, Macdonald; Fonds, 51:20, 427–8.

65 *Hansard*, 3d series, 186 (1867): 762–3.

66 Letter to the editor from J. Nelson, *Canadian News*, 4 April 1867, 217.

67 Ibid.

68 Roman, *Imperial Guarantees*, 4–11; Den Otter, *Philosophy*, 47–50, 91–
2,144–7; A.G. Bailey, "Railways and the Confederation Issue in New
Brunswick, 1863–1865," *Canadian Historical Review* 21 (1940): 367–83.
Don Roman's argument is that imperial loan guarantees were critical
in the formation of the Dominion.

69 Some Britons attributed this victory to American money. Adderley to
Monck, 8 October 1867, LAC, Monck Fonds.

70 Discussions of the possibility of forcible resistance to Confederation
are mentioned by Ken Pryke, *Nova Scotia and Confederation 1864–74*
(Toronto: University of Toronto Press, 1979), 65. Howe melodramati-
cally told John Young, a Montreal opponent of Confederation, that he
would never bring himself to fight "the Queen's troops." Howe to
Young, 11 May 1867, LAC, Howe Fonds, 9:366–8.

71 As William George Harcourt and Sir Roundell Palmer, two British
barristers told Howe it was extremely unlikely that a British court
would deem the BNA Act *ultra vires*. Joseph Howe to Sydenham
Howe, 9 April 1868, cited in Beck, *Howe*, 321. Palmer had been attorney general for England and Wales in 1863–66. David Steele, *Oxford
Dictionary of National Biography*, s.v. "Palmer, Roundell, First Earl of
Selborne (1812–1895)." For the rich pre-1776 history of the concept of
an imperial constitution constraining Westminster, see Mary Sarah
Bilder, *The Transatlantic Constitution: Colonial Legal Culture and the Empire* (Cambridge: Harvard University Press, 2004). For the Australian
judicial politics and other events leading to the passage of the Colonial Laws Validity Act, see David Swinfen, *Imperial Control of Colonial
Legislation, 1813–1865* (Oxford: Clarendon Press, 1970), 167–76.

72 *Hansard*, 3d series, 192 (1868): 1,658–76.

73 The Protestant church of Ireland was disestablished in 1869. Donald
Akenson, *The Church of Ireland: Ecclesiastic Reform and Revolution* (New
Haven: Yale University Press, 1971).

74 *Hansard*, 3d series, 192 (1868): 1,677–87.

75 There were 183 opposed. Howe to Stairs, 20 June 1868, in Burpee,
Joseph Howe, 465.

76 *Hansard*, 3d series, 193 (1868): 679–710.

77 Ibid., 689–94.

78 Ibid., 694–8.

79 Ibid., 704–5.

80 *Economist*, "The Dominion of Canada," 29 February 1868, 327.

81 Ibid., 20 June 1868.

82 Clement Francis Goodfellow, *Great Britain and South African Confederation, 1870–1881* (Oxford: Oxford University Press, 1966), 19. In 1867 Carnarvon also promoted a federation in the West Indies. C.S.S. Highman, "The General Assembly of the Leeward Islands," *English Historical Review* 41 (1926): 387–8.

83 See J.H. Aitchison, "The Municipal Corporations Act of 1849," *Canadian Historical Review* 30 (1949): 107–22.

84 Paul Romney, *Getting It Wrong: How Canadians Forgot Their Past and Imperilled Confederation* (Toronto: University of Toronto Press, 1999), 75–108.

85 Garth Stevenson, *Ex Uno Plures: Federal Provincial Relations in Canada, 1867–1896* (Montreal: McGill-Queen's University Press, 1993), 15.

86 Bruce W. Hodgins, "Democracy and the Ontario Fathers of Confederation," in *Profiles of a Province: Studies in the History of Ontario*, edited by Edith G. Firth (Toronto: Ontario Historical Society, 1967), 83–91.

CHAPTER EIGHT

1 J.C. Dent, *The Last Forty Years: The Union of 1841 to Confederation*, introduction by Donald Swainson (Toronto: McClelland and Stewart, 1972), 293.

2 For the high emigration rate see Alan Green, Mary MacKinnon, and Chris Minns, "Dominion or Republic? Migrants to North America from the United Kingdom, 1870–1910," *Economic History Review* 55(200): 666–96, 667. The general political situation is discussed in Peter Waite, *Canada 1874–1896: Arduous Destiny* (Toronto: McClelland and Stewart, 1971).

3 Canada, House of Commons, *Debates*, 1st Parliament, 3d session (1870), 6 April 1870, 906.

4 Ibid., 902.

5 Ibid., 22 April 1870, 1,145.

6 "An Act Respecting Interest and Usury in the Province of Nova Scotia," 36 Vic., cap. 71, in Charles Peers Davidson, *A Compilation of the Statutes Passed since Confederation Relating to Banks and Banking: Government and Other Savings Banks, Promissory Notes and Bills of Exchange, and Interest and Usury in New Brunswick and Nova Scotia* (Montreal:

Gazette, 1876), 72; "An Act Respecting Interest," 49 Vict. c.127, in Frank Weir, *The Law and Practice of Banking Corporations under Dominion Acts* (Montreal: J. Lovell, 1888), 415–20.

7 Currie, *Grand Trunk*, 115–16.

8 Goldwin Smith mocked the Intercolonial for its lack of traffic in *Canada and the Canadian Question*, 202. Ken Cruickshank points out that interregional traffic on the Intercolonial was light even decades after its opening. He argues against those who see the railway as having had a major impact on the place of the Maritimes in the Canadian economy. Kenneth Cruickshank, "The Intercolonial Railway, Freight Rates and the Maritime Economy," in *Farm, Factory and Fortune: New Studies in the Economic History of the Maritime Provinces*, edited by Kris Inwood (Fredericton: Acadiensis Press, 1993), 171–96, especially 175.

9 The nationalization of the Grand Trunk as a whole had been advocated by the *Manchester Guardian*, "Intercolonial Railway Bill," 12 March 1867, 7. The paper had argued that nationalization would benefit both the ordinary investor and Canada, as "a generally economical system under state control" would allow the government to "recoup itself much of its annual payments and to work the two lines of railway advantageously together." It also seems to have assumed that the Intercolonial would be built as an integral part of the Grand Trunk.

10 Currie, *Grand Trunk*, 132, 158.

11 Glazebrook, *History of Transportation*, 239–49. The Pacific Scandal of 1873 resulted in the loss of power by the Conservatives after the revelation that Sir John A. Macdonald had accepted money from one of the syndicates bidding for the contract to build the railway to British Columbia.

12 Brian J. Young, *Promoters and Politicians: The North-Shore Railways in the History of Quebec, 1854–85* (Toronto: University of Toronto Press, 1976), 41, 45, 50–2.

13 Currie, *Grand Trunk*, 115–219.

14 Ibid., 220–98.

15 See map in Ibid., 246.

16 Glazebrook, *History of Transportation*, 323–30, 361–9.

17 Quoted in D.E. Moggridge, *Maynard Keynes: An Economist's Biography* (London: Routledge, 1992), 423. Keynes was referring to the dispute over the valuation of the Grand Trunk, an issue pitting shareholders against the Canadian government that was not fully resolved until 1924.

18 Cartier to Watkin, 23 August 1867, 22 September 1867, 24 November 1867, 15 February 1868; Tupper to Watkin, 22 April 1868; Cartier, to

Watkin, 28 May 1868; Watkin to Cartier, 12 August 1868, in Watkin, *Canada and the States*, 459–73; Tupper to Macdonald, 25 April 1868, LAC, Macdonald Fonds, 282:129095–129101.

19 Watkin to Macdonald, 24 March 1887, LAC, Macdonald Fonds, 439: 217007–217012.

20 Watkin, *Canada and the States*, 4.

21 Brydges to Macdonald, LAC, Macdonald Fonds, 191:79548

22 Watkin's various post-1867 activities are discussed by David Hodgkins, *The Second Railway King: The Life and Times of Sir Edward Watkin, 1819–1901* (London: Merton, 2002), 309–668.

23 Morton, *Critical Years*, 234–5. Arthur Silver argues that in 1867 French Canadians were preoccupied with their homeland in Lower Canada and only later became interested in the West; A.I. Silver, *The French-Canadian Idea of Confederation, 1864–1900* (Toronto: University of Toronto Press, 1992), 33, 71.

24 *Oxford Dictionary of National Biography*, s.v. "Wodehouse, John, first earl of Kimberley (1826–1902)."

25 *Oxford Dictionary of National Biography*, s.v. "Northcote, Stafford Henry, First Earl of Iddesleigh (1818–1887)."

26 *Globe*, "Hudson's Bay Claims," 4 June 1868. The *Globe* based its reports on the London *Daily News*, a Radical publication.

27 Lytton to Head, 13 May 1859, LAC, Governor General's Office Fonds.

28 Charles W. Snyder, *Liberty and Morality: A Political Biography of Edward Bulwer-Lytton* (London: Peter Lang American University Studies 1995), 157.

29 Elaine A. Mitchell, "Edward Watkin and the Buying-Out of the Hudson's Bay Company," *Canadian Historical Review* 34 (1953): 219–44, 219.

30 Newcastle to Gladstone, 2 February 1863, University of Nottingham Library, Newcastle Papers, NEC 10,891.

31 Mitchell, "Edward Watkin," 221.

32 C.B. Adderley to Kimberley, 1 December 1868, HBC Papers A-8/12, cited in Galbraith, *Imperial Factor*, 420. Adderley, the under-secretary for the colonies, was merely communicating Buckingham's ideas, but they were congruent with his own. In 1868 he called the company an "absolute obstruction to the exertion of British enterprise." *Times*, "House of Commons," 10 June 1868, 6.

33 Galbraith, *Imperial Factor*, 417.

34 *Times*, "On Wednesday Lord Granville's Proposals," 22 March 1869, 8.

35 See the attacks on the HBC, W.B. Cheadle, "The Last Great Monopoly," *Westminster Review* 88, Old Series, and 32, New Series (1867):

85–119; *Financial Reformer*, "The Hudson's Bay Company and the Government," October 1866, 403–4.

36 *Times*, "The Hudsons Bay Company," 9 December 1868, 4.

37 *Money Market Review*, 4 June 1864, "The Canadian Pamphlet on Hudson's Bay Affairs," 657–8.

38 John S. Galbraith, *The Hudson's Bay Company as an Imperial Factor 1821–1869* (Toronto: University of Toronto Press, 1957), 389–94.

39 Watkin to Macdonald, 18 February 1865, LAC, Macdonald Fonds, 339:154752.

40 Kerr, *Scholarly Governor*, 228; Galbraith, *Imperial Factor*, 365–7, 396.

41 *Globe*, "The New Hudson's Bay Company," 18 July 1863, p.2.

42 Galbraith, *Imperial Factor*, 400.

43 Watkin to Macdonald, 18 February 1865, LAC, Macdonald Fonds, 339:154752.

44 McEwen to Head, 18 January 1866; Thomas Fraser to McEwen 24 January; W.E. Forster to Head, 20 February; Head, to Forster 1 March 1866, in Canada, *Sessional Papers*, 1867–68, no. 19, 3–13; Galbraith, *Imperial Factor*, 403.

45 Morton, *Critical Years*, 60–3.

46 Careless, *Brown of the Globe*, vol. 2, 178–9.

47 Galbraith, *Imperial Factor*, 401.

48 Cardwell to Monck, 17 June 1865, in *Papers relating to the Conference which have taken place between Her Majesty's Government and a Deputation from the Executive Council of Canada* (London: HMSO, 1865); *Economist*, "Mr Cardwell's Account of His Negotiations With Canada," 24 June 1865, 752.

49 *Herapath's*, "Hudson's Bay Company," 13 July 1867, 694–5.

50 When the coalition broke up in 1865, McDougall and several of Brown's other followers had failed to follow him back into opposition. See "Memoirs of William McDougall," LAC, William McDougall Fonds. McDougall acknowledged George Brown's important role in the beginnings of the Canadian campaign against the company.

51 Sir Edmund Head to Buckingham, 15 January 1868, in "Papers Relating to Rupert's Land," reprinted in *Irish University Press Series of British Parliamentary Papers* (Dublin: Irish University Press, 1971), vol. 27;109–13.

52 Ibid.

53 Morton, *Critical Years*, 233.

54 There was, however, opposition to a motion made by Sir H. Verney for a commission to investigate the agricultural and other potential of the territory, R.S. Aytoun calling the possession of large territories with

small populations a liability rather than an asset. *Hansard*, 3d series, vol. 194 (1868): 308–11.

55 Galbraith, *Critical Years*, 419.

56 Even though the BNA Act had provided for the admission of Rupert's Land to the Dominion, Buckingham felt that another piece of legislation was required in light of the Hudson's Bay Company's long tenure in the territory. *Times*, 9 June 1868, 8.

57 Galbraith, *Critical Years*, 422–6.

58 Granville to Gladstone, 11 March 1869, British Library Manuscripts Room, Gladstone Papers, Add MSS 44166, f. 34.

59 *Times*, "The Hudson's Bay Company," 17 March 1869, 12.

60 In 1866 one aggrieved shareholder had argued that the company's assets were worth five million pounds but that the management was deliberately undervaluing them. James Dodds, *The Hudson's Bay Company, its Position and Prospects*, (London: E. Stanford, 1866), 56.

61 *Times*, "On Wednesday Lord Granville's Proposals," 22 March 1869, 8.

62 Ibid., "The Hudson's Bay Company and the Governments of Canada," 25 March 1869, 4.

63 Ibid., "The Hudson's Bay Company Yesterday Accepted," 10 April 1869, 9.

64 *Economist*, "Business Notes," 17 April 1869, 443.

65 *Times*, "On Wednesday Lord Granville's Proposals," 22 March 1869, 8.

66 Recognition of its property rights did not necessarily result in the protection of those of the people to whom the company had granted land. Canada promised to recognize all land grants made before March 1869, but numerous practical problems stood in the way of individuals having their titles registered. See Archer Martin, *The Hudson's Bay Company's Land Tenures and the Occupation of Assiniboia, by Lord Selkirk's Settlers, with a List of Grantees under the Earl and the Company* (London: W. Clowes, 1898), 89.

67 *Dictionary of Canadian Biography*, vol. 14, s.v. "Smith, Donald Alexander, 1st Baron Strathcona and Mount Royal."

68 Alan Wilson, "'In a business way': C.J. Brydges and the Hudson's Bay Company, 1879–89,"in *The West and the Nation: Essays in Honour of W.L. Morton*, edited by Carl Berger and Ramsay Cook (Toronto: McClelland and Stewart 1976), 114–39; J.S. Galbraith, "Land Policies of the Hudson's Bay Company, 1870–1913," *Canadian Historical Review* 32 (1951): 1–21.

69 D.M.L. Farr, *The Colonial Office and Canada, 1867–1887* (Toronto: University of Toronto Press, 1955), 79–85.

70 *Hansard*, 3d series, 196 (1869): 877–8; ibid., 197 (1869): 1,145–8.
71 Ibid., 297 (1869): 1,450–2.
72 *Hansard*, 3d series, 198 (1869): 1,327–8.
73 Ibid., 1328.
74 Charles Wentworth Dilke, *Greater Britain: A Record of Travel in English-Speaking Countries during 1866 and 1867* (London: Macmillan, 1868), 63, 75, quotation from 66. The enthusiasm for democracy and dislike of oligarchy expressed in *Greater Britain* won him the support of J.S. Mill, who assisted his efforts to get into Parliament. *Oxford Dictionary of National Biography*, s.v. "Dilke, Sir Charles Wentworth, Second Baronet (1843–1911)." David Nicolls, *The Lost Prime Minister: A Life of Sir Charles Dilke* (London: Hamledon Press, 1995).
75 *Hansard*, 3d series, 198 (1869): 1,329–30.
76 C.P. Stacey, *Canada and the British Army, 1846–1871: A Study in the Practice of Responsible Government* (Toronto: University of Toronto Press, 1963). Although troop withdrawal can be seen as the logical extension of the principle of responsible government, this decision should not be viewed as a part or corollary of Confederation. After all, in the early 1860s, Watkin and Newcastle, two important supporters of colonial federation, were fierce opponents of the doctrine of colonial self-sufficiency in military matters. Watkin and Newcastle both believed in maintaining British garrisons in Canada. Eldridge, "Colonial Policy," 260; Bruce Knox, "The Concept of Empire in the Mid-Nineteenth Century: Ideas in the Colonial Defence Inquiries of 1859–61," *Journal of Imperial and Commonwealth History* 15 (1987): 242–63.
77 Watkin advocated a two-track approach to defending Canada that involved both defensive works and diplomacy. In 1865, when Anglo-American relations were at a low point, he suggested that a speaking tour by Cobden and Bright in the United States might generate good will and decrease the chances of war. See Ashworth to Cobden, 13 February 1865, British Library Manuscripts Room, Cobden Papers, Add MSS 43654, f. 342.
78 Watkin, *Canada and the States*, 18 (Watkin's italics).
79 Knox, "The Earl of Carnarvon, Empire, and Imperialism, 1855–1890," in *Managing the Business of Empire: Essays in Honour of David Fieldhouse*, edited by Peter Burroughs and A.J. Stockwell (London: Taylor and Francis, 1998), 48–67, 52.
80 Maureen M. Robson, "The Alabama Claims and Anglo-American Reconciliation, 1865–71," *Canadian Historical Review* 42 (1961): 1–22.
81 Farr, *The Colonial Office and Canada, 1867–1887*, 86.

82 W.F.D. Jervois, *Report on the Defence of Canada* (London: G.E. Eyre, 1864).
83 See William H. Lee, Report of a Committee of the Privy Council approved 20 January 1872, and Kimberley to Lisgar 18 March 1872, in Canada, *Sessional Papers*, 1872, no. 18, 51–4.
84 *Hansard*, 3d series, 216 (1873): 1,313–20. Robert Baxter, the railway solicitor who had been a founding member of the BNAA, was one of the bill's other sponsors.
85 *Hansard*, 3d series, 216 (1873): 1,320–6.
86 Farr, *The Colonial Office and Canada, 1867–1887*, 86. For the difference of opinion on economic policy between Lowe and Gladstone, see H.C.G. Matthew, *Gladstone, 1809–1874* (Oxford: Oxford University Press, 1986), 217–25. Reminiscent of the disagreement between Gladstone and Palmerston, the clash between Lowe and Gladstone suggests that whoever became prime minister would be forced to compromise their earlier financial principles.
87 *Hansard*, 3d series, 216 (1873): 1,326–9.
88 These subsidies in land and money are discussed in Harold A. Innis, *A History of the Canadian Pacific Railway* (London: P.S. King, 1923), *passim*; Peter James George, "A Benefit-Cost Analysis of the Canadian Pacific Railway"(PHD dissertation, University of Toronto, 1967).
89 Gibbon, *Steel of Empire*, 311–12.
90 This figure has been derived from "Statistical Abstract for the United Kingdom, 1865–1878,"in *Parliamentary Papers* (1880), vol. 76, 30–2, Table 14. British North America includes all British possessions in North America excluding Bermuda. These figures included goods produced in Britain and Ireland as well as foreign and colonial goods shipped to British North America through Britain.
91 Michael Hart, *Trading Nation: Canadian Trade Policy from Colonialism to Globalization* (Vancouver: University of British Columbia Press, 2002), 68; Innis, *Economic History*, 95–6. Davis and Huttenback *Mammon*, 159–61, stress the unimportance of exports to the colonies of settlement.
92 Forster, *Conjunction of Interests*, 69, 143, 154.
93 Farr, *The Colonial Office and Canada, 1867–1887*, 192–201.
94 Michael Hart, *A Trading Nation: Canadian Trade Policy from Colonialism to Globalization* (Vancouver: University of British Columbia Press, 2002), 72–5.
95 Andrew Carnegie, *The Gospel of Wealth and Other Timely Essays* (New York: Century, 1900), 125. Originally published in *North American Review* 167 (1898): 239–48.

96 Debt figures are taken from Section H: "Government Finance," in *Historical Statistics of Canada*, edited by M.C. Urquhart (Ottawa: Statistics Canada, 1983). Gross national product figures are from O.J. Firestone, *Canada's Economic Development, 1867–1953* (London: Bowes and Bowes, 1958), Table 9, 65.

97 Ranald C. Michie, "The Canadian Securities Market, 1850–1914," *Business History Review* 62 (1988): 35–73, 38; emphasis added. Michie argues that the City's commanding lead in the business of trading Canadian public obligations reflected the fact that most of the purchasers were British. The overwhelming majority of the purchasers of provincial bonds were also British. However, British predominance was less marked in the field of Canadian railway securities, with Britons holding only sixty percent of CPR shares in 1913. Most of the 45,000 people who owned Grand Trunk shares in 1907 were residents of the United Kingdom. In contrast, bank shares were normally owned by Canadians and traded locally.

98 Ziegler, *Sixth Great Power*, 302. The action the Bank of England took to rescue Barings is described by Cain and Hopkins, *British Imperialism*, 153–8; Ziegler, *Sixth Great Power*, 244–6.

99 Ranald C. Michie, *The London and New York Stock Exchanges, 1850–1914* (London: Allen and Unwin, 1987).

100 Ranald C. Michie, "The Canadian Securities Market, 1850–1914," 35, 50. Other works on the history of Canadian stock markets include John F. Whiteside, "The Toronto Stock Exchange and the Development of the Share Market to 1885," *Journal of Canadian Studies* 20 (1985): 64–81; Armstrong, *Blue Skies and Boiler Rooms*.

101 Michie, "The Canadian Securities Market, 1850–1914," 41.

102 Irving Stone, *Global Export*, Table 1, Table 2.

103 D.C.M. Platt, *Foreign Finance in Continental Europe and the United States, 1815–1870: Quantities, Origins, Functions, and Distributions* (London: George Allen, 1984), 141.

104 B.W. Wilkinson, "Section G: The Balance of International Payments, International Investment Position and Foreign Trade," in *Historical Statistics of Canada*, edited by Urquhart; Kenneth Buckley, *Capital Formation in Canada, 1896–1930*, introduction by M.C. Urquhart (Toronto: McClelland and Stewart, 1974), 101; Kenneth Norrie, Douglas Owram, J.C. Herbert Emery, *A History of the Canadian Economy*, 3d ed. (Toronto: Thompson-Nelson, 2002), 232.

105 Naylor, *History of Business*. His viewpoint reflects the Canadian left nationalism of the 1970s. See Leo Panitch, "Dependency and Class

in Canadian Political Economy," in *Studies in Political Economy* 6 (1981): 7–33.

106 Niall Ferguson, *Empire: The Rise and Demise of the British World Order and the Lessons for Global Power* (New York: Basic Books, 2003), 206.

107 Langhout, "Public Enterprise," 169.

108 Innis described Confederation as a "widening of the credit structure." Harold Adams Innis, *An Economic History of Canada*, edited by Mary Quayle Innis (Toronto: Ryerson Press, 1935), 237.

109 In their study of the Glorious Revolution, Douglas North and Barry Weingast argue that changing political institutions in England promoted this virtuous circle. Douglass North and Barry Weingast, "Constitutions and Commitment: The Evolution of Institutions Governing Public Choice in Seventeenth-Century England," *Journal of Economic History* 49(1989): 803–32; John Wells and Douglas Wills, "Revolution, Restoration, and Debt Repudiation: The Jacobite Threat to England's Institutions and Economic Growth," *Journal of Economic History* 60 (2000): 418–41; Gregory Clark, "The Political Foundations of Modern Economic Growth: England, 1540–1800," *Journal of Interdisciplinary History* 55 (1996): 563–87.

110 John Brewer, *The Sinews of Power* (Cambridge: Harvard Press, 1988); Peter Dickson, *The Financial Revolution in England* (New York: St Martin's, 1967). Stephen Quinn, "The Glorious Revolution's Effect on English Private Finance: A Microhistory, 1680–1705," *Journal of Economic History* 61, no. 3 (2001): 593–615.

111 Peter George, "Canadian Pacific Railway," did not attempt to estimate the social rate of return on the Canadian Pacific and merely looked at the question whether a smaller subsidy could have incented the construction of the railway by private capital. The importance of the development of the railway network in American economic growth was ably questioned by Robert W. Fogel, *Railroads and American Economic Growth: Essays in Econometric History* (Baltimore: Johns Hopkins Press, 1964).

112 Canada's lacklustre economic performance relative to the United States' in the decades after Confederation suggests that there was something wrong with the economic policies the Dominion government pursued. It is unusual for a New World society to experience net emigration, but from 1861 to 1896 Canada was a net exporter of people. O.J. Firestone, *Canada's Economic Development, 1867–1953: With Special Reference to Changes in the Country's National Product and National Wealth* (London: Bowes and Bowes, 1958).

113 Fenn's Compendium of the Funds, 12th ed. (London: Effingham Wilson, 1874), 253.

114 H.G.J. Aitken, "Defensive Expansionism: The State and Economic Growth in Canada," in *Approaches to Canadian Economic History: A Selection of Essays,* edited by W.T. Easterbrook and M.H. Watkins (Toronto: McClelland and Stewart, 1967), 183–221.

115 Alberto Alesina and Enrico Spolaore, *The Size of Nations* (Cambridge: MIT Press, 2003), 81–94, 155–74.

116 Gordon Tullock, "Federalism: Problems of Scale," in *The Economic Approach to Public Policy,* edited by Ryan C. Amacher, Robert Tollison, and Thomas D. Willett (Ithaca: Cornell University Press, 1976), 213–24; 19–29; Robert L. Bish, *Local Government Amalgamations: Discredited Nineteenth-Century Ideas Alive in the Twenty-First Century* (Toronto: C.D. Howe Institute, 2001); Richard E. Wagner, "Grazing the Federal Budgetary Commons: The Rational Politics of Budgetary Irresponsibility," *Journal of Law and Politics* 9 (1992): 105–19.

117 Barry R. Weingast, Kenneth A. Shepsk, Christopher Johnsen, "The Political Economy of Benefits and Costs: A Neoclassical Approach to Distributive Politics," *Journal of Political Economy* 89 (1981): 642–64.

118 Jane Jacobs, *Canadian Cities and Sovereignty Association* (Toronto: Canadian Broadcasting Corporation, 1980).

Index